Capitalism and Confinement

Praise for *Capitalism and Confinement*

"A tour de force of critical theorizing. By putting the widely discussed notion of the carceral into communication with the once-again salient concept of capitalism, A. J. Bohrer says something new and revelatory about both." – Nancy Fraser, author of *Cannibal Capitalism*

"In an age obsessed with global flows—of capital, goods, people—*Capitalism and Confinement* shifts our attention to the walls, borders, and enclosures underpinning all that movement. Drawing on everything from the plantation to the prison to the West Bank, A. J. Bohrer offers a unified theory of capitalism as a system of confinement, one that helps explain why freedom remains so elusive even as the world grows ever more interconnected. This is not just an important book—it is an urgent one." – Eman Abdelhadi, co-author of *Everything for Everyone*

"Bohrer's book on carcerality makes a singular contribution to a fast-growing field of prisons, detention, and abolitionist scholarship. This timely work offers a compelling and well-documented argument that geopolitical considerations, including different histories of colonialism, race, gender, and other social vectors of power, all inform the forms of capitalism we see, and that no analysis of prison institutions can be comprehensive without this kind of multifaceted framework." – Judith Butler, author of *The Force of Nonviolence*

"Recasting capitalism through the lens of confinement, A. J. Bohrer illuminates the articulation of labor, property, borders, policing, prisons, and care in the production and governance of social life. Far from opposing mobility and confinement in abstract terms, they show how capitalist expansion continuously operates through differentiated regimes of movement, containment, and capture. And they open new vistas for struggle within and against these regimes. This is a timely and much-needed book in an age of war and genocide." – Sandro Mezzadra, author of *The Rest and the West*

"The border. The factory. The ghetto. The prison. The plantation. The Indigenous reserve. All these spaces of enclosure and confinement are foundational to capitalism, as A. J. Bohrer shows in this profound study. Perhaps nowhere is this social logic of capitalist confinement more evident today than in the genocidal occupation of Palestine. *Capitalism and Confinement* provides a meticulous dissection of this brutal logic. But more than this, it calls us to a project of solidarity and presents a stirring alternative: abolition communism." – David McNally, author of *Capitalism and Slavery*

Capitalism and Confinement

A. J. Bohrer

VERSO
London • New York

First published by Verso 2026

The manufacturer's authorized representative in the EU for product safety (GPSR) is LOGOS EUROPE, 9 rue Nicolas Poussin, 17000, La Rochelle, France
Contact@logoseurope.eu

1 3 5 7 9 10 8 6 4 2

Verso
UK: 6 Meard Street, London W1F 0EG
US: 207 East 32nd Street, New York, NY 10016
versobooks.com

Verso is the imprint of New Left Books

ISBN-13: 978-1-80429-791-9
ISBN-13: 978-1-80429-793-3 (US EBK)
ISBN-13: 978-1-80429-792-6 (UK EBK)

British Library Cataloguing in Publication Data
A catalogue record for this book is available from the British Library

Library of Congress Cataloging-in-Publication Data
A catalog record for this book is available from the Library of Congress

Typeset in Minion Pro by MJ & N Gavan, Truro, Cornwall
Printed in the UK by CPI Group (UK) Ltd, Croydon, CR0 4YY

For Awdah

Contents

Acknowledgments

A book is always a collective project, one that accumulates unpayable debt and, when we are lucky, forges community. I have been extremely lucky in that, over the decade I worked on this book, my thinking benefitted from too many conversations, organizing meetings, comradely questions, and reading suggestions to name.

I presented pieces of this research to audiences at: Fordham University, Historical Materialism London, European University Viadrina, the University of Connecticut, University of North Carolina at Chapel Hill, University of Essex, Hofstra University, Villanova University, European University Institute (Florence), and Universidade Federal Fluminense (Rio de Janeiro). An early version of chapter 6 was published in *Crisis and Critique* as "The Class Politics of Abolition." I thank everyone at those institutions for the opportunities to deepen my analysis in intellectual community. Jishnu Guha-Majumdar, Sarah Balakrishnan, and I organized a symposium on capitalist confinement in 2022 that was generously supported by the Academy for Global Humanities and Critical Theory; thanks to them and to the participants in the conference.

Deep gratitude to everyone who read drafts of the book, in whole or in part: members of the Longfellow (Michelle O'Brien, Wilson Sherwin, and Aaron Jaffe), Will Paris, Mati Klitgård Sørensen, Alex Stein, Joy Wang, and Andrés Fabián Henao Castro. My research assistant, Siena Mann, was truly a hero. This project would never have been completed without its commissioning editor, Rosie Warren, to whom I remain forever grateful. Thanks also to the rest of the Verso team who brought it over the finish line.

In addition to those named above, deepest thanks to the personal support from my dearests, including: Eman Abdelhadi, Ari Bloomekatz, Scout Bratt, Nate Cohen, Brian Grady, Andrés Fabián Henao Castro, Dan Kroop, Becca Lubow, Gil Morejón, Jimmy Rothschild, Alex Stein, and Joy Wang.

The bulk of this project was written during the ongoing genocide in Gaza, and I would have drowned in grief without the vibrant and tireless community of Palestine solidarity activists in Chicago and around the world who helped me get up every day to fight again. They are too numerous to name here, but without them, I would surely have succumbed to the unspeakable despair that wells in my chest every day.

In this project, I write a lot about my time in Palestine. I traveled and organized in the West Bank and East Jerusalem primarily as an organizer with the Center for Jewish Nonviolence, and I am grateful to everyone who worked with me in that project. Over the course of many solidarity trips, protective presence missions, direct actions, and community conversations, I have had the unique privilege of learning with and from activists in Umm al-Khair, Susiya, Batan al-Hawa, Hebron, al-Walajay, Bethlehem, Beit Sahour, Tuwani, Beida, and others. In this book, I speak most often about one activist in particular, my dear friend and comrade Awdah, from whom I have learned so much about what a liberated world would look like and how to build the communities we need in order to achieve it. But there are so, so many more people, organizations, communities, conversations, and acts of resistance in these places that also shaped my analysis here and my own biography of theory and struggle. It has been the greatest honor of my life to be welcomed into these communities and to be changed by being in solidarity with them.

I write because it feels selfish to hoard the learning of these incredible communities, who know better than anyone what it means to resist, to remain, to push against the suffocating strictures of the capitalist world. To thank them is so much less than they deserve—for them, we must win the entire world. So rather than a thanks, a promise I made to Awdah many times: I am with you.

Introduction

I stood at the edge of a small metal building in Palestine while my friend Awdah spoke to an assembled group of international activists. The sun was scorching, even though it was morning, and the one-room village community center offered only minimal relief from the heat. I had heard Awdah speak about the history of his village, Umm al-Khair, many times before, on many such convergences of anti-occupation Jewish activists to the West Bank. Umm al-Khair sits deep in Area C, the part of the West Bank controlled entirely by the Israeli Army after the Oslo "Peace" Accords carved up historic Palestine into a new series of borders in the early 1990s. Umm al-Khair, unlike some of the other villages in the South Hebron Hills (Masafer Yatta), remains, to this day, an unrecognized village, meaning that it is illegal to build new structures, repair old ones, or set up electricity or running water. The community center we stood in had been demolished since my last visit and already had a new pending demolition order. Awdah explained the daily reality of living under Israeli occupation: segregated roads, a draconian permit system that restricts Palestinian movement, the imposing border wall. Some West Bank Palestinians do pass into Israel without permits, he tells the group, but just to work under the table; they return at night, across the sections of land where the so-called Separation Barrier has not yet been completed.

He spoke of the many barriers to movement that he and his community face: checkpoints at frequent intervals that sometimes delay even routine errands into multi-hour ordeals; the overnight appearance of large concrete roadblocks that cut off Palestinian villages from essential services like doctors, schools, and grocery stores; the declarations of large swaths of land (often where protests have converged) as "closed military zones";

the settler-operated drones that surveil from overhead to ensure compliance to its apartheid order or, sometimes, just to intimidate, or in the words of Israeli military policy, to "make their presence known."[1] He also speaks about how, originally, his people (Bedouins) moved around, and how various waves of occupation (Ottoman, British, Jordanian, Israeli) made their traditional, movement-based form of life impossible. To the violence and cultural erasure of forced settlement, the Israeli government adds yet more cruelty, asserting that the relative recency of his family's forced settlement "proves" that they aren't *really* from there, and hence are not entitled to the protections of Indigenous peoples.

I experienced many of these barriers in a momentary way, and with significantly more privilege as a Jew, as a white person, and as a US passport holder. A few days earlier, I had shepherded this particular group of activists through a checkpoint near Bethlehem—for many of them, the first military checkpoint they had ever experienced. We had walked along the part of Apartheid Wall running through Bethlehem and met with a family whose home is surrounded by the Wall on three sides. I remembered stories of Israeli activist friends who were beaten by Israeli passersby for marking the Green Line through downtown Jerusalem in green chalk—an imaginary but real border, whose presence and invisibility each carry their own forms of violence.[2]

I watched Awdah explain his story and the story of his community to this group of activists, as he had explained to so many groups of activists, international monitors, foreign legislators, NGO employees, tourists, and church groups before. I don't know whether he found the repetition exhausting, but he was as animated as always.

He told a different story this time, about his desire to go to the beach. It was his lifelong dream to dip his toes in the salt water of the Mediterranean, to hear the waves crash against the sand. From his home, the sea

1 Former Israeli soldier (now activist with Breaking the Silence) Shay Davidovich explains this policy: "As soldiers, when we would receive orders to 'make our presence known,' we understood it to mean that we must ensure the Palestinians feel our presence, that they are scared . . . Disrupting routine is exactly what they sent us to do. In the middle of a training exercise, and it doesn't matter what type of training, Palestinians are nothing more than cardboard targets. At the same time, however, the soldiers are 'making their presence known.' We are teaching Palestinians an important lesson: the army is always there. They soon come to understand that we can shoot artillery rounds, enter homes, drive our vehicles over their fields, arrest anyone we please. This is the nature of the occupation." Shay Davidovich, "For Israeli Soldiers, Some Palestinians Are Little More than Props," *+972 Magazine*, November 5, 2013, 972mag.com.

2 The Green Line marks the Armistice Line from 1949, Israel's de facto border until it captured (and occupied) East Jerusalem, Gaza, the West Bank, and the Golan in 1967.

is only about thirty miles (forty-eight kilometers) or so as the crow flies. But the system of checkpoints, segregated roads, and required permits (as he sometimes says, "When they say we need a permit, we know it is impossible") means that Awdah has never moved that far. As he spoke, I feared he may never be able to move that far.

It would have been easy to look at the scene through the lens of movement. Though I grew up in Los Angeles, I traveled to Masafer Yatta from Bologna, Italy, where I was living at the time. In order to stand in that community center, I had taken an Italian city bus, two planes, a train, a taxi, and two private busses (one with blue Israeli plates, one with green Palestinian plates). I had crossed multiple international borders in person and flown over perhaps a dozen more. I was standing in a room of activists who had come from London, Australia, Canada, New York, Pittsburgh, San Francisco, and New Orleans, in addition to several activists from Jerusalem and Tel Aviv and a dozen Bedouin Palestinian residents of the village. In order to get to this point, where I had helped organize this convergence, there were many other trips, many other planes, so much movement of bodies, ideas, and information across the globe over a period of years. As the product of Zionist schools, summer camps, and family, my own politics had to *move* a lot for me to be in that room in the first place.

But interpreting that scene or Awdah's story as one of movement would miss the real truth: that Awdah's life, like all Palestinians' lives, like so many people's lives under capitalism, is defined much more through confinement than movement. And while the confines are not at all equivalent, despite all the planes, trains, and busses that the international activists took to get to that room, their lives—and mine—were also defined through confinement.

In many ways, this book is about unfurling many of the layers in Awdah's story and about the ways that it interacts with and differs from my own. Contemporary settler colonial capitalism impacts us in different ways, activating different parts of our identities and our families' distinct histories of confinement and forced relocation; we also inhabit different relationships to power in navigating and resisting structures of domination. But for both of us, in different ways, what appears as movement is often a story of confinement, capture, borders, limitations, and enclosure. Awdah's story and mine thus appear at many points in the text; as Nietzsche once wrote, all theory is autobiography.[3] I am ultimately

3 He writes, "It has gradually become clear to me what every great philosophy up til now has consisted of—namely, the confession of its originator, and a species of involuntary and the unconscious auto-biography; and moreover that the moral (or

interested in philosophical analysis precisely *because* it explains and clarifies the real experiences of real people, including my own.

This book is also about what it means to move together in the face of these differences against the many forms of confinement we face, whether we experience them as shared or not. When we stand together in the face of domination, as we have many times in the past and as we must do again and again until we are all free, we activate a long history of others who, since the perverse twin birth of capitalism and colonialism, have moved against confinement, evading capture, pushing boundaries, crossing borders, tearing down enclosures, and embodying fugitivity. It has been one of the great privileges of my life to stand shoulder to shoulder with Awdah and with so many other Palestinians in the fight for a more just and liberated world. This book is thus also a story of resistance and the ineluctable joys of comradeship, solidarity, and co-resistance.

Capitalism and Confinement: Contours of a Problem

Palestine is hardly the only contemporary example of grotesque confinement. The world has never seen more prisons. Borders carve the world into pieces that prevent people from moving as they want or need to. Police decide who can move where, with terrifying punishments (including more confinement) for defying their orders. Fences and gates encircle homes, schools, workplaces, parks, and businesses, sending the resounding messages of "no trespassing" and "keep out." Institutions of confinement are basically everywhere.

We are more hemmed in than ever, and yet people across the world still attempt to move. They push against barriers, tear down walls. They organize movements to defund, disband, and dismantle the institutions that rain down confined misery on so many. Whether defiant or furtive, so many acts of resistance take aim at confinement. This book is partially about teasing out the lessons of those who resist capture, confinement, and closure, showing us how, even in the face of growing claustrophobia, the world can still be otherwise. This book also gives us an analysis of *why* confinement is such a common experience for so many. Our enclosed world is not an accident, a quirk, or a coincidence. Confinement is a

immoral) purpose in every philosophy has constituted the true vital germ out of which the entire plant has always grown." Friedrich Nietzsche, *Beyond Good and Evil: Prelude to a Philosophy of the Future*, trans. Helen Zimmern (Macmillan, 1907), 10. For just one more piece of autobiography, I wrote my undergraduate thesis on Nietzsche.

patterned, produced outcome that follows a particular logic. That logic is capitalism.

As much as Awdah's story is obviously one of confinement and colonization, it is also one of the rapacious expansion of capitalism across the globe—even if it might not seem like it at first glance. Awdah's isn't the typical narrative of direct capitalist exploitation; he doesn't work in a factory, and most of the violence he's experienced has nothing to do with his job (he's a teacher). And yet capitalism is a central part of how and why Awdah, like all Palestinians, like so many people across the world, cannot move or cannot move freely. Confinement is only increasing, encircling us at every turn, a snake coiled around us, squeezing us more and more tightly.

This book offers a theory of why—why confinement seems to be increasing over time, who profits, and what we can do about it. I show that even when it doesn't appear as such, capitalism is often a central part of how violence works in the contemporary world. To do so, this book weaves a narrative through many obvious institutions of extreme confinement—like chattel slavery, settler colonies, and prisons—exposing the multiple and crosscutting ways that capital produces and profits from them. I also look at forms of collective life that we might not always think of as confining—like wage work and care—to show how confinement is lodged deeply within them, often disavowing its own presence. Overall, I show that confinement is more capitalist than it often seems, and capitalism relies on confinement more than we realize. This book shows that if we want to abolish the many forms of confinement we face, we need to destroy capitalism. And at the same time, if we want to dismantle capitalism, we need to move with abolitionist intentions, demolishing the carceral structures on which capital depends.

Defining Capitalism

At its core, capitalism is a kind of society whose animating logic is the accumulation of capital. Capital, money that is advanced for a return on investment, can accumulate in many ways: by exploiting wage laborers, by creating new financial instruments like derivatives and futures, by crushing working people with unpayable debts, by commodifying ever new areas of life. Capital*ism* is not only an economic process but a kind of society, one where, in the largest and most abstract sense, the ability for capital to grow, expand, and accumulate directs much of collective existence. In our own world, whether people live or die, whether they will be able to remain housed, access healthcare, buy food, or obtain clean water depends on whether, through those activities, someone else's capital grows. Where we will find structural investment—and whether that investment is in schools or prisons—also often follows the probability of profit. In our world, too, large global trends of war, genocide, ecological destruction, and politics follow the drive to accumulate.

One of capitalism's key features is its commitment to reproduction, its constant need for *more*. No profit, no return on investment, no capital growth will ever sate its rapacious appetite. The only future capital can offer is more of the same. While many argue that capitalism is a mode of production, primarily concerned with how things are *made*, I see capitalism as primarily a mode of reproduction, concerned with how people *survive*. If you live in a society where your survival is largely determined by someone making a buck, often someone you have never and will never meet, you live under capitalism. If you live in a society where you can access life's necessities only by paying for them, you live under capitalism. A society that subordinates survival to profit is one where many institutions, policies, and decisions will prioritize capital over people. A capitalist society is one where capital's accumulative drive influences social relations, political institutions, and economic realities so much that it (largely) determines whether human beings live or die (and what kind of life they can pursue). Thus, capitalism's central feature is the compulsion "to subordinate the substance of society itself to the laws of the market."[4]

Nancy Fraser explains that capitalist society depends on many "background conditions" in order to work.[5] Chief among these conditions are that workers must *need* to work in order to make their daily needs; we go to work, even when we don't want to, because we have no other way of paying rent, buying groceries, accessing medical care, or acquiring life's other necessities. We are, in other words, forced into working for a wage (or a salary) because we simply have no other options to survive, a very constrained form of life indeed. As Marx showed, for wage labor to become widespread, workers were systematically separated from land, the primary way most people survived before capitalism; private property secures this material insecurity. Through the historical process of enclosure, serfs and peasants lost access to land and were newly forced to turn to wage labor to buy as commodities the necessities they once produced

4 Karl Polanyi, *The Great Transformation: The Political and Economic Origins of Our Time* (Beacon Press, 2001), 75.

5 Nancy Fraser, *Cannibal Capitalism* (Verso, 2022), 28, 31.

directly. If we cannot find jobs, or if we violate private property, we are often met with punitive forms of confinement.

Capitalism also requires workers. "Social reproduction" names a whole host of activities that produce *the people* on whom capitalism depends. Pregnancy, childbearing, child-rearing, cooking, cleaning, laundry, and an endless list of other tasks are required for there to *be workers at all*, and for existing workers to be ready to return to work day after day, week after week, year after year. Traditionally, this very hard work has been taken for granted in capitalist societies, even though it is one of its most important background conditions. In much of the world, this work has been not only invisibilized and unwaged but also imposed on women and girls as uniquely feminized labor, naturalized as supposedly biological proclivity. The kind of life expected of women and girls becomes confined by these expectations of care, even when they can find joy in the family and in the work of caring for themselves and others. But once demanded (rather than chosen) and once others profit from this demand, care can become a violent constraint. No labor could happen without this care work, and it is thus a necessary, if often hidden, part of capitalist society—and capitalist confinement.

Once we see this labor as necessary, it becomes clear that not all labor under capitalism is waged, even if waged labor is its most visible component. Many kinds of societies have wage labor, and many kinds of societies are class societies in which the rich rule over the poor; neither on its own makes a society "capitalist." If the existence of wage labor does not make a society capitalist, what does? Whether people's survival is subordinated to the logic of capitalist accumulation. In other words, the core of capitalism is not the form that labor takes but whether the fundamental coordinates of life are set by the logic of capital accumulation.

This insight opens the ability to see an entire social, political, and economic fabric as part of capitalist society. Many institutions support capital's ability to continue accumulation—including some institutions, like racialized chattel slavery, that we might imagine are outside capitalism. The same might be said of the many people who can no longer find jobs at all. As worker productivity reaches its highest levels ever, and as more and more jobs are replaced by machines and AI, capital needs fewer workers to see a return on investment, making large swathes of the global proletariat unnecessary to the regime of dizzying profits. Marx referred to these people locked out of production altogether as capitalism's "surplus populations." Surplus populations, people who are simply unnecessary from capital's perspective, are a structural feature of capitalist societies.

Those who are unable to work are sometimes able to eke out an existence by relying on waged family members, by accessing constantly receding forms of public assistance, or by stitching together their survival with informal or criminalized work. Often, however, they are shunted into institutions of extreme confinement like prisons, psychiatric facilities, and elder homes, where corporations profit from their existence rather than their labor.

Just as capitalism requires private property, social reproduction, and surplus populations as necessary conditions of its accumulation, it also relies heavily on the state. Even as capitalist ideology insists on a neat division between the economic and the political, in practice, these areas are highly integrated. Even libertarians concede the necessity of a limited state to guarantee capital's continued existence, insisting on a central armed authority that can print money, enforce contracts, and make war. The state thus forms another background condition of capital, setting up the monetary system and deploying its armed repression for those who skirt the laws that govern economic accumulation. Concretely, this has also often meant the creation of many forms of confinement, including highly militarized borders, the policing of resistance, and the construction of an expansive system of prisons.

Taken together, these elements show that capitalism is a kind of society anchored by the logic of accumulation. In Fraser's words, capitalism, rather than a kind of economy, is best conceived as an "institutionalized social order" that inflects every aspect of collective life.[6] A capitalist society is thus one that integrates all of these aspects—property, several forms of labor (waged, unwaged, care), and the state—in an institutionalized social order anchored by the logic of profit. The very distinction between "the economy" and "the political" or "the social" is itself the effect of capitalist society; we must refuse this distinction, seeing the whole breadth of capitalist society as needing revolutionary transformation. If capitalism infects every part of life, surely it anchors the confinements all around us.

Capitalism, Movement, and Confinement

Capitalist society might appear to be uniquely based in movement rather than confinement. For capital to produce a profit, it must be extended out into the realm of circulation, make commodities, pay wages, and eventually return back, hopefully larger than when it first departed the

6 Fraser, *Cannibal Capitalism*, 33.

capitalist's bank account. Capital *circulates*; it *moves* throughout society. The rule of accumulation demands a constant increase in profits, and so it also *grows*. To do so, it often travels far and wide, finding new markets, new consumers, new materials. In *Capital*, volume 2, Marx explains that capital "is a movement, a circulatory process through different stages . . . Hence it can only be grasped as a movement, and not as a static thing."[7] Elsewhere, he writes, "The valorization of value takes places only within this constantly renewed movement. The movement of capital is therefore limitless."[8] Capital is, in the words of Beverley Best and David Harvey, "value in motion."[9] Joshua Clover highlights "the compulsions of capital's self-moving motion," arguing that this is what constitutes "the real movement of social existence" under capitalism.[10] Marxist feminist theorist Cinzia Arruzza describes capitalist societies as "moving totalities."[11]

This idea makes a lot of sense: an individual capital dollar might hopscotch across the world back and forth several times before it returns profit. Whether in the relentless search to accumulate capital or to survive others' attempts to do so, human beings, too, move around the world, more now than ever before; capitalism has produced the most mobile workforce and most transnational production chain in the history of the world. Goods, component pieces, and raw materials are shuttled around on trains, planes, and shipping containers, far from their sites of extraction or production. That I wrote this book on an Apple computer whose parts were manufactured in China, assembled in Texas, made from component pieces from several continents—semiconductors from the UK, tungsten from the Democratic Republic of Congo, glass from Japan, diodes from Germany—illustrates the unprecedented movement of goods and people that underlies even banal activities. And, it seems, every time capital encounters a limit to its ability to accumulate—whether in the form of people who refuse to be exploited, legal limits on accumulation, areas of non-commodified life, or market exhaustion—it attacks those barriers with force. In Nicholas De Genova's words, "Capital has made and relentlessly re-made the world in its own image, and according to its chaotic

---

7 Karl Marx, *Capital: A Critique of Political Economy*, vol. 2, trans. David Fernbach (Penguin Books, 1978), 185.

8 Karl Marx, *Capital: A Critique of Political Economy*, vol. 1, trans. Ben Fowkes, with Ernest Mandel (Penguin Classics, 1992), 253.

9 Beverley Best, *The Automatic Fetish: The Law of Value in Marx's Capital* (Verso, 2024), 110; David Harvey, "Value in Motion," *New Left Review*, no. 126 (December 2020).

10 Joshua Clover, *Riot. Strike. Riot: The New Era of Uprisings* (Verso, 2016), 12.

11 Cinzia Arruzza, "Logic or History?: The Political Stakes of Marxist-Feminist Theory," *Viewpoint Magazine*, June 23, 2015, viewpointmag.com.

requirements—bursting asunder every apparent barrier in the creation of an ever-more unobstructed global arena for profit-making."[12] Capital thus "tear[s] down all the barriers which hem in the development of the forces of production."[13] Capital "is the endless and limitless drive to go beyond its limiting barriers. Every boundary is and has to be a barrier for it. Else it would cease to be capital."[14] Capital sees each limit to production "as a necessity which it constantly tries to violate and beyond which it constantly seeks to go."[15] Movement is so central to capital's operation that Clover contends that, for capital, "the moment of immobility is the moment of crisis."[16] At every level, movement seems central to capital's ability to accumulate.

Capital is the endless expander, the ceaseless motion, the driver of physical movement, and the breaker of barriers. Surely, then, capital*ism*, the form of society anchored in this boundless movement, must be a form of society uniquely committed to movement. But is it?

Sort of. As in the opening scene, movement under capitalism is rarely so simple. Accounts that emphasize capital's movement are not wrong, but they are misleading. They may, in the end, hide just as much as they illuminate.

In addition to capitalism's innate tendencies toward movement, it also cultivates confinement as a central part of its reproduction. Since the dawn of capitalism in the fifteenth and sixteenth centuries, confinement has been a common fate of land and human beings alike. Beyond enclosures, capitalism continued to invent ever-new strategies of confining the global working class. Workhouses and poorhouses mushroomed in the sixteenth century to manage the newly impoverished workers, especially women and children; this phenomenon was so widespread during the time of capitalism's initial rise that Yann Moulier-Boutang refers to it as the "Great Fixation."[17] As waged labor became the norm in Western Europe, women often found themselves confined to the domestic sphere, their care work invisiblized and undercompensated. At the same time, European powers ushered in world-historical creation of race in the modern sense

12 Nicholas De Genova, "A Racial Theory of Labour: Racial Capitalism from Colonial Slavery to Postcolonial Migration," *Historical Materialism* 31, no. 3 (2023): 241.

13 Karl Marx, *Grundrisse: Foundations of the Critique of Political Economy*, trans. Martin Nicolaus (Penguin Classics, 1993), 409.

14 Ibid., 334.

15 Ibid., 345.

16 Clover, *Riot. Strike. Riot*, 137.

17 Yann Moulier Boutang, *De L'esclavage au salariat* (Presses Universitaires de France, 1998), 291–3.

through its use of confinement strategies of colonial capitalism in Middle Passage ships, mines, and large-scale plantations to expropriate the land and labor of African and Amerindian peoples for the benefit of Europe's rising bourgeoisie (and enduring gentry). After the end of de jure slavery, tactics of redlining, segregation, and slum creation instituted new forms of racialized control and accumulation. The rise of the modern nation-state as the default form of political governance included the creation of national borders, which have only become more tightly controlled and heavily militarized as capital grows. In our contemporary moment, police, prisons, and border detention confront so many people as a limitation on their ability to move and to live the lives they desire. So much of capital's rushing movement of goods, people, money, and ideas across the planet is shaped by a consistent structure of confinement, captivity, and restriction. Movement and confinement are two sides of the same coin.

My provocation is that the imbrication of movement and confinement is not unique to the transition from feudalism to capitalism in Europe but rather a central part of how capitalism unfolds, spreads, and reproduces itself. That is, if we looked hard enough at any of capitalism's flows, circulations, or seemingly ceaseless movements, we will find, underneath it, various modes of confinement as their condition of possibility.

The Contours of Confinement

As might already be clear, confinement can come in many forms. In its broadest sense, confinement involves limitations on or barriers to movement, development, growth, or change, or the imposition of forms of control that constrain, contain, or fix in (physical or conceptual) place. Confinement need not always *prevent* movement entirely; confinement can also introduce increased *friction* in the pursuit of movement, by raising the costs of mobility or levying penalties for pursuing it. Confinement may be overt and physical—like being put in a cage—but it may also take less obvious forms: constricting our ability to think or imagine or pursue the lives we desire, restricting possible pathways of social change, and creating social, economic, and political conditions that force us into, in the grand scheme of things, a pretty limited menu of life options.

Confinement is not the mere opposite of movement, though it does sometimes make motion impossible. Movement and confinement are more in a dynamic and evolving relationship with each other rather than in a death match. Often the movement of capital and goods depends on the confinement of human beings. Some people's movement might depend on the confinement of others. Sometimes, techniques of confinement narrow the possibilities of movement, or force the adoption of clandestine, furtive, or insurgent motion as the only avenue of maneuver. Often, movement faces severe punishment and repression, creating barriers or friction to movement rather than complete blockage. Though I see confinement as form of domination, this does not imply that movement is always a natural, unambiguous good. Many communities, especially in Palestine, have fought valiantly to remain in place against an onslaught of dispossession, colonial domination, deportation, gentrification, and dispersion. Those fights to stay, I contend, are often also struggles against confinement.

Across capitalism's history, many groups—the poor, the disabled, the feminized, the racialized, the colonized, the vagrant, the rebellious, the criminal—have faced brutal forms of confinement. But private property is not the prison, and the psychiatric ward is not the colony. These differences are important. In fact, the *differences* in confinement are part of how they work, how they are profitable for capital, and why they are so frequently reproduced. In short, this book looks at the *commonality of a capitalist strategy* of confinement through a *differential analysis* of the multiple logics of confinement produced over the history of capitalism. I trace this across many key institutions of capitalism's history and present: chattel slavery (chapter 1), wage labor (chapter 2), property (chapters 3 and 4), nation-state borders (chapter 5), police (chapter 6), prisons (chapter 7), and the home (chapter 8). In each chapter, I show that confinement enables the free flow of capital accumulation. Taken together, this book shows that technologies of confinement ground capitalist society in nearly all aspects of its existence.

Confinement is both exceedingly common and unequally distributed. Capitalism frequently recycles similar tactics against different groups, across time and space, mutating as it goes. While attending to the specific domination of particular groups ("intersections") is always important, Patricia Hill Collins reminds us that we can also learn a lot about violent systems looking at repeated tactics across contexts of oppression and exploitation, what she calls the "matrix of domination."[18] Identifying these patterns, in addition to the unique factors that make any struggle local and specific, helps us understand both the structures of domination we face and the tactics we might need to overcome them. In this book, which

18 Patricia Hill Collins, *Black Feminist Thought: Knowledge, Consciousness, and the Politics of Empowerment* (Routledge, 2000), 274–5.

looks at many places and times, I treat confinement as one crucial axis inside the matrix of domination that capitalism produces.

This book shows that we can only fully understand capital's laws of motion when we understand the forms of confinement that enable it. At the same time, we can only understand why so many of us confront confinement by seeing the pivotal role capitalism plays. Who and what is able to move, under what conditions, and to whose benefit only becomes visible when we understand movement in dynamic relation with who or what cannot move, the penalties or costs of movement, and the underlying social logic that valorizes some movements and condemns others. The real truth of movement is revealed through the analytic of confinement.

A Typology of Capitalist Confinement: Labor, Land, and Life

Across capitalism's history and present, confinement emerges in three areas: labor, land, and life. These three are interlocking and overlapping, working in and with each other, rather than as rigid separate spheres.

Marx considered labor and land the two "original sources of all wealth."[19] Confinement, I show, is central to *how* capital taps into these original sources of wealth, deploying them toward accumulation. Beyond labor and land, capitalism also channels confinement across many areas of social, political, intimate, and cultural life.

Labor confines and controls the possibility of our lives. At some points in capitalism's history, workers have been directly confined in order to more easily extract their labor, in workhouses, in prisons, in impressed navies and conscripted armies, and in racialized chattel slavery. At other points, confinement has been the punishment for *not* working, sending supposedly "idle" proletarians to prisons, dungeons, chain gangs, and psychiatric hospitals. By confining those who do not or cannot work, people are pushed into, confined into, forms of work and labor they might otherwise refuse. Since those who work for a wage certainly are not truly free to choose whether they work or the conditions of their work, capitalism confines many lives *to* the forced choice between wage labor and starvation. Exploitation is also confining, conscripting workers into accumulating capital (for others) against our will and to our detriment. In nearly every capitalist society, multiple forms of labor confinement coexist, working in and through one another. Sometimes confinement marks particular

19 Marx, *Capital*, vol. 1, 638.

groups of people out for particular kinds of labor exploitation, confining the possibilities of their lives in advance without any choice.

Capitalism's societal reproduction produces forms of social immobility that depend on the illusion of capitalist social *mobility*. Because most of us work to survive, labor constrains our overall life possibilities, including how and when we move or stay. Migration, deportation, family separation, and other forms of confined movement follow the dictates of capital accumulation. Waged workers also experience a general confinement of life possibility that trades on the illusion of freedom; for many, the existence of choice and mobility in certain areas of our working lives (where to work or live, what kind of job to pursue, what to study or train for) masks or hides a deeper form of forced choice between exploitation and death.

Labor confinement has often explicitly aimed at inculcating capitalist values and forms of life into those who had resisted them. These forms of labor confinement facilitated a process that French philosopher Michel Foucault has called "discipline": the control of the global working class that compels not only capitalist labor but capitalist *values* of hard work, individualism, and internalized surveillance.[20] The capitalist doesn't need us just to work but *to want to work, to need to work, to believe that our work is our life, to believe that our lives are only worthy if they are productive to the capitalist, to punish ourselves and others for failing to prioritize work.* In some circumstances, generalized social relations and ideology reproduce these ideas on their own, but the threat of physical confinement often acts as disciplinary backstop.

Capitalism also proceeds through controlling access to land. From Europe's first enclosures through today, access to land mediated by the ability to pay for it. Not only does capitalism restrict access to land, but through the imposition of private property, it imposes economic calculation as the "natural" relationship between humans and the environment. Private property itself functions as a kind of constraint, one that sets a constrictive grammar for how we think about and interact with land and its products; in other words, capitalist private property not only *encloses* land but *forecloses* many other ways we could think about and interact with land beyond the calculation of profit and economic value.

Privatization is only part of the problem. Even public, collective, and state-owned land are captured by capitalist confinement. Under the aegis of both private and public property, access to land under capitalism is

20 Michel Foucault, *Discipline and Punish: The Birth of the Prison*, 2nd edition, trans. Alan Sheridan (Vintage Books, 1995).

always deeply patterned. Land is not, it turns out, equally confined for all. Through land confinement, I show how capitalist land access and use are uneven and unequal, with different rules for different groups of people, whether explicit or implied. Land use and access is at the center of capitalism's intertwining with gender, race, colonial, and national forms of exclusion and subordination, which often involve their own complex web of confinements, physical and social.

Capitalism also takes control of collective social life. The way we meet our basic needs generates modes of being, living, and relating to one another, and these are powerful forces in our lives.[21] Social relations, ideology, culture, identity, and narrative are integral parts of what it actually means to *live* under capitalism. Capitalism influences, mobilizes, and uses these areas of life in complicated ways that cannot be simply derived from the control of land or labor. Social, political, cultural, and ideological life are not direct *outcomes* of the logic of capital, but capital vies for strategic control of these aspects of life. If we only have labor and land, we have an accountant's balance sheet, not an analysis of society and its social relations. The tripartite structure of labor, land, and life allows us to see the interpenetration of the material, ideological, and practical in the constitution of capitalism.

Capitalism suffuses many areas of life with confinement. Capitalism thrives on narrowing our understanding of *a life worth living*, just as much as it constrains the possibilities of life available to pursue. And since capitalism has always been entwined with various forms of oppression, it also produces *a differential valuation of life*. That some lives are seen as worthy of reproduction, protection, and valuation, and others are seen as disposable, violable, and exploitable is a core feature of the necessary hierarchies of capitalist social relations. Capitalism requires carceral social relations, which Genevieve LeBaron and Adrienne Roberts define as "the various ways in which people's current and future life choices and possibilities are being locked into hierarchical and unfree capitalist social relations, and, further, the ways in which the physical and social mobility of certain sectors of the population are being constrained through these

21 In Marx's words, "The production of life, both of one's own in labour and of fresh life in procreation, now appears as a double relationship: on the one hand as a natural, on the other as a social relationship. By social we understand the co-operation of several individuals, no matter under what conditions, in what manner and to what end. It follows from this that a certain mode of production, or industrial stage, is always combined with a certain mode of co-operation, or social stage, and this mode of co-operation is itself a 'productive force.'" Karl Marx and Friedrich Engels, *The German Ideology* (International Publishers, 1967), 17.

relations."[22] Of course, labor and land are part of how these unfree social relations are created, organized, maintained, and reproduced over time. But the character of an unfree and unequal social realm is not exhausted by them.

Since capitalism's inevitable outcome is that many toil while the few relax, that some starve even while we overproduce food, that many go without homes while apartments lie empty, that some are left to die of illnesses others cure with little effort, that some are confined to cages while others traipse across the globe with ease—all of this must be justified somehow. These justifications are rooted in the idea that some lives are more valuable than others, that some people deserve to live more than others, and that their lives deserve more choice, more comfort, and more consideration than others. The idea that many lives are expendable justifies many forms of confinement, limiting the physical and social mobility of so many people across time and space. It forecloses possibilities of life for so many and erects boundaries around the trajectories of the plausible and the imaginable. If your chances of going to university or to prison are easily predicted by your postal code, that is a form of confinement.

Capitalism has always marked out some people for different access, treatment, and violence from others. Gender, race, sexuality, ability, incarceration status, national origin, immigration status, and many other markers construct capitalism's differential distribution of life chances, responsibilities, and the (in)ability to move. In a very real way, *which* groups you belong to constrains *what you can do* and *who you can become*. These patterns of access and exposure come together to create a social anti-mobility that constricts the *kind of life* available from the outset on the basis of a series of imposed (and sometimes chosen) identities. For reasons I explained extensively in my previous book, *Marxism and Intersectionality*, this differential valuation of life is central to the reproduction of capitalist society.[23] In other words, we can see a combined and uneven development of capitalism's forms of subjectivity or forms of life.

The flip side of capitalism's enclosure of life is its ghoulish distribution of death. For many, *life itself* has become a privilege. Especially in our times of climate catastrophe, settler colonial genocide, and medical apartheid, it is clearer perhaps than ever that capitalism functions by allowing

22 Genevieve LeBaron and Adrienne Roberts, "Toward a Feminist Political Economy of Capitalism and Carcerality," *Signs: Journal of Women in Culture and Society* 36, no. 1 (2010): 1.

23 Ashley J. Bohrer, *Marxism and Intersectionality: Race, Gender, Class and Sexuality Under Contemporary Capitalism* (Transcript Verlag, 2019).

some to live and exposing many more to death, disease, and destruction. Capital's enclosure of life works in and through policing the boundaries between those who deserve to live and those whom capital can simply abandon. It is thus *both* that capitalism polices the boundaries of who is able to live *and* controls and confines *what kind of life* is available to those who survive. As Gary Fields puts it, drawing on the words of Reviel Netz:

> In the end, mobility and the prevention of movement are themes in a story about power and unequal rights in a world overlaid with lines of control where human beings confront friction. There are those with rights of free passage across such lines and through space; and there are those of less fortune, unable to circulate freely and access spaces beyond lines of control as a result of power imposed upon them, power often involving "bodily violence and the infliction of pain."[24]

The confinement of life erodes the range of choices we have available, but even those of us with relatively many choices are also constrained by capitalist social relations. We cannot equate relative ease or mobility under a regime of confinement with life beyond confinement. No one can be truly free under conditions of structural domination. Capitalist logic and confinement infect even those who secure relative advantages in it, and thus everyone has something to gain from organizing to destroy capitalist relations of confinement, even as the harms of capitalism's inequality and unfreedom are differentially distributed, unequally felt, and divergently positioned.

What's more, capitalism infects our capacity for imagining alternatives, making it seem as if this system, with all of its cruelties, is the only way—perhaps even the best possible way—to organize collective life. Capitalism's commitment to its own reproduction enacts a confinement of the imaginary, foreclosing many possible futures, often punishing and incarcerating people who attempt to shine a light on how we might organize society to the benefit of all. The imperative that the future look exactly like the present, that it follow the same rules and dictates, that it favor the class of owners against the rest of us, forecloses so many social, political, and economic possibilities. The late cultural critic Fredric Jameson once wrote, "It is easier to imagine the end of the world than to imagine the end of capitalism."[25] The closure of political possibility and

24 Gary Fields, "Lockdown: Gaza Through a Camera Lens and Historical Mirror," *Journal of Palestine Studies* 49, no. 3 (2020): 44.

25 Fredric Jameson, "Future City," *New Left Review*, no. 21 (May/June 2003).

political imagination is part of capitalism's constitution, part of the way it confines even without walls and bars.

Only by seeing how fully capital penetrates every aspect of social life can we truly understand how important abolishing capitalism is. If capitalism were merely an economic issue, we could mobilize, change, and abolish one set of institutions—an important and recalcitrant set of institutions but still only one among many. By seeing capitalism's capture of social life, desire, identity, and ideas, we can see just how much would have to change to abolish capitalism. If we see capitalism only where profit logics are obvious and direct, we will overlook the many deep, complicated, surprising, and clandestine chains that bind a society to the logic of accumulation. We risk underplaying how bad capitalism really is and how much work we really have to do.

Tracing confinement across the spheres of labor, land, and life thus illuminates many aspects of capitalist society that may remain hidden if we overly emphasize movement. Any individual practice or institution of confinement can and often does operate on more than one sphere. These groupings are thus heuristic and provisional, as each term weaves in and through the forms of confinement I analyze. Taken together, this book shows that across many times, spaces, and scales, confinement emerges as a fecund field of investigation for capitalist modernity, one that adds needed clarity and context to capitalism's frequent movement.

This book does not attempt to detail every mode of confinement deployed by capitalism across time and space; there are simply too many connections for one book to cover. I hope that by focusing on some cases, this book opens the door to thinking about many more. Through these investigations, I hope readers become newly attentive to seeing capitalism as a system rooted in confinement generally. I believe the question "Who or what is being confined here?" can emerge as kind of a heuristic to guide both our investigations into capitalism and our resistance to it.

The Abolition of Capitalism

If capitalism and confinement are intertwined, then anti-capitalist analysis and activism must be invested in opposing confinement. For centuries, the most developed grammar of anti-confinement politics has been *abolition*.

If Marxism has disclosed the shape of anti-capitalism, abolition gives us the grammar of anti-confinement politics. If capitalism and confinement are intertwined so as to be suffused, one may not be abolished without the other. We need both Marxism and abolitionism to ground us in theory, orient us in struggle, and help us imagine a liberated world.

"Abolition" as a named political orientation emerged with anti-slavery activists in the Atlantic World. Against milquetoast policies of reform that were much more in vogue, abolitionists demanded nothing less than an end to the evil (and we will see, uniquely capitalist) institution. Small changes, incremental wins, and petty concessions could not be accepted in the face of horrors so great as chattel slavery. They were right to insist, against the tide, on full emancipation. Of course, as we know, while the institution of slavery was abolished through the brave work and fearless organizing of many, especially of enslaved people themselves, the full dream of liberated humanity remains to be realized.

The book begins with an analysis of racialized chattel slavery as one of rising capitalism's banner institutions and as a testament to the ongoing necessity of abolition as a political framework to orient us in thought and in struggle. This book also traces how some of the ways people have tried to overcome capitalism have, sometimes despite themselves, often fallen short of the abolitionist horizon. Time and again, we have failed to fully extirpate capitalism, often, I show, because in one way or another, our solutions have mirrored rather than eliminated forms of confinement. This pattern, too, was set in racialized chattel slavery, where the abolitionist dream of a truly free world remained, in the words of Langston Hughes, "a dream deferred." Looking at capitalism's imbrication with confinement reveals the necessity of testing our proposed solutions for their abolitionist ethos. This book offers both a theory of what we must fight and an orientation for figuring out what it would mean to win.

Many struggles have taken up abolitionism's clarion call. In our own times, calls to abolish prisons, police, and borders boom from every corner of our confined world. At its root, abolition as a philosophy demands the elimination of confinement, recognizing that in order to really liberate the world, mere reforms will never succeed.

The tradition of abolition encompasses two important features I highlight over the course of this text. In the first place, abolitionist politics have a particular content: they are politics oriented toward the breaking of walls, barriers, and confinements of whatever kind, physical and social. From prison abolition to border abolition, we use the idea of abolition most often in the context of struggles against the very kinds of confinement at issue in this book.

Moreover, abolition not only names a set of desired social transformations, but also an orientation toward political praxis that refuses reformist compromises. While abolitionists sometimes accept what André Gorz and others have called "non-reformist reforms," ultimately abolitionist politics have a total and revolutionary horizon—they are committed to the emancipation of *all*, and they would not be abolitionist without this horizon. Abolitionist politics aim simultaneously at specific institutions of confinement *and* demand holistic changes in societies that would eliminate the tendencies to police, incarcerate, cage, and confine *in general*. As a kind of political ethic, abolition names a refusal to accept any arrangement that purchases some people's freedom with others' domination.[26]

Abolition has its own anti-capitalist history. Since Marx and Engels's publication of *The Communist Manifesto*, abolition has been a central demand of anti-capitalist thought and organizing. In that piece, Marx and Engels declare that "the theory of the Communists may be summed up in the single sentence: abolition of private property."[27] To prevent capital from accumulating across generations, instituting the confining social immobility of capitalist social life, they demand we also secure the "abolition of all right of inheritance."[28] In *The German Ideology*, they notoriously demand that care and social reproduction work be completely reorganized as well, noting that it is "self-evident" that the abolition of capitalism "is inseparable from the abolition of the family."[29]

While some have argued that these forms of abolition constitute two different "traditions of abolitionist thinking," Marx and Engels were deeply influenced by the abolitionist struggle against slavery.[30] Lurking

26 Thanks very much to Joy Wang for conversations and feedback around this distinction.

27 Karl Marx and Friedrich Engels, *The Communist Manifesto* (Pluto Press, 2017), 72.

28 Ibid., 83.

29 Karl Marx and Friedrich Engels, *The German Ideology* (International Publishers, 1967), 50.

30 M. E. O'Brien, *Family Abolition: Capitalism and the Communizing of Care* (Pluto Press, 2023), 54. The first use of the term "abolition" in reference to slavery emerges in 1788, a full sixty years before the *Manifesto*'s publication. Marx, who was opposed to slavery throughout his intellectual career, could hardly have been ignorant of this usage. Most of the writing on Marx and abolition, for example Sophie Lewis's, focuses on the German term *aufhebung* (which is translated into English as "abolition" in these texts, but in the larger philosophical canon may also be translated as "positive supercession" or "sublation") and on the way Marx inherits this philosophical term from G. W. F. Hegel. But as Susan Buck-Morss, Nick Nesbitt, and others have shown, Hegel's own thinking on questions of slavery, history, recognition, and right—all key areas through which he develops the concept of *aufhebung*—was deeply influenced by the global movement to abolish slavery in general and by the Haitian Revolution in particular. As O'Brien comments, "The Hegelian notion of abolition may also owe much to the Black radical struggle in the Americas" (O'Brien, *Family Abolition*, 57). Curiously, though, despite this

perhaps in the adoption of the term "abolition" is a latent recognition that the struggle against capitalism must be simultaneously a struggle against confinement in all its forms, a total abolition of the world as it presently exists. This book attempts to make good on this recognition, and to explore what it would mean to place abolition at the center of anti-capitalist theory and resistance.

To do so, I use Marxist and abolitionist ideas to examine many of capitalism's foundational institutions from the perspective of confinement. Bringing these ideas together shows that to abolish capitalism, we need to abolish enslavement, exploitation, property, the family, borders, police, and prisons. Abolition and Marxism also come together to give us glimpses into what this project would require of us in social movements for justice and liberation. In Ruth Wilson Gilmore's words, abolition "is not the absence of something but the presence of something."[31] Abolition requires we "change one thing: everything."[32]

Since these institutions are interconnected, we cannot abolish any one of them in isolation. The condition of real abolition, one that would not leave forms of unfreedom intact or merely altered, is the abolition of the entire kind of society that the term "capitalism" describes. As Fred Moten and Stefano Harney write:

> What is, so to speak, the object of abolition? Not so much the abolition of prisons but the abolition of a society that could have prisons, that could have slavery, that could have the wage, and therefore not abolition as the elimination of anything but abolition as the founding of a new society.[33]

---

insight, she does not discuss this link on the pages that directly discuss Marx's concept of abolition, where she talks extensively about how the term operates in Hegel's work and seems to position the anti-slavery and the Marxist traditions as two separate trajectories. On the etymology of "abolition" in the context of slavery see: "Abolition," Online Etymology Dictionary, accessed February 24, 2025, etymonline.com. For O'Brien's and Lewis's accounts of the *aufhebung*-abolition connection see Sophie Lewis, *Abolish the Family: A Manifesto for Care and Liberation* (Verso, 2022), 46–8. On the influence of slavery and Haiti on Hegel's thought see: Susan Buck-Morss, *Hegel, Haiti, and Universal History*, 1st edition (University of Pittsburgh Press, 2009); Nick Nesbitt, "Troping Toussaint, Reading Revolution," *Research in African Literatures* 35, no. 2 (2004): 18–33.

31 Ruth Wilson Gilmore, "Abolition Feminism," in *Revolutionary Feminisms: Conversations on Collective Action and Radical Thought*, eds. Brenna Bhandar and Rafeef Ziadah (Verso, 2020), 170.

32 Ruth Wilson Gilmore, "Foreword," in *The Jail Is Everywhere: Fighting the New Geography of Mass Incarceration*, eds. Jack Norton et al. (Verso, 2024), xi.

33 Stefano Harney and Fred Moten, *The Undercommons: Fugitive Planning and Black Study* (Autonomedia, 2013), 42.

To move toward this new society, we need an analysis of how confinement and capitalism work in and through each other, historically and in our own time. It is only by understanding the full scope of the problems we face that we have any hope of truly abolishing the complicated society of domination in which we all live.

From Capitalism and Confinement to Abolition Communism

By seeing confinement as a differential but generalized condition, I hope to widen the scope of what we see as "capitalist" society. Understanding capitalism in the expanded way I propose allows us to see many more aspects of contemporary life under capitalism *as capitalist*, even when they diverge from the economy, exploitation, or labor. Seeing unwaged labor, social reproduction, colonization, care, prisons, and other phenomena as part and parcel of capitalist society is urgent, especially as social movements for liberation increasingly target these institutions. Beginning from confinement's centrality allows us to see struggles against prisons, police, borders, gendered oppression, slavery, and other forms of domination as already anti-capitalist demands, even when they use a different kind of vernacular. Placing these struggles at the center of anti-capitalism opens new avenues of connection—what Angela Davis has called "the intersectionality of struggles"—and can facilitate a much-needed cross-pollination of resources, ideas, and strategies into a broad united front for liberation.

I hope it also shifts how we imagine whom capitalism dominates and where resistance might emerge. Not only factory workers but also enslaved people, caregivers, incarcerated people, and disabled people inhabit the pluralized center of capitalist harm and anti-capitalist resistance. Wage workers, prisoners, and caregivers are all enveloped by capitalist social relations; they all equally (but differently) respond to the dictates of capitalist accumulation. No single position can tell us everything we need to know about capitalism, just as no one institution could. By multiplying the starting points of anti-capitalist critique, a clearer and more nuanced view of capitalism emerges. We need such a view for both critique and for struggle.

My intervention is twofold: I show that confined subjects are more central to capitalism than is often supposed *and* that capitalism's "free" subjects are more confined than is often assumed. Doing so uncovers the possibilities of an abolitionist, anti-capitalist theory and practice. By simultaneously holding on to the differences across forms of confinement *and* exploring the *connections* between them, we bring the often overlooked features of capitalism into view and deepen our understanding of capitalism's most studied features.

As we theorize, analyze, and organize toward a more just and freer world, attention to the imbrication of capitalism and confinement can reorient us in new and important ways. As a heuristic device, the question of confinement can also help us test out the viability of our solutions. Does this vision, this proposal, this reform, this model of leadership combat or reinforce anti-capitalism as a struggle against confinement? Politically, I hope this project can help us reframe many of our movements in terms that are productive of transnational solidarity and intensive introspection as equally important elements of revolutionary politics.

Lastly, exploring the imbrication of confinement and capitalism illuminates urgent linkages between abolition and anti-capitalism as liberatory philosophies. Capitalism is a central part of the confinements so many people experience across the globe—and thus, abolishing these confinements will require dismantling capitalism. I hope this book contributes to the beautiful and growing literature that places anti-capitalism at the center of abolitionist thought and practice. The more we see capitalism and confinement as intertwined, the clearer it becomes that we cannot tear down walls without abolishing the entire capitalist society that built our confined world. By exploring how capitalism and confinement are brutal twin pillars of domination, I think we clear the ground for considering abolition and communism to be two joint beacons of light guiding our struggles.

When we are fighting for the overthrow of capitalism, we are fighting not only for the material conditions for freedom—non-proprietary and non-extractive relationships to land, non-exploitative and non-alienated relationships to individual and collective effort—but also for freedom itself, to live in a world wherein life chances are both open and equally open to all. To achieve that vision and to build that world, we need a clearer understanding of the restrictions, confinements, and enclosures that structure the current one.

1

Capitalism's Slavery

Direct slavery is the pivot of bourgeois industry just as machinery, credits, etc. Without slavery you have no cotton; without cotton you cannot have modern industry. It is slavery that has given the colonies their value; it is the colonies that have created world trade, and it is world trade that is the pre-condition of large-scale industry. Thus slavery is an economic category of the greatest importance.

—Karl Marx[1]

The slave is the object or the ground that makes possible the existence of the bourgeois subject and, by negation or contradistinction, defines liberty, citizenship, and the enclosures of the social body.

—Saidiya Hartman[2]

Over the course of a few centuries, 12 million Africans were captured and sold into slavery by European powers; 2 million perished before reaching the Western Hemisphere on the notorious Middle Passage, an accumulation of death at the time rivaled only by the campaign of extermination undertaken against Indigenous peoples in the Americas. Every year after 1570, more enslaved Africans arrived in the Spanish colonies than colonists. Slavery grew rapidly and exponentially. While 3,000 human beings a year were sold to Spanish America between 1550 and 1650, by the early eighteenth century, the English and French colonies were buying

1 Karl Marx, *The Poverty of Philosophy: A Reply to M. Proudhon's Philosophy of Poverty*, trans. H. Quelch (Charles H. Kerr & Company, 1920), 121. Translation modified.

2 Saidiya V. Hartman, *Scenes of Subjection: Terror, Slavery, and Self-Making in Nineteenth-Century America*, 1st edition (Oxford University Press, 1997), 62. Emphasis mine.

30,000 to 40,000 human captives annually, a figure that, by the turn of the next century, frequently topped 100,000. Transatlantic chattel slavery constituted the largest movement of human beings in world history. In Toni Morrison's words:

> The overweening, defining event of the modern world is the mass movement of raced populations, beginning with the largest forced transfer of people in the history of the world: slavery. The consequences of which transfer have determined all the wars following it as well as the current ones being waged on every continent.[3]

It may be tempting to read this history as a unique investment in movement. This would be a mistake. While human beings were certainly moved across the world, every step of transatlantic chattel slavery involved confinement of the most extreme varieties. The entire process of capture abounded with terrifying and sadistically varied methods of immobilization—intimidation, kidnapping, beatings, iron chains, physical restraints, coffles, barracoons—and this was just on the African continent. After the moment of capture, an interminable period of confined waiting, some in holding prisons like Elmina Castle, some sitting on the very ships that would inaugurate terrifyingly novel forms of confinement. Enslaved people were branded with hot irons on their sides and chests to communicate their condition of bondage was permanent, a physical mark that could return them to confinement should they ever manage escape. The Middle Passage, a confinement so brutal it killed one out of every six forced into it, was a prison with sails. Human beings were chained into hold for weeks and months at a time, packed side by side, unable to move even to defecate or vomit. Women and girls were occasionally removed from the hold and subjected to sexual violation, its own form of confinement that would mark slavery as an extreme form of sexualized discipline. After months of prolonged torture, docking in the Western Hemisphere brought no relief. Here, enslaved people would find the plantation and its myriad confinements, physical, social, racial. The Slave Codes that legalized this routinized brutality prioritized the regulation of movement: enslaved people could not leave plantations without permission, and the possibility of flight consumed the planter class to the point of near hysteria. Physical restraint in chains, in stocks, or on treadmills were commonplace. That enslaved people were fixed in

3 Toni Morrison, "Home," in *The House That Race Built: Black Americans, US Terrain*, eds. Wahneema Lubiano and Arnold Rampersad (Pantheon, 1997), 10.

place while their kin and loved ones were sold away was one of the most torturous implications of widespread confinement. Enslavement was, in Louis Althusser's words, "captivity without the possibility of flight."[4] Hortense Spillers emphasizes how this confinement constituted "a *theft of the body*—a willful and violent (and unimaginable from this distance) severing of the captive body from its motive will, its active desire."[5] This separation of body from will was a uniquely painful form of confinement.

In short, enslavement constituted "a cartography of boundaries that [enslaved people] were forbidden to transgress."[6] Any possible movement is best thought of as a "punitive mobility."[7] An entire infrastructure, legal, economic, and carceral, concreted to ensure the impossibility of transcending the enslaved condition. Legalized gangs of slave catchers emerged to enforce this confinement, ultimately birthing modern police forces, a consequence that continues to affect us all. If, against all odds, enslaved people found a way to cross boundaries and seize their freedom to move, they lived under constant threat of recapture. The regime of confinement was so severe that one slaveholder hysterically warned that even the sight of birds flying in the sky stimulated freedom dreams too radical to abide.[8]

It might also be tempting to read this history as a sadistic premodern holdover of a world that capitalism swept away. Isn't, after all, wage labor the very defining quality of capitalism? Whatever the grotesque horrors capitalism has wrought upon us all, surely we must all be able to agree that chattel slavery, the antithesis of free labor, was not one of them? Might we not count the abolition of slavery as capitalism's virtue—perhaps its only one?

This proposition does not survive much scrutiny. Racialized chattel slavery was central to the rise and expansion of capitalism and to many of the categories, like the commodity, that anchor capitalism's logic. Karl Marx opens *Capital,* his magnum opus, with the question of the commodity: "The wealth of societies in which the capitalist mode of production prevails appears as 'an immense collection of commodities'; the individual

4 Louis Althusser, *The Spectre of Hegel*, trans. G. M. Goshgarian (Verso, 1997), 25.

5 Hortense Spillers, "Mama's Baby, Papa's Maybe: An American Grammar Book," *Diacritics* 17, no. 2 (1987): 67.

6 Fields, "Lockdown: Gaza Through a Camera Lens and Historical Mirror," 46.

7 Florence Bernault, "The Politics of Enclosure in Colonial and Postcolonial Africa," in *A History of Prison and Confinement in Africa*, ed. Florence Bernault, trans. Janet Roitman (Heinemann, 2003), 6.

8 Walter Johnson, *River of Dark Dreams: Slavery and Empire in the Cotton Kingdom* (Harvard University Press, 2013), 209.

commodity appears as its elementary form."[9] Marx goes on to describe many commodities—iron, paper, reams of linen, coats, and so many "useful things"—that capitalism has transformed into sources of profit. He uses the commodity, a useful object produced with the explicit goal of making a profit, as the inroad to explain the whole of capitalist society, its anchoring logic, its history, and the misery it produces. But what if Marx had begun his inquiry with a very different kind of commodity, human beings treated as chattel, bought and sold for the very same rapacious profit that occupied his intellectual life for half a century? If capitalism deploys confinement across sites in the process of accumulation, if it organizes a spectrum of direct to indirect violence to produce profit, if it combines exploitation with oppression to stabilize a complex social order of reproduction, then chattel slavery might be more capitalist than often supposed.

Beginning from confinement, racialized chattel emerges in a new light: as the innovation of a specifically capitalist form of slavery, one that was constitutively and qualitatively different from every form of slavery that had come before it.

Racialized Chattel Slavery

Many societies have held human beings captive, but racialized chattel slavery was a slavery like no other. Like so many other forms of confinement, capitalism encountered slavery and constitutively transformed the institution into something nearly unrecognizable from its earlier forms. While all slavery involves confinement, racialized chattel slavery was a distinctly capitalist institution, subordinated to the rapacious search for profit, oriented toward commodity production. As Eric Wiliams shows, the gradual waning of chattel slavery over the course of the nineteenth century was due to capital's changing needs, not capitalism's incompatibility with slavery.

All slavery includes forced labor, but racialized chattel slavery was much more than a labor regime. There are, of course, many forms of forced labor in the world, both historical and present. In premodern times, people were enslaved as spoils of war, collateral for debts, or punishment for crimes. In the rising centuries of capitalism, forced labor was nearly ubiquitous, and not at all unique to enslaved people. Europeans

9 Marx, *Capital*, vol. 1, 125.

faced forced labor in the forms of serfdom, impressment, indentured servitude, and the workhouse. European colonizers instituted a wide variety of forced-work requirements as part of capital's global spread—the *encomienda*, the *mita*, the *corvée*, *prestations de travail*, the *chibalo*, and others.

Lest we think capitalism washed compulsory or uncompensated labor away, many of these practices outlasted the formal abolition of racialized chattel slavery and some continue in the present day. Forced labor in the British colonies in West Africa was not overturned until 1920 (and was conserved after that date for "political" labor). Across the French Empire, *prestations de travail* were de rigeur, forcing Indigenous peoples to work on public-works projects (roads, dams, railways), as well as in agriculture; this practice was not repealed until 1946. As Babacar Fall and Richard L. Roberts detail:

> Forced labour in twentieth-century Africa was a widespread means of building and maintaining infrastructure, supporting the mining sector and developing and servicing the export-oriented agricultural sector in French, German, Belgian, Portuguese, Italian and Spanish colonies, and, to a lesser degree, in the British colonies, where public labour ordinances, compulsory labour ordinances and communal labour ordinances served similar goals.[10]

Forced labor was a central aspect of Portuguese domination in colonized Angola, a practice only outlawed in the 1960s. In India, the abolition of slavery gave rise to a grueling system of forced and indentured labor, in which millions of Indians were transported to colonies across Africa, Asia, and the Americas, often to the very plantations at the center of the slave economy; within Indian borders, modern forms of forced labor were only addressed by the Bonded Labour System Act of 1976. Newly emancipated proletarians in the Americas often found themselves locked out of the wage market, pushed into coercive structures of sharecropping, indenture, public works, and imprisonment (where labor was a ubiquitous requirement). In many cases, the abolition of slavery meant, from a labor perspective, being caught up into slightly different forms of confined labor, often on the very same plantations of the pre-abolition period—far from the vision of the triumph of free labor over enslavement. Mauritania

10 Babacar Fall and Richard L. Roberts, "Forced Labor," in *General Labour History of Africa: Workers, Employers and Governments, 20th–21st Centuries*, eds. Stefano Bellucci and Andreas Eckert (Boydell & Brewer, 2019), 78.

was the last country to officially outlaw slavery, in 1981. Coerced labor continues to structure the lives of tens of millions of people, even at the height of global capitalist development and conditions of "real subsumption." Notoriously, the United States retained an exception clause to the Thirteenth Amendment that preserves the possibility of using slavery as punishment for a crime. The fact that slavery continues in some of the most profitable global industries should alone be enough to dispel any notion that it represents a "precapitalist" mode of production inimical to fully developed capitalism. Global estimates of so-called modern slavery vary (and some contain methodological issues that cast doubt on their specific estimates), but it is undeniable that unfree labor persists in mining, manufacturing, agriculture, domestic work, construction, and a variety of criminalized industries, including smuggling and sex work.[11] Forced labor thus continues under capitalism in many forms, even though racialized chattel slavery does not.

Unfortunately, in analyses of capitalism, racialized chattel slavery is too often simply equated with forced labor *in general.* As just one example, Nicholas De Genova defines racialized chattel slavery as "the reduction of human beings . . . into labour and nothing but labour."[12] In accounts like this, one gets the impression that slavery was a mere labor status, one thankfully abolished in the nineteenth century.

But racialized chattel slavery was not forced labor like any other. Scholars agree that it resembled no other form of forced labor seen before or since. It was, as we shall see, precisely in its *differences* from other forms of forced labor that racialized chattel slavery anchored a nascent capitalist world system and continues to set the coordinates for contemporary social relations. Any account of chattel slavery that reduces it to unfree labor will be unable to grasp the true character of the relationship between slavery and capitalism, between capitalism and race, and between confinement and capital.

So what distinguished racialized chattel slavery from other forms of forced labor? It was lifelong rather than time bound, it was hereditary rather than situational, it entailed the total elimination (rather than reduction) of rights, and it was (often) immutable. But most importantly, it was racialized, meaning that it inaugurated an entire, durable *social status* of inferiority that applied in every sphere of social, political, economic, intimate, and personal life, one that oppressed *all people of African descent,*

11 International Labour Organization et al., *Global Estimates of Modern Slavery: Forced Labour and Forced Marriage* (ILO Publications, 2022), 1–144, cdn.walkfree.org.

12 De Genova, "A Racial Theory of Labour," 219.

whether or not they were enslaved. It also subjected enslaved people not only to the despotic power of an individual slaver but to the whims of *all white people* generally (whether they participated directly in slavery or not). The racial grammar that chattel slavery inaugurated was unlike any other form of social domination, partially because of this generalized, hereditary, immutable status that transcended the formal relation; jailers had power over the debtors under their charge for their term of incarceration, but no generalized class of jailers could arrest, harass, whip, detain, or murder any current or former debtor (and their family) for the entirety of their lives. The social relations of slavery were thus extremely unique in contrast to other forms of forced or unfree labor.

It was this uniqueness, invented at the same time as capitalism itself, that made it so profitable. Transatlantic chattel slavery was a uniquely capitalist social form because it was oriented to the accumulation of profit at every turn, subordinating enslaved people's life and death to the cold, calculating pursuit of accumulation. To do so, racialized chattel slavery treated enslaved people as a unique combination of commodity, worker, and capital.[13] Chattel slavery was capitalist because of this specific

13 This account differs from every other account of slavery and capitalism in the Marxist canon, each of which has its own issues. On the one hand, there is the patent dismissal of slavery as capitalist, on the assumption that wage labor is the only truly capitalist form of labor (Robert Brenner, Ellen Meiksins Wood). A more nuanced version of this position is that while slavery was historically important to the concretion of capital (as primitive accumulation), or that it was integrated into the capitalist world market, it was not itself a capitalist form of labor (Nick Nesbitt, Dale Tomich, Charlie Post). From a completely different perspective, some scholars emphasize how the different position of worker and slave, especially the white worker's power over enslaved people, means that slavery cannot be captured by the analytic of capitalism (Frank Wilderson, Sidney Mintz). For reasons that will become clear, these positions fundamentally misrecognize what capitalism is and how it functions, cementing wage labor as the univocal model of capitalist labor. But the problems perhaps only compound if we look at the other side of the scholarly debate, in which capitalism and slavery are intertwined. Several of these accounts (Jairus Banaji, Immanuel Wallerstein, Edward E. Baptist, New History of Capitalism scholars like Sven Beckert) *also* misrecognize what capitalism is, seeing it merely as the development of markets or trade or industrialization; these accounts mostly prove that transatlantic chattel slavery was integrated into global trade or that it was profitable, which is a related but not entirely helpful claim. John Garrigus and Trevor Burnard represent another trend, which focuses on the extent to which enslavement followed an *industrial* rather than distinctly capitalist trajectory—often conflating these two in extremely confusing ways. Others emphasize the way that the historical invention of *race* was necessary to capitalism and that slavery was the means of this invention (Cedric Robinson, David Roediger, Theodore Allen), an elucidating claim that, as I discuss below, moves in the right direction, but ultimately underestimates the relationship between slavery and capitalism. Others highlight how enslavement was a historically necessary realm of noncapitalism on which capitalism was parasitically dependent (Rosa Luxemburg and other "ongoing primitive accumulation" theorists);

and unprecedented capital-oriented position to which enslaved people were confined. Commodification, super-exploitation, and capitalization together anchored slavery's world-historical confinement toward the reproduction and expansion of capitalist accumulation.

Commodification: Many have remarked that enslavement treated human beings as objects, instituting social relations of dehumanization rather than mere inequality. In his classic *Discourse on Colonialism,* Aimé Césaire describes this phenomenon as "thingification."[14] "Among the other violences," Ian Baucom reminds us, slavery involved "the violence of becoming a 'type': a type of person, or, terribly, not even that, a type of nonperson, a type of property, a type of commodity, a type of money."[15]

Racialized chattel slavery treated enslaved people not only as inhuman but specifically as *commodities.* As Marx explains, a commodity is not simply any kind of property; it is a distinctive form of property that is produced to be sold for a profit, for accumulation. For workers who sell their own labor on the market, capitalism commodifies their labor power; but enslavement commodifies *life itself.* When employing a worker is no longer profitable, they are fired, forced to find another way to make ends meet; when capitalist slavers fear a financial loss, they commit mass murder.

Let us explore just one example of this grotesque history. In August 1781, a ship departed from Cape Coast Castle in present-day Ghana. Originally a Dutch vessel, the ship was under new ownership, a syndicate of Liverpool businessmen, after it was captured in the Anglo-Dutch War. The ship sailed under the name *Zong,* a transformation of its original Dutch name *Zorg* (meaning "care"), and though it brandished a new flag, it contained the same cargo it always had: human captives destined for European plantation colonies in the Western Hemisphere. Three months into the sickening journey, the floating prison encountered new peril: navigational incompetence had extended the journey so long that not enough water remained to sustain the 442 enslaved people and seventeen crew on board. With their destination of Jamaica nearly two weeks away and fewer than four days' water, the crew decided to throw fifty-four enslaved women and children into the sea. Their reasoning? The human cargo was

---

this position combines the normally opposed assertions that slavery is both, strictly speaking, noncapitalist *and* necessary to capitalism. While there is deep insight in each account, I find each of these positions to contain their own flaws.

14 Aimé Césaire, *Discourse on Colonialism* (Monthly Review Press, 1973), 42.

15 Ian Baucom, *Specters of the Atlantic: Finance Capital, Slavery, and the Philosophy of History* (Duke University Press, 2005), 11.

insured at thirty pounds per head and so there was no "real loss." Over the next several days, 132 enslaved people would be jettisoned into the ocean, abandoned to drown; ten leapt into the water in acts of defiance. The ship's owner filed an insurance claim on the 142 lost lives, which he considered cargo, and attempted to recoup his loss. The subsequent court case litigated whether the insurers indeed had to pay up, but what both insurance company and slavers agreed on was that the massacred human beings were simple cargo, mere investment. From the perspective of the courts and capital, the human beings were commodities.

To say that enslaved people were commodified means that their treatment and legal status followed the logic of accumulation. Whether enslaved people were allowed to live or die depended on whether their survival would be profitable. As C. L. R. James details, the massacre on the *Zong* was not an isolated incident; throughout the regime of chattel slavery, many enslaved people were simply murdered if, "held up by calms or adverse winds," their deaths became more profitable than their lives.[16] On the plantation, market conditions dictated whether the next generation of enslaved people would be secured through sales or mass rape.[17] The capitalist commodification of enslaved life meant that market mechanisms and the rapacious search for profit dictated life and death—and the conditions of that life or death. Enslaved people were treated not only as objects or property generally but as commodities in particular, as property produced for the sole purpose of return on investment. As soon as their lives were seen as "surplus," they were summarily extinguished. Their lives were confined to the market in the direst way imaginable. All of this differed greatly from other forms of slavery throughout history and from other forms of forced labor during the same time period.

It took an entire industry to produce human beings *as commodities*. Slavers and banks extended capital at many points in the macabre industry, which promised a massive return on investment. The industry of "slave production" employed a wide variety of death-producing workers (slave catchers, ship captains, shackle producers, overseers) and machinery (ships, prisons, chains, spades, cotton gins) in order to produce this commodity. Producing human beings as commodities also required new *legal*, *social*, and *political* structures, most notably white supremacy, as integral parts in the "production process" of people as "slaves." The industry was thus also the real work of many lawyers, judges, legislators,

16 C. L. R. James, *The Black Jacobins: Toussaint L'Ouverture and the San Domingo Revolution*, 2nd edition (Vintage, 1989), 8.

17 Ibid., 14.

and writers. Capital transmogrified human beings into not *things* or *property*, but *commodities*—part of what made transatlantic chattel slavery distinctly *capitalist*.

Super-exploitation: Slavers also treated enslaved people *as workers*, to produce further commodities. The plantation's raison d'être was the production of saleable commodities. The orientation toward commodity production significantly differentiated racialized chattel slavery from other forms of forced labor. As all workers under capitalism, enslaved people produced commodities they could not control for a boss who reaped all the rewards. As workers, then, enslaved people were certainly exploited in the ordinary Marxist sense, though their exploitation was so severe that it may be more accurate to describe it, as Ruy Mauro Marini does, as "super-exploitation."[18] The conjunction of super-exploitation and commodification produced a unique kind of society unseen in other regimes of forced labor.

Capitalization: Beyond commodification and super-exploitation, enslaved people were also used *as capital* itself, yet another unique element of racialized chattel slavery.[19] Slavers treated enslaved people as "highly flexible capital investments . . . Planters could sell them, use them as collateral, or hire them out to planters who needed additional labor."[20] Through the abolition of chattel slavery in the 1880s, enslaved people were deployed *as capital*: a form of investment advanced to generate further profit. Enslaved people were seen and treated as initial investments who could generate a profitable return in a variety of ways.

The most grotesque form of capitalization came in the form of sexual violence. Slavers saw enslaved people's pregnancies as unique investment opportunities that could return extremely high profits. They turned to systematic rape as a mechanism of profit accumulation. As Hartman explains, "the ravished body," unlike other forms of violent injury inflicted by the lash, the chain, or the treadmill, "did not decrease productivity or diminish value—on the contrary, it might actually increase the captive's magnitude of value."[21] Despite prevailing patriarchal European norms, nearly all colonial

18 Ruy Mauro Marini, *The Dialectics of Dependency* (Monthly Review Press, 2022).

19 While most often, capital emerges in the form of money, the universal equivalent, this is not an immutable or necessary feature of capital itself. That money, as the universal equivalent, can take many concrete forms is hardly debatable. What distinguishes money from capital is that the latter is advanced with the specific aim of a return on investment, that as it circulates, it will return to its owner a larger quantity than at the outset.

20 Trevor Burnard and John Garrigus, *The Plantation Machine: Atlantic Capitalism in French Saint-Domingue and British Jamaica* (University of Pennsylvania Press, 2016), 7.

21 Hartman, *Scenes of Subjection*, 95.

powers adopted maternal descent as the basis for determining one's status as free or enslaved; by the principle of *partus sequitur ventrem* (literally "offspring follows the belly"), any person born to an enslaved mother became legally enslaved. Functionally, sexual violence became a direct "means of increasing property."[22] As Jennifer Morgan has shown, slavers used the language of "increase" to name how their capital investment would grow through biological reproduction, including through the constant sexual violation of enslaved people.[23] Notorious slaver Thomas Jefferson once wrote, "I consider the labor of a breeding woman as no object, and that a child raised every 2 years is of more profit than the crop of the best laboring man."[24] Sexual violence was a direct tool of capital accumulation, creating new enslaved people who could be exploited (as a worker), sold (as a commodity), or raped (as capital).[25] It is no exaggeration to say that the institution of racialized chattel slavery constituted an economy of rape for profit, perhaps the most condensed and monstrous meeting point of social and societal reproduction. The capitalization of enslaved people was thus simultaneously racialized and gendered.[26]

In this way, chattel slavery created an unprecedented and unduplicated site in capitalist accumulation in which a single person was transformed into a combination of commodity, worker, and capital. In

---

22 Cheryl I. Harris, "Whiteness as Property," *Harvard Law Review* 106, no. 8 (1993): 1719.

23 Jennifer Morgan, *Laboring Women: Reproduction and Gender in New World Slavery* (University of Pennsylvania Press, 2004).

24 Thomas Jefferson, "Letter of Thomas Jefferson to Joel Yancey," January 17, 1819, National Archives (Founders Online), founders.archives.gov.

25 It is true and worth remarking that the intense *investment* in sexual violence as a tool of accumulation was more marked in the United States than in other places, especially following the abolition of the slave trade. Across the slaving world, many different attitudes toward reproduction were adopted, and these broadly corresponded to the dictates of capital accumulation. Where it was more profitable to import new human beings, less emphasis was placed on reproducing the enslaved population through rape and pregnancy; the sustained correlation between sexual violence and the dictates of capital should make abundantly clear how much enslaved life was subordinated to the logic of capital accumulation.

26 It is worth raising, as Hortense Spillers has, whether sexual violence against enslaved people is, properly speaking, "gendered." Spillers argues that the social relation of gendering and gender differentiation we normally associate with gender was absent in chattel slavery, even though forms of torture were indeed sexed. For this reason, Spillers and others who follow her prefer to think about this violence, rather, as a form of "ungendering," raising a deep and continuing question in gender studies as to whether Black people (and other racialized/colonized people) are *gendered differently* than white people, or whether *gender* as a category is predominantly a white category. For more see Spillers, "Mama's Baby, Papa's Maybe"; Marquis Bey, "Black Fugitivity Un/Gendered," *The Black Scholar* (San Francisco) 49, no. 1 (2019): 55–62.

Achille Mbembe's words, enslaved people inhabited a unique combination of human and nonhuman properties; they were "human-objects, human-commodities, human-money."[27] New forms of social, political, and legal domination emerged to buttress the emergence of this new capitalist melding of commodification, super-exploitation, and capitalization.[28] Enslaved people's simultaneous status as labor, capital, and commodity accounts for some of the peculiar ambivalences plantation society produced, especially as regards personhood. While denied the legal status of personhood, enslaved people's humanity was often also undeniable and unavoidable, even at the heart of white supremacist ideology and institutions. Courts were often forced to recognize enslaved people as responsible, rational persons in order to punish and discipline them, a point Hartman emphasizes. White supremacist institutions recognized enslaved personhood only at the moment of its denial, one of the chief "scenes of subjection" Hartman traces.[29] Capitalist slavery requires the dispossession of humanity, a faint recognition that contradictorily undermines itself. Contortionist logics such as these arose precisely because of the multiple, overlapping, mutually reinforcing positions that enslaved people were forced to occupy under chattel slavery.

This combination produced made chattel slavery unlike any form of slavery before or since. It created what Robin Blackburn called "slaveholder capitalism."[30] Capitalist slavery was not only, as Piero Sraffa once described, a system of "commodities producing commodities" but a system *to produce* commodities (commodification) and capital (capitalization) who produce commodities (through super-exploitation).[31] The rule of capital was suffused to every part of the new regime of racialized chattel slavery; no part of its systematic confinement could be understood outside the capitalist dictate of accumulation. Recall that *capitalism is a form of society*, one in which capital's drive to accumulate sets the general shape of compulsion, especially though not only through its control of how we produce life's necessities. A society is capitalist if survival (of human and nonhuman life) is largely controlled by the logic of capital accumulation.

---

27 Achille Mbembe, *Critique of Black Reason* (Duke University Press, 2017), 2.

28 There is always something suspicious in Marxist accounts that continue to insist that enslaved people were "just" variable capital, inputs to production, the same as machinery.

29 Hartman, *Scenes of Subjection*.

30 Robin Blackburn, *The Reckoning: From the Second Slavery to Abolition, 1776–1888* (Verso, 2024).

31 Piero Sraffa, *Production of Commodities by Means of Commodities: Prelude to a Critique of Economic Theory* (Vora & Co. Publishers, 1960).

Many capitalist societies, including our own, make ample use of unfree labor. Many societies, including noncapitalist ones, have used wage labor. Rather than ask whether any institution—wage labor, enslavement, or the family—is capitalist *generally*, it is more helpful to explore the ways that the practice or institution grows, thrives, and reproduces itself under a society dominated by the rule of capital. It is not clear to me what it could mean for a noncapitalist institution to be central to a capitalist society, nor is it clear to me what it could mean to say that societies with unfree labor (like our own) are by definition not capitalist. The relevant question is whether, however they labor, people's material conditions of life were embedded in capital accumulation. Enslaved people's lives were undeniably so. As Achille Mbembe describes the social relations that emerge from enslavement:

> The slave condition produces a contradiction between freedom of property and freedom of person. An unequal relationship is established along with the inequality of the power over life. *This power over the life of another takes the form of commerce*: a person's humanity is dissolved to the point where it becomes possible to say that the slave's life is possessed by the master.[32]

If, as Mbembe writes, chattel slavery's social relations subordinate enslaved people to marketized commerce, this is a unique form of slavery that is, through and through, capitalist. If capitalism confines human beings into the reproduction of capital at the expense of freedom, nowhere is this confinement more visible than in transatlantic chattel slavery. Slavery thus dramatizes the most extreme forms of confinement that capitalism can make use of in its drive toward the reproductive expansion of capital.

Rather than the question of "How can unfree labor be capitalist?" new questions emerge: what kinds of unfree labor might be useful to or compatible with capitalism, and under what conditions? How can we understand the relationship between unfree and waged work in actually existing capitalist societies? Once we understand capitalism as a society in which survival (or death) is dictated by capital, we can begin to see how many different forms of labor and many different forms of life can be captured and *put to work* to this end. As Siddhant Issar writes, "This excision of 'unfree' labour from capitalism's logics of accumulation results in the inability to grasp how a *continuum* of labour regimes from 'unfree'

32 Achille Mbembe, "Necropolitics," trans. Libby Meintjes, *Public Culture* 15, no. 1 (2003): 22. Emphasis added.

to 'free' power expanded reproduction, and the ways racial slavery and its afterlives serve as the foundation against which 'free' wage labour is posed."[33] In most capitalist societies, labor exists on a continuum of free to unfree, or in Marx's terms, indirectly to directly coerced.

Direct and Indirect Compulsion

Chattel slavery's attempted dissolution of humanity in the triad of commodification, super-exploitation, and capitalization positions enslaved people very differently than waged workers. As I will explore more thoroughly in the next chapter, capital can command wage labor so effectively partially because its compulsion is not obvious—because workers have certain kinds of choices (where to work, what to study, what kind of job to pursue), labor often *appears* as a site of freedom. It isn't really, since all these choices are suspended in a larger forced choice of wage labor or starvation. Marx thus describes wage labor as a particular form of indirect compulsion. But enslavement was made possible by direct confinement, compulsion, and violence. What does it mean if, at least in some places, the accumulation and reproduction of capital depended on the whip?

It means that resistance was constant. The gradual recession of direct violence against wage laborers signals their effective incorporation into capitalism. Though new proletarians resisted mightily in the process of transition, gradually repression won out—they were, in Foucault's terms, "made docile," with only occasional spurts of resistance occasioning the use of direct force. As I hope is clear, this is not a moral or political failing of these proletarians, but a structural condition of the wage: it is hard to resist the conditions that secure your survival, no matter how harrowing those conditions.

But enslaved people confront capitalism as the means of their deaths and so have a unified interest in its abolition. And pursue this interest they did, constantly and all the time. Enslaved people resisted capture, fought slavers, ran away, sometimes purchased their freedom. They resisted transportation, staged mutinies, and when that failed, jumped overboard. Enslaved people organized rebellions, riots, strikes, work stoppages, and slowdowns. They broke tools, reappropriated property, and poisoned enslavers. Enslaved people resisted with every available means, including various forms of what Banu Bargu calls "necro-resistance," like

33 Siddhant Issar, "Theorising 'Racial/Colonial Primitive Accumulation': Settler Colonialism, Slavery, and Racial Capitalism," *Race & Class* 63, no. 1 (2021): 36.

infanticide, abortion, and suicide.[34] They conserved cultural, religious, and family ties where they could; they cared for each other in the face of extreme brutality and incentives to abandon community. They fled the plantation at every opportunity—they took to the mountains and swamps, sometimes alone, sometimes in groups. In fugitivity, they joined free communities of Indigenous peoples and founded their own maroon societies. For every repressive rule and every attempt to turn humans into capital, there was resistance. The intense and systematic resistance to enslavement underscores how and why it was met with such systematic and continuous direct force. Direct violence implies continued rebellion, the sign of human beings who would not be made docile.

How are the threats faced by enslaved people (the whip, the chain, the treadmill, systematic rape) different from those faced by waged workers (the growling belly or eviction)? There is no denying a difference between the impersonal violence of the market and the direct, personal violence of enslaver; the question is what difference does this difference make?

Marx returned to this question over and over again throughout his life, even as his answers were inconsistent and ultimately unsatisfying. His constant interest demonstrated that, in some way, slavery revealed the truth of wage labor, even if the exact nature of that truth was somewhat in flux. Overall, Marx continually contrasts slavery and wage labor "precisely to underscore the affinities between the two."[35]

These affinities should not be altogether surprising; free and coerced labor were materially interlinked in the global economy for centuries. Long chains of production connected commodities produced by enslaved and waged labor alike with the valorization of capital dependent on the seamless connection between, for example, slave-produced sugar, urban English manufacturers, and slavers in the infamous Triangular Trade. The market integration of free and enslaved labor created material connections between these different statuses, ultimately creating a reinforcing system of mutual dependence, at least for a while.

These material connections were intensified by the imperial circulation of mechanisms of repression. Slavers and factory owners exchanged techniques of pacification, of efficiency, and eventually of policing, along with the commodities they traded. As Amy Dru Stanley explains in the context of the United States, "just as the ideal of free labor was transported south, so its coercive aspects—articulated in rules governing the freed

34 Banu Bargu, *Starve and Immolate: The Politics of Human Weapons* (Columbia University Press, 2014).

35 De Genova, "A Racial Theory of Labour," 229.

people—were carried back north."[36] This was far from an eccentricity of an internally divided colony-cum-nation: Hartman argues that this characterized a multinational, "transatlantic capitalist system that traded information and strategies of labor management between the plantation and the factory."[37]

At the same time, chattel slavery was also deeply implicated in other forms of direct compulsion, especially the genocide of Indigenous peoples in the Western Hemisphere. Slaveholder capitalism was a distinctly *colonial* capitalism. Approximately 55 million Indigenous people were systematically exterminated in the century following Columbus's first voyage to the Americas, and European capitalism sought to dominate Indigenous people and Indigenous land as sources of profit and accumulation. The brutal confinement of the capitalist plantation enacted further confinements of Indigenous peoples, linking the violence of chattel slavery with the murderous practices of settler colonialism, which instituted its own forms of racial and gender domination. Plantation-based chattel slavery was impossible without the widespread land theft and genocide of settler colonialization, linking multiple forms of direct compulsion in a compounding circuit of profit-motivated brutality. Settler colonization was the ground of chattel slavery.

In other words, capitalism worked through the relationship between free and bound labor, as well as between the confinements of labor, land, and life. Capitalism pursued a multifaceted strategy that subjected different groups of people to different forms of domination for one unified goal: the accumulation of capital. Issar explains that the world system brought together capitalists, wage laborers, and enslaved people into one global economy:

> In the context of the capitalist world-system, these two layers of political-economic and gendered, reproductive expropriation congealed in the institution of chattel slavery, accumulating profit not for only planters and slave owners, but also a vast intercontinental network of merchants, financiers, industrialists, state, and corporations. In a direct sense, capital's exploitation of wage labour in the North and in Europe was premised on the expropriation of Black slave labour, including the reproductive capacities of Black women.[38]

36 Amy Dru Stanley, *From Bondage to Contract: Wage Labor, Marriage, and the Market in the Age of Slave Emancipation* (Cambridge University Press, 1998), 130.

37 Hartman, *Scenes of Subjection*, 138.

38 Issar, "Theorising 'Racial/Colonial Primitive Accumulation,'" 37.

Capitalism thrived precisely by creating a system in which different groups of people were defined, confined, and controlled in different ways. Part of capitalism's resilience was precisely its internal differentiation, condemning Black people to enslavement and Indigenous peoples to expulsion, as it pushed white people into waged exploitation. Thus, not only was enslavement directly profitable but it also stabilized the rising regime of waged exploitation and expanded the settler colonial control over land. The ravages of chattel slavery made the violences of wage labor seem a comparatively lucky lot in life, diffusing much of the resistance against it. Enslavement constituted a labor discipline on wage workers that combined the threat of worse treatment and an offer of "wages of whiteness" in exchange for incorporation into capitalism.[39] Enslavement also provided an ideological contrast that allowed wage labor to *seem like* freedom. In Hartman's words, "Slavery is less the antithesis of free labor than an intemperate consort, a moral foil, a barbarism overcome, and the pedestal on which the virtues of free labor are decried."[40]

It was not just that the *labor conditions* of the wage could appear as "free" when compared to more obviously unfree forms of labor. Chattel slavery and settler colonialism inaugurated race in the modern sense, as a foundational and unchangeable social hierarchy. Slavers and colonizers variously proclaimed white supremacy as divinely ordained, scientifically proven, and universal, despite its obviously modern emergence. Compared to the supposedly eternal and unbreakable stability of race, capitalism's *social immobility* became mystified. In addition to its subordination to capital's metabolism, modern slavery was distinguished from previous forms through the invention of race. The simultaneous demonization of feudal power and invention of race entrenched the ideological construction of wage labor as the guarantor of mobility, choice, chance, and upward possibility, at least for the select few white proletarians who fully submitted to the dictates of capitalist discipline. Increasingly, submitting to capitalism would mean betraying any form of solidarity with racialized proletarians, accepting the role as the dominator of others. These dynamics continue to condition the reproduction of capital to this day.

Once chattel slavery ceased to be profitable for capitalism, it largely disappeared, while wage labor remained or, perhaps, was strengthened.[41]

39 David R. Roediger et al., *The Wages of Whiteness: Race and the Making of the American Working Class* (Verso, 2007); Theodore W. Allen, *The Invention of the White Race*, vol. 2; *The Origin of Racial Oppression in Anglo-America*, 2nd edition (Verso, 2012).

40 Hartman, *Scenes of Subjection*, 139.

41 Eric Williams, *Capitalism and Slavery*, 1st edition (The University of North Carolina Press, 1994).

The elimination of slavery at the height of European industrialization has led some to conclude that slavery was simply not capitalist, that it was merely a holdover from a previous, premodern regime of accumulation almost destined to be abolished.

If only that were true. Transatlantic chattel slavery was not so much eliminated as transformed, reconfiguring social relations that, as we shall see, conserved many of these elements. Racialized chattel slavery inaugurated a grammar of domination and a series of confinements that reshaped the trajectory of everything that followed, not only for formerly enslaved people, but also for Indigenous people and waged workers. As such, chattel slavery, though abolished, set some of the major dynamics of capitalist modernity. It is to the enduring effects of capitalist slavery, its "afterlives" to use Hartman's phrase, to which we now turn.

The Capitalist "Afterlife" of Slavery

It is no exaggeration to say we live still in the world built by racialized slavery. So many of the dynamics and social relations we live through—in every facet of life, from economics to politics to global institutions to interpersonal relations—are shaped by the social relations inaugurated by chattel slavery. Chattel status was indeed abolished throughout the nineteenth century, but the "afterlife" of slavery conserved, expanded, and reproduced global and domestic racisms, neocolonialisms, and necropolitics. In Rinaldo Walcott's words:

> The plantation isn't, as so many of us, Black and otherwise, think or at least wish to believe, a thing of the past; rather, the planation persists as a largely unseen superstructure shaping modern, everyday life and many of its practices, attitudes, and assumptions, even if some of these have been, over time, transformed.[42]

It is precisely because we still live in the world racialized chattel slavery created, in its "afterlives," that abolition remains an unfinished project. The abolitionist horizon, the imaginary of a world beyond confinement, mechanized death, and profitable torture, continues to animate our collective freedom dreams.

If the historical abolition of slavery produced "the afterlife" rather than true "emancipation," we must understand contemporary social relations

42 Rinaldo Walcott, *On Property: Policing, Prisons, and the Call for Abolition* (Biblioasis, 2021), 21.

to be saturated with the logics chattel slavery created. Wholly capitalist in its origin and abolition, chattel slavery can no longer be conceived as a precapitalist mode of production destroyed by capital's ascendance to global power. We should be skeptical of any narrative that positions capital as liberator. Just as capital's claim of liberating serfs from feudal despotism is a narrative of half-truths, so too is the idea that capitalism emancipated Black labor from the bondage of precapitalist domination as chattel. But moreover, understanding the continued structural power of slavery's afterlife recasts the relationship between capitalism and abolition.

The nineteenth-century abolitionist movement achieved something incredible, and it took centuries of resistance and organizing, mostly by enslaved people themselves, to transform the world so drastically. Despite the tireless efforts of more radical formations, a liberal and legalistic approach to abolition ultimately triumphed. This version of abolition focused on extirpating forced labor, which it did mostly though incompletely. Liberal reformers proclaimed that all of slavery had been swept away to the dark annals of a history, thanks to the law and capital, ignoring the many ways that slavery's social relations were conserved, even if transformed. Rather than seeing slavery and capitalism as successive modes of production, we can understand historical emancipation as a technique shift within capitalism: a capitalist abolition that transformed a capitalist slavery.

What did this capitalist abolition ultimately entail? Emancipation, in the broad sense, opened up three pathways for formerly enslaved people, each of which deployed confinement technologies: (1) the *incorporation* into the wage-labor market, always at a relative disadvantage to white wage workers, (2) the *substitution* of one unfree labor status for another, such as debt peonage, indenture, or sharecropping, and (3) the *expulsion* from capitalist labor market, often through expanded use of workhouses and prisons. Each of these pathways buttressed capitalism in different ways, but all confined the life chances of racialized people. It is worth exploring each of these pathways in greater detail.

Incorporation: In some cases, formerly enslaved people did join the ranks of the exploited working classes, always at a disadvantage compared to white workers. They were paid less and worked longer hours, with fewer labor protections, often in the most dangerous industries. Nearly universally, Black women entered the labor market at much higher rates than even white working-class women, often shunted into highly devalued work in the social reproduction sector. They would soon find that waged exploitation fell significantly short of true liberation. In and beyond their working conditions, capitalist abolition instituted racist laws around work, property, education, citizenship, literacy, and disenfranchisement across the Americas, shaping the confinement of the Black working class in particular ways. When and where these explicit restrictions are removed, capital's reliance on societal reproduction means that, all over the world, Black workers are structurally hemmed in by lower inheritances, less housing stability, higher unemployment rates, and less access to basic necessities like education and healthcare. Even when capitalism pursued post-abolition incorporation, Black people remain doubly confined: to the general confinements of wage labor (discussed in the next chapter) and to the specific disadvantages and life circumstances produced by white supremacy.

Some critics—liberal and Marxist alike—have incorrectly diagnosed the partial and unequal incorporation into wage labor or the bourgeoisie as evidence of a lessening racial regime of confinement.[43] As both the waged and ruling class diversify, as governments outlaw (at least some forms of) explicit racism, capitalism begins to seem neutral on questions of race—or even anti-racist. However, these incorporation practices are always partial at best. Racialized workers simply do not enter into the wage market on the same terms as white workers.

But moreover, some forms of inclusion conceal confinement. The (unfulfilled) promise of equal inclusion into capitalism is not only illusory, but ideological. It produces the illusion of social mobility, suggesting that capitalist success or failure hinges on individual decision-making rather than collective structures of racist power that confine Black communities from the outset. That capitalism sometimes pursues an inclusionary strategy works to disavow the social immobility that truly patterns life possibilities and experiences, what Keeanga-Yamahtta Taylor calls "predatory inclusion."[44] When inclusion stabilizes domination rather than unsettles it, diversification testifies to the entrenchment of oppression rather than its overcoming. Queer activists, feminists, and anti-racists have long called out these incorporation strategies as oppressive in

43 For example, in Nancy Fraser's latest book, she argues that racialized distinctions under capitalism are best conceived by the distinction between exploited (white) labor and expropriated (racialized) labor. Since this neat population-level distinction no longer holds, with more white people experiencing expropriation (primarily through debt) and more racialized people folded into waged exploitation, her analysis "suggests the crumbling, if not the full demise, of what has served historically as racism's structural basis in capitalist society." Nancy Fraser, *Cannibal Capitalism* (Verso, 2022), 48.

44 Keeanga-Yamahtta Taylor, *Race for Profit: How Banks and the Real Estate Industry Undermined Black Homeownership* (University of North Carolina Press, 2019).

their own right. Homonormative capital is not evidence that capital has abandoned heteropatriarchy; homonormativity is one *form of heteropatriarchy.* A "feminist" politics of "lean-in" girlbossing is a neoliberal form of misogyny. In the same way, the capitalist embrace of racial inclusion or colorblindness remains a form of white supremacy, one that relies on the structural disempowerment of Black people. It leaves intact a power structure premised on the devaluation of Black life, Black flourishing, and Black being. White supremacy, Eurocentrism, and coloniality are baked into the fundamental organization of capitalism, which continues to create multiple forms of confinement by reproducing structures that treat racialized peoples, cultures, lands, and work as something less than fully human. Incorporation into the wage economy did not deliver racial equality, much less Black liberation.

In social forms that eschew overt and codified racial difference, the illusion of universal social mobility conserves and deepens the illusion of capitalism's commitment to equality and freedom. Colorblind capitalism has not eliminated the structurally racist conditions of accumulation in our own time.

Substitution: At the same time capitalist emancipation pursued these incorporation strategies, it also created racially specific forms of unfree labor. Examples from across the world abound. In the United States, the white southern elite created the sharecropping system, wherein formerly enslaved people worked on the same plantations they had before abolition, but now had to pay their former enslavers for seeds, tools, and housing at high interest rates. A similar system emerged around the Caribbean, where it was variously called *metayage*, *metairie*, and *mezzadria*. The system plunged Black workers into deeply entrenched debt, which meant that these nominally free workers were confined to the same plantations as their forebearers. If they left, they faced imprisonment, in which the system of convict-leasing rented out incarcerated labor to private corporations. Both states and corporations made exorbitant profits while incarcerated people remained unpaid and super-exploited. Across the British colonies, in places like Jamaica, Guyana, and Barbados, capitalist abolition brought a new system of "apprenticeship" in which formerly enslaved people were forced to work without pay for their enslavers for a period of six or four years, during which time they were unable to leave the plantation. Failure to comply with this forced servitude was met with harsh labor in the workhouses. After this period, the British planting classes turned to South Asia for indentured labor on the plantations, which continued until the 1920s. While capitalist abolition entailed continued confinement and forced labor for racialized people, across the British, French, Dutch, Danish, Spanish, and Portuguese Empires, white slavers were often compensated for their "financial losses." Even abolition was profitable for slavers.

Expulsion: Some formerly enslaved people found themselves expelled from the capitalist labor market altogether. When colonizers, slavers, and capitalists determined it was profitable, formerly enslaved people were simply abandoned. For individual people, this often meant unemployment, starvation, and precarity; with the expansion of laws criminalizing vagrancy and idleness, they found themselves confined to institutions like workhouses and prisons in higher numbers than ever before, inaugurating contemporary racialized dynamics of mass incarceration. At the same time, entire colonies faced what Christopher Taylor has called an "empire of neglect" after European powers faced diminishing profits in the post-abolition era.[45] Without lessening the large, structural controls over Black communities or Indigenous lands, white supremacy also took the form of systematized abandonment and disinvestment, creating a ballooning "surplus population" that constantly struggled to survive. To this day, white supremacy justifies structural neglect through the idea that Black people in particular and racialized people more generally deserve less, need less, are capable of less, and *are* lesser than.

Whatever pathway abolition took, it everywhere conserved white supremacy. The white supremacy of the post-abolition world is folded into the fabric of capital accumulation and continues to produce necropolitical effects in every area of life and survival. Hartman describes this constellation of factors as "the afterlife of slavery—skewed life chances, limited access to health and education, premature death, incarceration, and impoverishment. I, too, am the afterlife of slavery."[46] The highly racialized contemporary composition of the global class of expelled, neglected, and "surplus" people also has its roots here.

These three pathways disclose something important: slavery's afterlives circulate between strategies that incorporate formerly enslaved people into capitalism's "normal" operation of the wage market and those that innovate unique confinements for racialized people. Capitalist abolition not only innovated these three pathways but inaugurated a system of cycling between them in order to more profitably confine. Through

45 Christopher Taylor, *Empire of Neglect: The West Indies in the Wake of British Liberalism* (Duke University Press, 2018).

46 Saidiya V. Hartman, *Lose Your Mother: A Journey Along the Atlantic Slave Trade Route Terror* (Farrar, Straus and Giroux, 2007), 6.

incorporation, substitution, and expulsion, capitalist abolition set the stage for the contemporary logic of capitalist domination, taking elements of slaveholder capitalism into the post-abolition world.

In this way, we can see that capitalist abolition did not wholly eliminate the key features of capitalist slavery (commodification, super-exploitation, and capitalization); it rather transformed them. Where the lives of enslaved people had been directly commodified, capitalist abolition offered some the commodification of labor power instead. But for others, who capital could not accommodate with wages, life itself would continue to form a direct source of profit. Conditions of super-exploitation continued apace; wages simply lowered the rate of exploitation. Thus, capitalism did not abandon commodification; it simply redirected it.

The logic of capitalist slavery is conserved, too, in the production of some people's lives as "surplus populations" who can simply be abandoned to death and disinvestment, sacrificed on the altar of capital's growth and restructuring. Just as enslaved people were sometimes seen to be worth more dead than alive, many other groups have been exterminated for profit. In the ghoulish system of death-dealing we call capitalism, people are routinely either abandoned to or actively exterminated. Indigenous peoples in the Americas and Palestine know too well the grotesque violence that can come from capitalism's macabre accounting. The entire notion that *people* and their *lives* should be valued according to a capitalist logic is rooted in the commodification of human life that capitalist slavery produced. That some people can become simply "null" from capital's perspective, worth neither investment nor exploitation, continues to produce death on a widespread scale across the world. This, too, is the afterlife of slavery. As I will discuss in much more detail in the chapters on prisons and policing, contemporary capitalism continues to *capitalize* on the parts of the population made surplus.

At the same time, conditions of accumulation still shaped the possibilities of life and death for racialized people, who continued to face the terror of white supremacy. Legendary Black activist and journalist Ida B. Wells-Barnett revealed that widespread practices of lynching were directly linked to the search for profit. It was perhaps capitalization that shifted the most dramatically in capitalist abolition—or seemed to. Though rape no longer directly expands capital, rampant sexual violence continues to structure Black women's lives and experiences of the capitalist world, a particularly gendered element of slavery's afterlife that continues to confine life chances and possibilities.[47]

47 Danielle L. McGuire, *At the Dark End of the Street: Black Women, Rape,*

Perhaps the most important mutation of capitalist abolition was that the three aspects of racialized chattel slavery became separable: individuals no longer faced all three at the same time. Capitalism disarticulated these strategies, pulling on them one and a time, cycling through them as market conditions sought to maximize profit. While enslaved people were commodified, capitalized, and super-exploited at one and the same time, capitalist abolition created a world in which these were different strategies that could be pursued independently. *This* is the world we still live in, one in which, when convenient, capital will pursue accumulation through exploitation, death, and commodification (of both labor and life), and will decide between these strategies on the basis of profit maximization.

Centering Capitalism's Confinements

Placing chattel slavery at the center of capitalism's history allows us to better understand not only slavery and its afterlives but also what capitalism is and how it works. While some tell the history of capitalism through the emergence of wage labor, in reality, the history of capitalism involves many other forms of labor. By also understanding the nonlabor elements of slavery, we can see how capitalism also creates forms of social domination which are not rooted in labor at all, creating space to center those who are, in Saskia Sassen's words, "expelled" from the realm of waged labor, who lack access to even basic social protections and services.[48] It also allows us to see how forms of oppression like rape and sexual violence permeate the fabric of capitalist life, even when they cannot be reduced directly to accumulation. Beginning our analysis of capitalism in confinement also allows us to see how many forms of coercion coexist, including many—like indentured prison labor, debt peonage, and the many forms of contemporary slavery—that outlasted formal abolition. Rooting in capitalism's plurality can widen anti-capitalist organizing beyond traditional mechanisms of unionization and workplace struggle, mobilizing the unique anti-capitalist potential in classes of people who are literally being killed by capitalism.

This perspective also illuminates how anti-capitalism must simultaneously attend to differences and see connections across difference. The logic of racialized chattel slavery was enmeshed with wage labor and settler

---

Resistance—A New History of the Civil Rights Movement from Rosa Parks to the Rise of Black Power (Vintage, 2011).

48 Saskia Sassen, *Expulsions: Brutality and Complexity in the Global Economy* (Harvard University Press, 2014).

colonial genocide from the outset. Capitalism's shift from accumulation by slavery to accumulation by abolition forms a central part of the accumulative strategy and its tenacious expansion. Capitalism's ability to mask the violence of the wage hinges on the creation of more visible, grotesque, and obvious forms of violence that, by contrast, produce the illusion of the wage as guarantor of freedom, equality, and justice, no matter how ideal or unattainable. The important point here is that whether capital will pursue strategies of accumulation based in incorporation, differentiation, or death is part of how capitalism works. It is not the choice of one tactic or the other that makes a system 'capitalist'; it is that the choice will be made in order to maximize the growth of capital. Slavery and its abolition are not the only terrain on which this choice appears, but rather, form a world-historical anchor for the way these choices would be pursued in many different forms.

When Hartman talks about the present as "the afterlives of slavery" or when Patrick Wolfe describes settler colonization as "a structure not an event," when Fred Moten insists we continue to live "in the break" inaugurated by chattel slavery, or in Christina Sharpe's words "in the wake," they are pointing to the way that the past continues to rule the present.[49] This is not accidental or incidental; it is what the societal reproduction of capitalism produces. It is not an anachronistic holdover from a fully eliminated premodern or precapitalist social form parasitically clinging to an emancipated or enlightened modernity; the continued reproduction of the *social relations of enslavement* are partially constitutive of modern, enlightened capitalism. As Alexis Shotwell explains:

> The present we move through . . . is a reliquary of the past, holding traces of everything that has happened and everything that has been erased. The present is also necessarily a continually receding seed of the future. Whatever happens *now* shapes the conditions for what can happen in any given *then*.[50]

To truly overcome capitalism, we would need to transform the full gamut of social relations that structure slavery's afterlife in a real and total abolition.

---

49 Patrick Wolfe, "Settler Colonialism and the Elimination of the Native," *Journal of Genocide Research* 8, no. 4 (2006): 387–409; Christina Sharpe, *In the Wake: On Blackness and Being* (Duke University Press, 2016); Hartman, *Lose Your Mother*; Fred Moten, *In the Break: The Aesthetics of the Black Radical Tradition* (University of Minnesota Press, 2003).

50 Alexis Shotwell, *Against Purity: Living Ethically in Compromised Times* (University of Minnesota Press, 2016), 77.

Conclusion: The Unfinished Promise of Abolition

In the face of perhaps the most extreme confinement experienced in human history, enslaved people not only resisted explicitly but also kept alive the dream and possibility of a world beyond confinement. Hartman continues:

> The ambulant expressions of freedom are consistently detailed in slave testimony. The search for a parent, child, poor lover, and the longing to return to the place of one's birth or simply instantiate being free through the exercise of this new mobility. Locomotion was definitive of personal liberty. Blackstone's *Commentaries* defines personal liberty in terms of the power of locomotion: "Personal liberty consists in the power of locomotion, of changing one's situation, of removing one's person to whatever place one's inclination may direct, without restraint, unless by due course of law." As itineracy, nomadism, migration, roving, or simply walking, moving about occurred below the threshold of formal sexuality and rights and articulated the limits of emancipation and the constrained terms of agency. It is clear that the freedom experienced was in the search and not the destination.[51]

Though the form of mobility gained in the wake of nineteenth-century abolition was not negligible, it unfortunately did not materialize a society of true emancipation. White supremacist, heteropatriarchal, colonial capitalism repressed that possibility wherever it could, conserving many forms of confinement and leaving the promise of abolition partially unfulfilled. A capitalist abolition could only ever have been partial at best; in order to make good on the abolitionist dream, we must abolish the capitalist system that created so grotesque a regime of confinement.

The unfulfilled promise of abolition remains a powerful analytic in the struggle against capitalist confinement. In the name of a movement yet incomplete, contemporary abolitionists envision reorganizing society beyond the forms of confinement entrenched in slavery's afterlives. The resurgence of contemporary abolitionism signifies not the triumph of a previous movement but how the forms of domination we face in the present—capitalism, debt, racism, police, prisons, and more—inherit structural dominations rooted in slavery. The abolitionist horizon demands we finally eliminate these forms of violence from the world, not only for Black people but for us all.

---

51 Hartman, *Scenes of Subjection*, 151.

Abolition is thus an indispensable orientation for the revolutionary anti-capitalist. In the example of racialized chattel slavery, we all should learn a harrowing lesson: structures of domination can persist beyond the institutions that supposedly produce them. As we envision what it would mean to fully extirpate capitalism, we must learn from past abolitionism how easy it might be for our wins to be partial and incomplete. The ruling class clings tenaciously to domination, finding ways to conserve in practice even what it supposedly concedes. To birth a truly liberated world, we must both deal with the afterlives of slavery that continue to frame the present and adopt an abolitionist approach to anti-capitalism that would not leave behind an "afterlife" of capitalism.

Liberal "abolitionism" saw the legalistic elimination of chattel status as a completed victory, oblivious to or uninterested in the ways that capital would morph to continue accumulating through novel forms of confinement. Chattel slavery generated the impression of wage labor as the ultimate freedom, as a mode of life beyond confinement. Newly proletarianized people around the world—both formerly enslaved and formerly enserfed—would over and over again learn that this was a dastardly trick. As we will see in the next chapter, the liberal capitalist's vaunted remedy for the confinements of chattel slavery would turn out to offer only new forms of confinement, now packaged as freedom. Like so many other human attempts to eliminate confinement, capitalism co-opted the abolitionist struggle, deploying toward its own ends, ultimately entrenching yet another form of capitalist confinement: the wage. That wage labor did not deliver true emancipation for Black people or for any of us demonstrates the necessity of integrating *both* abolitionism and anti-capitalism into our horizon of liberatory praxis. It is a confinement we continue to fight today, and one we can truly overcome only by understanding wage labor as it really is: not a mode of freedom, but a mode of confinement.

2

Wage Labor and the Price of Mobility

There's a better life and you think about it don't you. / It's a rich man's game no matter what they call it. / And you spend your life puttin' money in his wallet. / Nine to five, what a way to make a livin'. / Barely getting' by, it's all takin' and no givin'.

—Dolly Parton[1]

In September 1977, agents of the United States Immigration Naturalization Service (INS), the precursor of today's Immigration and Customs Enforcement (ICE), descended on a garment factory in Southern California. Suspecting that the factory employed undocumented people—but not having any individual names—armed INS agents raided the workplace, questioning everyone. They positioned several agents at each exit while other officers moved systematically through the factory, questioning each worker about their citizenship status, eventually making arrests. Four questioned workers filed suit, arguing that because they were not free to leave, the questioning violated their rights against unreasonable search and seizure.

Any reasonable person would have likely felt unable to leave, surrounded and harassed by armed agents of the state. The Ninth Circuit Court of Appeals concurred with this assessment, finding the searches to be unconstitutional in 1982. INS appealed the ruling, and the case came before the United States Supreme Court in 1984.

Ultimately, the Supreme Court found in favor of the immigration cops but perhaps not for the reason one might imagine. The workers *were* likely

1 Dolly Parton, "9 to 5" (RCA Records, 1980).

unfree to leave the site of the raid, the Court reasoned, but not because of the scary armed men in uniform. They were unfree to leave because they were at work.

Chief Justice William Rehnquist, writing the majority opinion, explained: "When people are at work their freedom to move about has been meaningfully restricted, not by the actions of law enforcement officials, but by the workers' voluntary obligations to their employers."[2] The workers had to stay in the factory during the raid because their employer said so, not because the state did. The boss controlled the workers' movements, not the state.

While there is something obviously ridiculous about the Court's reasoning here, it speaks also to a deep truth experienced by many across the world: waged work is a site of confinement. It is not only that once we clock in, the boss decides when we clock out; we are compelled to go to work regardless of whether we are tired or sick or whether our kids need care, because the rent needs to be paid, groceries must be bought, loans must be repaid. Though Rehnquist calls work a "voluntary obligation," there is hardly anything in this world that feels *less* voluntary than the day-in-day-out compulsion of going to work and staying there until a petty despot allows you to leave. As unfree as this feels, capitalism thrives on the ideology that labor is voluntary, free, and chosen simply because it is contracted. Workers the world over know that nothing could be further from the truth. What we can hear in Rehnquist's opinion is that the ruling class knows this too, and that the confinement of work is an important part of how capitalism operates.[3]

Thinking about wage labor as a form of confinement might appear to be a very strange claim indeed. After all, wage labor is at least partially defined by how workers gained *mobility* as they left the status of serfdom or enslavement behind. But as we shall see, this form of physical mobility came at the high price of confinement in a variety of other senses.

The History of Confinement and the Rise of the Wage

To hear bourgeois political economists tell the story, one would imagine that feudal peasants, crushed under the weight of their immobilized subjection to the despotic whims of the feudal lord, joyously clamored for the wage as the means of their emancipation. This revisionist narrative is

2 *INS v. Delgado*, 466 U.S. 210 (United States Supreme Court 1984).

3 Thanks very much to Alex Stein for bringing this case to my attention.

largely based on the gradual political enfranchisement of waged workers, which in most European countries occurred only in the late eighteenth and early nineteenth centuries (and for white women, workers of color, and colonized workers, well into the twentieth). A political ideology of free work and free men (always *men*) has projected into the much more distant past a fusion of waged work as contract and the political equality of personhood assumed by contemporary contract theory.

Subtending this narrative lies a theoretical equation between mobility and freedom in the Western philosophical canon. As Hagar Kotef shows, liberal philosophy conceives of the ability to *move* as a central element of what freedom means.[4] But freedom must mean something *more* than movement, since as we will see, movement can be imbricated in confinement; movement and confinement are less opposed than the liberal philosophers would have us think.

The freedom at issue in the concept of "free" labor designated mobility in two distinct but related ways. In the first place, it meant that workers, unlike feudal serfs, were not tied to any piece of land in particular. They could move to find better opportunities, to seek out the bustle of city life, to detach themselves from complicated domestic arrangements, or for whatever other reason struck their fancy. From the perspective of the newly proletarianized worker, what had for generations appeared as an ironclad relationship between labor and land was severed—in ways that increased their life choices in some ways and constrained them in others. This newfound mobility came at the expense of the relative material security of land access and was often experienced not as a form of freedom but as forced displacement. In another way, the freedom of free labor meant a few specific employment rights: the ability to choose your employer and to quit your job if you pleased. Here there is a different kind of mobility at issue. As any job seeker knows, this mobility depends on the state of the labor market, so how much one can actually exercise this "freedom" varies greatly.

In reality, serfs resisted the rise of wage labor in literally every way they could. Confining land under private property separated producers from their means of subsistence and reproduction, a loss so dire it imperiled many people's survival. The destruction of peasant families, communities, and ways of life were hotly contested by peasants of all genders and ages. After protracted battles with a reorganizing ruling class, the majority of

4 Hagar Kotef, *Movement and the Ordering of Freedom: On Liberal Governances of Mobility* (Duke University Press, 2015).

peasants were violently evicted from their land and forced to fend for themselves, selling their labor for a pittance in order to survive.

In addition to violent displacement, new forms of confinement awaited any proletarian who could not find waged work or refused to. New laws mushroomed criminalizing nearly every form of subsistence or resistance. Across the European countryside, new penalties for hunting ("poaching") and collecting food or wood ("thieving") came into effect in attempts to further force new proletarians into meeting their needs through wage labor. At the same time, the ruling classes invented new crimes targeting those who simply didn't want to sell their labor for a wage: idleness, vagabondage, and vagrancy were particularly common charges. And what was the frequent penalty for all of these crimes? Confinement.

The English founded "houses of correction" in the fourteenth century, through the Poor Laws that sought to rectify the "problem" of labor shortages caused by peasants' resistance to waged work. Also called the "workhouse" or the "spike," these institutions persisted through the nineteenth century. In 1536, King Henry VIII dissolved the monasteries, the bedrocks of charitable support for the indigent; from then on, workhouses became newly important, as the numbers of poor, sick, disabled, widowed, and orphaned people seeking state support swelled. The Poor Relief Acts of 1576 and 1601 divided the poor into three categories: the able-bodied, who were sent to workhouses for hard labor and physical punishment; the impotent (elderly and sick), who were placed in indigent housing; and others, primarily widows, who could receive small amounts of money or food in the form of "outdoor relief" in their own homes. A 1776 Parliamentary Report placed the total number of British workhouse occupants at 90,000.[5] The workhouse model inaugurated a work requirement for assistance that would shape much of the subsequent development and management of the working classes, in Britain and beyond.[6]

In France, the system of royal prisons, galleys, and workhouses massively expanded during the reign of Louis XI (1461–1483) and continued to grow through the Revolution (1789).[7] In Spain, vagrants and itinerant poor were increasingly pressed into galley servitude from 1500 on. Across

5 Great Britain Overseers of the Poor, *Abstract of the Returns Made by the Overseers of the Poor: In Pursuance of an Act, Passed in the Twenty-Sixth Year of His Present Majesty's Reign, Intituled, an Act for Obliging Overseers of the Poor to Make Returns upon Oath, to Certain Questions "Specified Therein, Relative to the State of the Poor"* (London, 1787).

6 Derek Fraser, *The Evolution of the British Welfare State*, 4th edition (Palgrave Macmillan, 2009), 38–40.

7 Norval Morris and David J. Rothman, eds., *The Oxford History of the Prison: The Practice of Punishment in Western Society* (Oxford University Press, 1997), 36.

Europe, prisons increasingly supplanted galley service in the early seventeenth century, especially following the establishment of large prisons in Lyon and Madrid in the 1620s.

Workhouse discipline was deeply gendered and left a lasting impact on the heteropatriarchal gender relations of rising capitalism in the colonial metropole. Anne McClintock explains that "many of the inmates of the houses of correction were women, suggesting that the houses were threshold institutions, mediating the gradual transfer of productive labor from the family to the factory."[8] In England, it is estimated that over two-thirds of those committed to workhouses were women.[9] In Spain, the mistress of one of the largest workhouses explained the cause of the growing number of women confined to her care: "There are many vagabond and idle women, including some girls sixteen and younger, who are supported by nothing other than a bad life . . . These lazy women . . . do not wish to work or serve."[10] The remedy she proposes

> is to attack the problem at its roots . . . In all cities where this is possible, there should be houses or schools where . . . they can be taught virtue, Christianity and decency . . . making them practice Christian virtue and doctrine, and learn work decency and good habits so that in due time they may serve in proper and honest houses.[11]

The transition from feudalism to capitalism fueled a decisive split between productive and reproductive labor, and crucially, reproductive labor ceased to be thought of as work at all. Women often entered the sex trades to support themselves and their families, a solution met with rising criminalization and confinement to prisons and workhouses.

In sum, the process of creating proletarians involved being "first forcibly expropriated from the soil, driven from their homes, turned into vagabonds, and then whipped, branded, and tortured by grotesquely

---

8 Anne McClintock, *Imperial Leather: Race, Gender, and Sexuality in the Colonial Contest*, 1st edition (Routledge, 1995), 252.

9 J. Innes, "Prisons for the Poor: English Bridewells, 1555–1800," in *Labour, Law, and Crime: An Historical Perspective*, eds. F. Snyder and D. Hay (Tavistock, 1987).

10 Magdalena de San Jerónimo, "Vagabond Women (1608)," in *Early Modern Spain: A Documentary History*, ed. Jon Cowans (University of Pennsylvania Press, 2003), 141; Magdalena de San Jerónimo, *Razón y Forma de La Galera y Casa Real, Que El Rey, Nuestro Señor, Manda Hacer En Nuestros Reinos, Para Castigo de Las Mujeres Vagantes y Ladronas, Aclahuetas, Hechiceras, y Otras Semejantes* (Francisco Fernández de Córdova, 1608).

11 San Jerónimo, "Vagabond Women (1608)," 142; San Jerónimo, *Razón y Forma de La Galera y Casa Real, Que El Rey, Nuestro Señor, Manda Hacer En Nuestros Reinos, Para Castigo de Las Mujeres Vagantes y Ladronas, Aclahuetas, Hechiceras, y Otras Semejantes.*

terroristic laws accepting the discipline necessary for the system of wage labour."[12] Intense violence and threats of confinement formed the historical conditions of possibility of wage labor's spread.

Several themes emerge here. First, the supposed new mobility of wage workers was coupled with new forms of confinement. True, these new proletarians were free to move around (in order to work), but this is a mobility of an obviously deeply limited kind. Second, because refusing to work (or failing to find it) was punished by confinement, proletarians learned that work secured freedom and mobility. The wage, mobility, and freedom become tied together ideologically, not because workers were actually free to do as they pleased or go where they wanted, but because *not* working was thoroughly associated with confinement in workhouses, galleys, and prisons. In this sense, we could say that it was the *new regimes of confinement* that disciplined workers into the acceptance of waged labor and that anchored the ideological association of waged work and freedom. Third, as explored in the previous chapter, new proletarians, especially in the settler colonies, saw firsthand how much different wage labor was from the forms of enslavement imposed on colonized and racialized people. Wage labor appeared "free" or at least closer to freedom in contradistinction to *both* the prisons they faced for resisting it *and* the more torturous and obvious confinement of slavery. *Institutions of confinement thus appear as the necessary double to the wage from its earliest manifestations*, a trend that continues to the present day.

The idea of wage labor as a mechanism of mobility and freedom was thus not immediately apparent to workers; this impression had to be created and imposed at every turn. If wage labor were so obviously in the natural interest of the workers, if it so clearly represented the triumph of freedom over bondage, of mobility over confinement, why were so many forms of violence required for them to accept it?

The Structural Violence of the Wage

European peasants resisted the incorporation into wage labor for the same reason that people all over the world resist it now: they understood (even if they did not always articulate it) that there was something fundamentally violent about working for wages.

At the individual level, waged work constitutes a kind of theft. Every worker produces more value than they are paid; this basic principle makes

12 Marx, *Capital*, vol. 1, 899.

capitalist production profitable. Every wage worker must produce profit that they do not share. Why do they accept this theft? Mostly because they have no other choice. Their lives are confined to the dictates of the market. Because life's necessities must be bought or rented, workers need money to survive, and most of us access money only by selling our labor. Capitalism thus severs us from our own survival, forcing our incorporation into a system built on violence, theft, displacement, and brutality for the mere chance at accessing basic necessities. This is why Marx describes proletarians as "doubly free" under capitalism: they are "free" to sell their labor on the market and "free" of accessing the means of (re)production. But this freedom, at base, is a freedom to be exploited—a freedom unworthy of the name.

Defenders of capitalism often locate its supposed freedom in the worker's "consent" to their conditions of employment. Because workers have a certain amount of mobility, they choose where they work, and they have the ability to choose to quit their jobs if they please. This extremely constricted idea of mobility and a deeply anemic notion of freedom is ubiquitous in microeconomics, where scholars assume that workers would simply refuse bad working arrangements. But this ignores the fact that under capitalism, we always make these choices under duress. Capitalism forces us to choose between two bad options: exploitation or starvation. Hardly the notion of consent and freedom so valorized in political theory! Max Weber explains that the vast power asymmetry between worker and employer makes these choices coercive rather than free by definition:

> The formal right of the worker to enter into any contract whatsoever with any employer does not in practice represent for the employment seeker even the slightest freedom in the determination of his own conditions of work, and it does not guarantee him any influence on this process. It rather means, at least primarily, that the more powerful party in the market, i.e. normally the employer, has the possibility to set the terms, to offer the job "take it or leave it," and, given the normally pressing economic need of the worker, to impose his terms upon him. The result of contractual freedom, then, is in the first place the opening of the opportunity to use, by the clever utilization of property ownership in the market, these resources without legal restraints as a means for achievement of power over others . . . In the labor market, it is left to the "free" discretion of the parties to accept the conditions imposed by those who are economically stronger by virtue of the guaranty of their property . . . Formally, the market

> community does not recognize direct coercion on the basis of personal authority. It produces in its stead a special kind of coercive situation.[13]

This "special kind of coercive situation" of the wage is a structural feature of capitalism; this coercion sets the capitalist rules of the game in advance, rules that individuals are not free to ignore. Because the very survival of the worker depends on responding to this foundational coercion, it will condition (though not automatically determine) workers' choices. The idea that people's ability to meet their needs (broadly conceived) conditions their choices is the commitment of historical materialism.

It may be obvious, but bears repeating, that the theft of labor and theft of time (surplus value) is violent. It is so structurally and thoroughly violent that Marx once called it "indirect forced slavery."[14] A capitalist society is a society directly committed to theft, an idea that the anarchist Pierre-Joseph Proudhon famously stylized as the claim that "property is theft." Marx showed that wage labor is also theft. A society based simultaneously in private property and wage labor is a society based in the widespread, structural reproduction of theft.

The structural violence of waged labor does not eliminate the direct physical violence from proletarian life; Marx explains that it just makes it more infrequent:

> The [mute] compulsion of economic relations seals the domination of the capitalist over the worker. Extra-economic, immediate violence is still of course used, but only in exceptional cases. In the ordinary run of things, the worker can be left to the "natural laws of production," i.e. it is possible to rely on his dependence on capital, which springs from the conditions of production themselves, and is guaranteed in perpetuity by them.[15]

A lot of the direct violence needed to maintain capitalist society is taken up by the state itself, in the form of police, prisons, political repression, border control, and the military, which I discuss more thoroughly in subsequent chapters. The incredibly suspect division of capitalist society into separate political and economic realms separates the direct coercion of state violence from the "indirect" coercion of the market, when in reality, they function in tandem. The threat of physical confinement that

13 Max Weber, *Economy and Society: An Outline of an Interpretive Sociology*, eds. Guenther Roth and Claus Wittich (University of California Press, 1978), 2: 729–31.

14 Marx, *Grundrisse*, 326.

15 Marx, *Capital*, vol. 1, 899.

established wage labor remains a constant threat and consequence for failing to properly assimilate into the regime of waged work.

Capitalist wage labor relies on the synergistic split between structural and direct violence. Søren Mau emphasizes the role of "mute compulsion" in capitalism, that is, how its violence, though ever present, is continually denied, covered over, made invisible. He draws attention to Rosa Luxemburg, who writes:

> When the ancient slave, crucified by his master, writhed in ineffable agony, when the serf collapsed under the rod of the corvée overseer or under the burden of labor and misery, at least the crime of man against man, of society against the individual, lay open, exposed, atrocious in its nakedness, blatant in its brutality. The crucified slave, the martyred serf, died with a curse on his lips, and his dying gaze met his tormentors with hatred and a promise of revenge. Only bourgeois society draws a veil of invisibility over its crimes.[16]

Going to work for a wage does not usually *appear* as violent; it is normalized and internalized, even valorized. This dissimulation is a crucial element of how capitalism accomplishes its societal reproduction, by packaging structural violence as freedom.

Social Immobility and Societal Reproduction

The violence of the wage only compounds as we analyze capitalism's endurance over time. A society's ability to reproduce itself over time is called "societal reproduction"; capitalist societal reproduction confines workers *to a capitalist future.*

Any mobility that workers gained through proletarianization relied on confinement to the capitalist system as a whole. A worker can move to a new city or exchange their carpentry tools for the doctor's stethoscope (if they can afford more school), but they cannot choose to organize their life beyond the dictates of capital; in this sense, they are confined, locked in, controlled to respond to a society that was made by human choices, but which they are not free to alter.

16 Quoted in Søren Mau, *Mute Compulsion: A Marxist Theory of the Economic Power of Capital* (Verso, 2023), 1.

This is precisely what Marx means when he writes that the worker can leave their specific place of employment, but they

> cannot leave the whole class of its purchasers, that is, the capitalist class, without renouncing his own existence. He does not belong to this or that particular employer, but he does belong to the employing class; and more than that, it is his business to find an employer; that is, among this employing class it is his business to discover his own particular purchaser.[17]

The mobility of wage labor thus entails a huge cost: the confinement to a system of organized violence that brands itself as liberation. We cannot opt out of the capitalist system—at least not individually.

Capitalist societal reproduction also structurally produces class divergence. In sum, because the rich steal money, time, and labor from proletarians, capitalism entails that the rich get richer and the poor get poorer. That is, in general and with few exceptions, working-class people have no path beyond their lot and will remain, regardless of their individual choices, confined to this legalized predation while the bourgeoisie expand their wealth at the expense of people and planet.

What this produces overall is *social immobility*. While capitalist ideology continually emphasizes the possibility of social mobility—if you just work hard enough and save your pennies, you too can exploit other human beings!—this is mostly an illusion (individual exceptions notwithstanding). It is not in any way surprising that the richest families of the Renaissance still constitute most of the wealthiest Italian families today.[18] It is not surprising that entire countries accumulate capital at the expense of others by continuing to impose a regime of labor exploitation, stolen land, resource extraction, and cultural imperialism.

An individual person may move from worker to unemployed and back again; in exceptional cases, they may even claw their way into the ranks of the bourgeoisie, but capitalism *capitalizes* on proletarian misery, and exploitation produces class immobility; which is to say, class confinement. Even the image of upward class mobility that exerts so much pressure on working-class people is usually the intense desire for (and occasional achievement of) middle-class comfort: easeful consumption, relative job and housing security, and reduced existential stress. A far cry from actual class mobility, these desires *actually* name better proletarian working

17 Karl Marx and J. L. Joynes, *Wage-Labor and Capital* (Twentieth Century Press Limited, 1893), 4.

18 Guglielmo Barone and Sauro Mocetti, *Intergenerational Mobility in the Very Long Run: Florence 1427–2011*, Temi di discussione 1060 (Bank of Italy, 2016), 42.

conditions with a lower rate of exploitation. The middle class is the part of the working class with personal property and moderate savings; they are not the bourgeois owners of the means of production. The desire or achievement of middle-class stability is *not* class mobility. It is rather, the appearance of mobility that further entrenches the societal reproduction of confinement to the proletarian condition, in a way that reinforces a form of manufactured consent.

Discourses of class mobility intersect with other forms of social immobility, notably, with race. Race, unlike many other forms of group membership, is a social construction based in its supposed *immutability* and *heritability*. Scholars of race and racism generally agree that whatever forms of ethnic, national, religious, and regional parochialisms dominated social imaginaries before the sixteenth century, it was global capitalism, through its reliance on enslavement and colonization, that created race in the modern sense. Though the shape of race has shifted over the last five hundred years, taking on morphological, biological, scientific, cultural, and colorblind forms, all these modern ideas of race are rooted in a supposedly immutable and biological inheritance.[19] At the same time that the social determinism of feudalism was supposedly waning, the racialization of enslaved and colonized peoples cemented a new form of naturalized human hierarchy.

Racialization forms a technology of confinement in several ways: on the one hand, the most brutal forms of confinement were reserved for racialized peoples, and on the other, people became confined by race, meaning that their life chances and possibilities were marked out by the boundaries of racial classification. But perhaps one of the most important functions of race alongside (rather than opposed to) the wage was that the introduction of extreme immobilization made the class system seem comparatively mobile. Anyone could become rich—at least in theory—but no one could change their race (Rachel Dolezal notwithstanding!). That is to say, one of the main ways that race is valuable to capitalism is as a system of stable confinement that makes the confinement of the wage *appear* free and mobile.

Marx famously declared that "labor in white skin cannot emancipate itself where it is branded in black."[20] Many have interpreted this passage as a commentary on the linked fate of Black and white workers or on the

19 Ladelle McWhorter, *Racism and Sexual Oppression in Anglo-America: A Genealogy* (Indiana University Press, 2009); Eduardo Bonilla-Silva, *Racism Without Racists: Color-Blind Racism and the Persistence of Racial Inequality in America*, 3rd edition (Rowman & Littlefield Publishers, 2009).

20 Marx, *Capital*, volume 1, 414.

intertwined institutions of wage labor and transatlantic chattel slavery. We might also read this line as an insight that capitalism, which is predicated on an illusory social mobility, can never be overcome where other forms of durable social hierarchy continue to exist, where some are *branded* and *marked* out as a permanent underclass subjected to brutality and violence. The project of overcoming capitalism would entail eliminating *all forms* of social branding; some kernel of capitalist logic would have remained if we eliminated wage labor but left intact systemic and naturalized hierarchies of any kind, especially those that sustain the accumulation of capital.

Thus, in addition to thinking about the wage worker as "doubly free," we might also think about the wage worker as "doubly confined": confined to being exploited, confined to reproducing the system that exploits them. And when we seek to overcome these forms of confinement, through the refusal to work or organizing for a world constituted otherwise, other forms of confinement await as punishment, repression, and deterrence. If we read capitalism through the lens of confinement, we see new dimensions of wage labor, emphasizing the limits of worker mobility rather than its promise. The wage, both for the individual worker and for the class, emerges as a mechanism of confinement to the precarity and exploitation of waged work.

Investment in Domination

This violence is more apparent in some situations rather than others. When Awdah spoke to the group of activists described in the Introduction, he emphasized the ways that Palestinians are confined, both in and beyond work. He described a racist system of checkpoints and permits that inhibit workers' free movement, no matter where they work. But he also talked about how some Palestinians are forced to work for Israelis, either outside the West Bank or, increasingly, in the very same settlements that encroach on Palestinian land. Though the Israeli settler colonial regime sometimes attempts to eliminate, exterminate, and expel Palestinians, it also at times requires Palestinian workers. As explored in the previous chapter, capitalism can and does cycle through attempts to incorporate, exterminate, and abandon racialized workers, depending on market conditions. This pattern has been particularly devastating since the Nakba.

Over the last century, the Israeli state and proto-Israeli Zionist settlers have at times very much depended on Palestinian labor, especially in construction and agriculture. In the wake of both the First and Second Intifadas, the Israeli government increasingly pursued foreign workers as a way of decreasing its reliance on Palestinian workers. Palestinians know clearly that wages do not bring freedom, just as they know well that survival often compels proletarians to seek employment from Israelis actively expanding settler colonialism. In a situation that seems only to get more dire every year, Palestinian workers are often forced with an impossible choice: starvation or survival through exploitation by those who will, at every turn, support their annihilation.

In some sense, all workers under capitalism face some version of this impossible choice—starvation or survival through exploitation. But at the same time, the colonial and racial character of capitalist accumulation introduces specific differences within the global proletariat. Across the world, racialized and colonized people have often faced specific barriers on their physical mobility: pass laws, visa requirements, checkpoints, health inspections, and more. Incorporation into the capitalist wage market deepened rather than eliminated these barriers to supposedly free movement. At the same time, the colonial character of capitalist accumulation further entrenches additional forms of social immobility for racialized peoples. It matters that Palestinian workers are forced to accumulate profit not only for a *capitalist* but for a *settler capitalist*. If all workers confront the wage as a double bind, racialized and colonized workers find themselves hemmed in by still more forces.

That all waged workers depend on the capitalist system for survival is part of its sticky power and the seemingly intractable strength of its compulsion. Capital confronts the waged worker *simultaneously* as the source of their unfreedom *and* as the condition of the possibility of their survival. In other words, capitalism creates workers with *split interests*, who simultaneously have an interest in overcoming capitalist domination and who reproduce themselves through capitalism.[21] This knot forms part of the challenge of proletarian anti-capitalist struggle.

If you depend on something for your survival, even if it is a violent thing, you become *invested* in its reproduction in some ways. As Marx reminds us, proletarians *have nothing* to sell but their own labor, and the threat of starvation, death, and imprisonment are obvious motivators. Because the capitalist system is *both* the source of anti-proletarian structural violence *and* the means of avoiding a different (and worse) fate, workers' interests are *actually*—not only ideologically—split, carved in two.

21 The language of split interests has been deepened and nuanced in many conversations with Will Paris.

Considered from a long-term structural perspective, it is of course in our interest to overturn the systematic theft reproducing our precarity and threatening us at every turn with death and state violence. But we also have an interest in survival—a real, material, immediate interest. This is why most of us who *understand* the wage as the source of our exploitation (and who organize with others against it) are not free to desist from it and will make (forced, not free) choices to ensure that we remain employed. Thus, proletarians *also* have an interest in the perpetuation of capitalism, even if it is a split interest. Wage labor's unique power is its production of *split interests* in the working class, which makes resistance a particularly difficult and dangerous endeavor. Workers who meet anti-capitalist analysis with skepticism, anxiety, or fear are not simple dupes of a system of naked lies, but are rather responding to a real material force, and they recognize, *as do the bourgeoisie and state powers*, the dangers of anti-capitalism to the current system of reproduction.

Precisely because of the "veil" over the violence of capitalism, the worker's immediate interest *seems* to be the reproduction of the system—and they actually aren't wrong about this. I do not want to dismiss how terrifying anti-capitalist analysis and organizing must seem for a large part of the working class, a fact overlooked by too many organizers. Even if we have "a world to win," anti-capitalism requires assailing *your basic means of survival.* It is not altogether surprising that this is a hard sell. This is perhaps the lesson we should learn from the massive resurgence of mutual-aid projects in the contemporary world (and in previously successful programs like the Black Panthers' Free Breakfast Program). The basic principles of materialism tell us that workers cannot live on the revolutionary idea alone; they also need bread (and roses too). For people to give up on their means of survival—that is, in order for people to refuse the role of societal reproduction—they must see another path toward that survival in a real and concrete way. Part of capitalism's confinement of life is to foreclose both the material possibilities of surviving beyond a wage *and* the imaginative possibilities of dreaming a world constituted otherwise.

Søren Mau sums up one part of this knot, highlighting how capitalism's structural violence functions: "Mute compulsion only works because the worker *wants to live.* Only because of this can capital succeed in demanding surplus labour in exchange for the means of life."[22]

Capitalism is defined by this seizure of life. More so than any form of labor in particular, capitalism defines any society in which the

22 Mau, *Mute Compulsion*, 134.

reproduction of life becomes dictated by the whims of the market, the logic of accumulation, and a class of bourgeois exploiters who own the means of production and for whom workers are fundamentally interchangeable and eminently replaceable.

In a concrete sense, capital transformed how life was managed. In the eighteenth and nineteenth centuries, the state and bourgeoisie developed a keen interest in understanding and knowing more and more about common people in order to make them more profitable. Equipped with new practices of tracking, optimization, and data collection, the state and bourgeoisie alike attempted to reshape all aspects of society to facilitate the growth of capital. As more of our lives have transitioned online, this trend is only intensifying. To this end, states (rather than parishes) begin to implement birth and death registries, censuses, and the entire edifice of what Dean Spade calls "administrative life": identity documents (including passports), state certifications, imposed health checks, and the list goes on. Armed with new information about its population, state and capital make decisions about which populations to invest in (in terms of infrastructure, social services, and so on) and which to leave to what Ruth Wilson Gilmore calls "organized abandonment."[23] They mobilize new population-level knowledge in order to better confine, to enact a differential valuation of populations' lives, a process Michel Foucault once described as "biopower" or control over life and its character. Capitalism divides the population into those worthy of investment and, in Jacques Rancière's words, "the part that has no part."[24] This division was, from the beginning, a racist project, one suffused with a eugenicist philosophy baked into the central functions of the state.[25]

Severed from the means of (re)production, proletarians are forced to accept a different form of life, a capitalist form of life. This process is directed at proletarians as a *population*, as a whole, rather than at individual workers. But since, as we saw above, *not everyone* who depends on the wage will indeed have access to it, some will simply be allowed

---

23 Dean Spade, *Normal Life: Administrative Violence, Critical Trans Politics, and the Limits of Law* (Duke University Press, 2015); Ruth Wilson Gilmore, *Abolition Geography*, eds. Brenna Bhandar and Alberto Toscano (Verso, 2022), 92, 102, 233, 305.

24 Jacques Rancière, *Disagreement: Politics and Philosophy*, trans. Julie Rose (University of Minnesota Press, 2004), 30.

25 For Foucault, this eugenicist orientation of state policy both is racial in the normal sense we use the term and also applies to many groups of people who we wouldn't often call "racialized." Eugenics as a philosophy and as fascist state policy *always* applied to both racialized populations and other groups of people like LGBTQ people, Jews, and Muslims (who are sometimes though not always *also* racialized), disabled people, and so on.

to die. Capital thus splits the proletarian population in two: those who secure their survival by producing as much value as possible for capital, and those whom capital and the state deem "bad investments." This latter population will face one of two fates: either they will be subjected to more direct forms of confinement *or* they will be simply abandoned, left to die, their deaths treated as individual failures and cautionary tales. In settler colonial states, extermination and abandonment often clear the way for further settlement, land grabs, and resource extraction, further incentivizing the "making surplus" of Indigenous peoples.

What does it mean, in a real sense, for institutions of power to say some lives should be reproduced while others lay abandoned? In a material sense, some populations will have access to schools, libraries, safe housing, hospitals, parks, recreational facilities, and grocery stores, while others must do without. It will manifest in a divide in infrastructural investment, public works, building or maintaining access to key utilities. It will also determine where police will invade to enforce organized abandonment. The wage thus forms one important mechanism of capital's confinement of life, but the distribution of the population into those who may live and those who may die is inscribed in the working of capitalist *society* far beyond the workplace, reflected in a dense web of institutional arrangements, political and financial investments, and deployments of direct violence.

Capital's relationship with waged workers is thus *bi-directional.* Capital depends on the successful capture of proletarians into the system of capital accumulation; in general, it is directly invested in proletarian life and in making us live in the way most conducive to the continued accumulation of capital. *At the same time that capital depends on workers, proletarians depend on capital to live.* It is thus a bi-directional (though profoundly asymmetrical) relationship, one that severely confines the possibilities and character of proletarian life.

When workers exhort their fellows that "you don't need the boss, the boss needs you," they are dramatizing the parasitic nature of capitalist exploitation. Antonio Gramsci's great insight was that for the wage worker, capitalism relies on the production of consent.[26] His analysis shows the importance of creating new counter-hegemonic ideas that can expose the violence of the capitalist system. The interruption of ideological domination is, of course, a necessary element of anti-capitalist struggle; but it is equally important to recognize that consent is not manufactured

26 Antonio Gramsci, *Selections from the Prison Notebooks* (International Publishers, 1971), 100.

from thin air. Consent correlates to the waged worker's material reality: our dependence on capitalism as a means of our immediate survival.

Conclusion: Confinement and the Societal Reproduction of Wage Society

Wage labor illuminates four distinct modes of capitalist confinement. The first is capitalism's imperative of societal reproduction. For capital to accumulate, capitalism must continue, week after week, month after month, year after year. Capitalism as a form of society must reproduce itself for capital to grow. The reproduction imperative constrains the kind of future we can enact, inhabit, and imagine. The basic premise of societal reproduction is that we continue on the same path forward, that the kinds of violence that structure our society be extended, doubled, intensified. In capitalism, it often seems as though "anything is possible"—as long as the future looks exactly like the present. We are harnessed into this confined vision of the future, often against our will, often without even realizing it. This may be true of all societies that compel reproduction, but it takes on new meaning under capitalism.

Second, what capitalism reproduces is a form of generalized social *immobility*. Wage labor is one important piece of capitalism's overall immobility, the reproduction of massive asymmetries of power and the means of survival. This constitutes one key element in the confinement of life: what we can aspire to is only more of the same, the eternal return on capital's investment.

Third, wage labor constitutes a unique form of confinement in capitalist society. As wage laborers survive through their incorporation into the capitalist system, mobilizing against it appears as their death. The wage is a delicate instrument of domination, one so finely tuned that it turns violence and exploitation into the thing we clamor for rather than a violence we are able to reject. By producing a direct *interest* in capital's reproduction, waged workers face extreme barriers to mobilizing against capitalism. We want to survive. Hardly anyone could be faulted for such a desire. But because capital confines our means of survival to the system of exploitation, workers have interests that are constitutively split: while we would benefit from the abolition of capitalism in the largest sense, mobilizing against capitalism entails militating against our means of survival. The idea that workers have nothing to lose but their chains is a brilliant agitation, but it may not tell the whole story.

Lastly, capitalism's intertwining with forms of racial, gender, and colonial power means that the expansion of waged labor often entails unique confinements for certain sectors of the global proletariat. As much as capital pits workers against one another, forcing us to compete for access to survival, it continues to harness the power of multiple oppressions to ensure that we do not all compete on equal ground. Capitalism divides the working class as a central part of its strategy, including by dividing workers from those made "surplus."

For those locked out of the wage market, however, the balance of power looks much different. As explored in the previous chapter, capital will often engage in wanton and rapacious campaigns of murder; for enslaved and colonized people, as well as for those made "surplus" to capital's accumulation, capital promises death much more than survival. For this reason, resistance historically took on a much different trajectory among enslaved and colonized people. When capitalism promises death rather than survival, people often recognize that in a very real sense, they have nothing to lose but their (often physical) chains.

Wage labor is thus capitalism's preferred form of domination, not because it is the *only* way to concrete capital but because it has proven *the most stable form of capitalist domination.* In drawing proletarians into the system, in folding them into the system, in capturing their *interests*, capitalism appropriates, domesticates, defangs, and disciplines. *For that reason, wage workers might, contrary to accepted Marxist wisdom, be the least likely position to initiate revolutionary action against the capitalist system as a whole.* Workers are so confined by this logic that they may believe they have nowhere to move, no space to maneuver, no possible way out.

This split—between workers and other proletarians—is itself a central part of capital's divide-and-conquer strategy. It bribes workers to accept their domination as a comparatively better lot than their neighbors' and feeds an ideology of moral (or biological) superiority to prevent the recognition of shared interests. It has often seeded mutual distrust, convincing workers to pursue our liberation at the expense of or in isolation from those abandoned by the state and capital. The wage is thus an extremely precise instrument of capitalist domination: on the one hand, it splits our interests, limiting our radicalism in the name of our own survival, and on the other, it splits us off from truly understanding and resisting the production of others' death from which we are exempt. This trap has ensnared workers and theorists alike. It has made us liable to believe that exploitation is the worst fate proletarians experience, and it has occluded a clearer understanding of just how bad things are—and how much worse they are likely to get if we cannot overcome capitalism.

In this context, communists' demand for the abolition of wage labor takes on new meaning. When communists demand the abolition of wage labor, it is not only a demand for the end of private property in the means of production, the end of exploitation, the end of a system that compels toil from the many for the benefit of the few. But a liberated society must also demand the elimination of a society that splits worker interests so fatally, and that splits workers off from other proletarians. The opposition of liberation and survival is woven deep into the character of capitalist society; the abolition of wage labor speaks to the desire for a society in which survival and liberation go hand in hand.

Truly revolutionary organizing must eliminate two different organizations of confinement: the multiple confinements of the wage and the confinement of life to capitalist reproduction. Achieving the latter requires making good on the unfinished promise of abolition explored in the previous chapter. Liberation from capitalism must not cease at the elimination of exploitation, but at the full range of institutions, practices, and social narratives that support capitalism's death machine.

The abolition of waged exploitation is a central demand for anticapitalists, as is the abolition of the entire society that relies on it. To abolish wage labor, however, we must also abolish the private property that undergirds the social system of exploitation. It is not only that wage labor takes place *somewhere*—and that somewhere is private property—but also that the entire ability of the capitalist class to engage in systematic predation depends on the legal and social relations of private property, the subject of the next chapter. If the creation of a liberated society depends on overcoming wage labor *and* the social relations of the wage, it surely also requires the communists' original proposal: the abolition of private property.

3

Private Property and the Confinement of Land, Labor, and Life

Class war does not happen on an abstract board toting up profit and loss, it is a war that needs a terrain.

—Midnight Notes Collective[1]

The law locks up the man or woman / Who steals the goose off the common, / But lets the greater villain loose / Who steals the common from the goose.

—English Folk Poem[2]

In 1829, the verdant hills and valley surrounding the Pyrenees Mountains shook into revolt. Though conditions had been deteriorating for the local peasants for some time, a new set of regulations passed by King Charles X threatened to make life so untenable that the residents of Bellongue, Bethmale, Biros, and Massat finally said "enough." Armed with guns, threats, and fire, the peasants began organizing, first in small groups and later in much larger ones. The War of the Demoiselles had opened, and it would continue in earnest for the next two and half years.

The peasants contested many effects of rising state consolidation and the Industrial Revolution, but the immediate cause of revolt was the Forest Code of 1827. Under the pretense of forest conservation, the Forest Code prohibited local residents from using the woods and its products as they always had by banning wood collecting, felling, grazing, hunting,

1 Midnight Notes Collective, "Introduction," *The New Enclosures*, no. 10 (1990): 9.

2 Quoted in Peter Linebaugh, *Stop, Thief!: The Commons, Enclosures, and Resistance* (PM Press, 2014), 153.

fishing, and gathering. In essence, the Code took the forest out of the common and attempted to sever the local population from their means of basic survival.[3]

Facing this existential threat, residents banded together and fought back. They began by rounding up forest guards and forcing them out of the area. So united were they that guards complained that innkeepers would no longer let rooms to them. By the summer of 1830, the entire region in and around Ariège was in open revolt. The army was sent in to quell the resistance, but to no avail. By September, authorities realized that the peasants wanted "the removal not of particular, abusive guards, but of the entire forest administration from the mountain forests and the recovery of the forests for themselves."[4] In other words, they demanded the reopening of the forest commons against the newly instituted policy of its confinement.

The villagers appeared at night, wearing long white skirts and scarves, and some of them in wigs. They often covered their faces with pieces of cloth or hid their identity by painting their faces with black ash. They attacked landowners, forest wardens, and local police. They called themselves *les demoiselles*, a term roughly equivalent to "young ladies." Historians seem convinced that all the protesters were men dressed up as women, but it seems likely that women were among the organizers, as they so often are. The War of the Demoiselles was not the first uprising to defend communal land rights in the region; resistance swelled against previous enclosure attempts in 1707, 1801, 1806, and 1820.[5] It was, however, the movement that lasted the longest. Over the course of their battle, the Demoiselles united a region of peasants across linguistic and cultural differences to fight state encroachment on their common provisioning.

About a decade later, in the summer of 1841, the fight around forest enclosures flared again, this time in Western Prussia. After a series of conversations from May to July, the Rhine Provincial Assembly voted on a seemingly minor statutory change concerning dead wood in the forests. Little did they know they were about to change the world.

The law redefined "theft of wood" as a crime (rather than a civil offense) and levied harsh penalties for taking any piece of wood, dead

3 Jean-Marie Ballu, Gustave Huffel, and Georges-André Morin, *Histoire des forêts françaises. De la Gaule chevelue à nos jours* (Centre national de la propriété forestière, 2019), 93.

4 Peter Sahlins, *Forest Rites: The War of the Demoiselles in Nineteenth-Century France* (Harvard University Press, 1994), 3.

5 Ibid., 21.

or alive, from any forest, private or communal. In effect, the law made all forests private property, severely upending the rhythms of common life. For centuries if not millennia, residents had ventured to the forests for dead wood to heat their homes in the bitter winters; if they collected extra, they might sell a cord or two. Even as capitalism encroached on their survival, dead wood furnished a modicum of material security for even the most destitute. Beginning on that fateful day in 1841, however, these customary practices would be met with steep fines and forced labor. Fines were increased if an offender followed the example of the Demoiselles and "concealed or had blackened his face."[6]

This law and the debates around it became a near-obsession for a twenty-four-year-old journalist. While the legislators were predominantly concerned with the "restitution" of property owners, the journalist saw the other side: transforming this vital resource into private property would surely lead to the deaths of those who depended on it. He meticulously documented the debates and published five articles about the so-called theft of wood law. Immediately recognizing the class violence of the new law, he wrote, "You should have called it murder of wood and punished it as murder."[7] That young journalist was Karl Marx.

Witnessing the enclosure of the forests and the subsequent misery they caused left a lasting impact on the young Marx. He later reflected that witnessing the collusion between landowning interests and the judicial system "gave me the first impulse to take up the study of economic questions."[8] While his philosophy would mature over time, the question of private property would remain a central anchor in his critique of capitalist society for the rest of his life.

Private property constitutes an anchoring form of confinement upon which all of capitalism's apparent movement depends. Capitalism inaugurated new forms of private property, both in Europe and through colonization, giving rise to multiple forms of overlapping and crosscutting confinement. Capitalism also installed new ideas about property at the heart of what it means to be a human being, with devastating consequences for people around the globe.

---

6 Quoted in Daniel Bensaïd, *The Dispossessed: Karl Marx's Debates on Wood Theft and the Right of the Poor*, trans. Robert Nichols (University of Minnesota Press, 2021), 7.

7 Ibid., 62.

8 Karl Marx, *Contribution to the Critique of Political Economy*, trans. N. I. Stone (Charles H. Kerr & Company, 1904), 10.

Private Property and Capitalist Society

Although, as political theorist C. B. Macpherson contends, "in current common usage, property is *things*," the reality is much more complicated: "Property is not things but *rights*" in things.[9] This could be said of all forms of property, but what makes private property unique is the specific character of those rights, that is, "the exclusive rights of possession, use, and disposition. Its attributes are the right to transfer or alienability, the right to use and enjoyment, and the right to exclude others."[10] Importantly, private property centers the right of exclusion, which many other forms of property lack. As a set of rights (rather than objects), private property is a social relation, and it, too, has a history. Understanding the unique features of capitalist private property illuminates the distinctive violence of capitalist society. "Modern private property, which is my right to exclude you from something" differs substantially "from any form of common property, which is the right of each individual not to be excluded from something."[11] In the words of Michael Hardt and Antonio Negri, the entire system of private property "grants a monopoly of access and decision-making to an individual owner to the exclusion of others."[12] The "private" character of private property signifies the ability to exclude as legal entitlement.

The legal right to exclude is foundational to the logic of capital. A capitalist society produces commodities, goods that are produced not for direct use but to make a profit. Commodity production relies on private property in several ways. In the first place, the capitalist owns *the means*

---

9 C. B. Macpherson, "The Meaning of Property," in *Property: Mainstream and Critical Positions* (University of Toronto Press, 1978), 2. Emphasis in original. The (incorrect) idea that property is about *things* is itself produced by capitalism. As Macpherson explains this trajectory: "As rights in land became more absolute, and parcels of land became more freely marketable commodities, it became natural to think of the land itself as the property. And as aggregations of commercial and industrial capital, operating in increasingly free markets and themselves freely marketable, overtook in bulk the older kinds of moveable wealth based on charters and monopolies, the capital itself, whether in money or in the form of actual plant, could easily be thought of as the property. The more freely and pervasively the market operated, the more this was so. It appeared to be the things themselves, not just rights in them, that were exchanged on the market." (Macpherson, "The Meaning of Property," 7).

10 Harris, "Whiteness as Property," 1730. While in legal practice, courts have sometimes recognized property rights in ways that don't precisely coincide with this definition, my primary concern is not about how individual courts relate to this idea.

11 Macpherson, "The Meaning of Property," 4.

12 Michael Hardt and Antonio Negri, *Assembly* (Oxford University Press, 2017), xvi.

of production (the factory, the machinery, the material inputs) as private property. The capitalist also owns *the product* (the commodity) as private property; this allows profit to proceed directly into their hands rather than to the laborers who made it. In another way, capitalism turns labor into the private property of the worker, something they can contract out in exchange for a wage. Usually, production occurs on land that is also private property, bought and sold by an individual proprietor. Macpherson thus explains that private property "in land and capital" are unique from other forms of property because "they carry with them, when they are held in quantities larger than an individual can work by himself, a power to control in some measure the lives of others."[13] What initially appears as a private right of enjoyment, in practice becomes a right to command the labor of others, to confine the possibilities of others' lives under a form of private despotism. As philosopher and activist Daniel Bensaïd explains:

> The very meaning of the concept of property was thus transformed, gradually and in proportion to the extension of market relations, as capital penetrated into the sphere of production and separated the worker from the means of production. For early liberalism, this signaled the founding of individual autonomy and the transition from feudal subjection to modern citizenship. For rapidly maturing capitalism, this signaled the right to private appropriation of the means of production and the dispossession of the worker, not only from his land or his tools, but his own personhood, which he was then forced to sell at market.[14]

Private property is thus the source of the worker's exploitation—it is because they make but do not profit from production that their wages always undercompensate, that they always produce more value than they are paid. They must then survive by using underpayment to purchase food, water, housing, medicine, and whatever they need to survive, all of which generate profit for members of the bourgeoisie. In the words of Proudhon: "Property, after having robbed the labourer by usury, murders him slowly by starvation . . . Without robbery and murder, property cannot exist."[15] For this reason, Proudhon declared that property is theft.

---

13 Macpherson, "The Meaning of Property," 12.

14 Bensaïd, *The Dispossessed*, 28–9.

15 Pierre-Joseph Proudhon, *What Is Property?*, eds. Donald R. Kelley and Bonnie G. Smith (Cambridge University Press, 2008), 140.

Waged workers must produce commodities to survive because they have no other choice; the wage depends on a prior dispossession from commonly held lands. Private property confronts ordinary people as a barrier to meeting their basic needs, which for Bensaïd means that it always stands in opposition to "the inalienable right to existence (to 'life'!)."[16] Private property thus undercuts the possibilities of living and surviving as a matter of course.

Because private property requires enforcement, it is a paradigmatically political relation steeped in violence (or its threat). As Macpherson continues, "To have property is to have a right in the sense of an enforceable claim to use or benefit of something," meaning that "a claim that will be enforced by society or the state."[17] As David Correia and Tyler Wall write:

> Private property does not merely describe a relation between an owner and a thing. It is a social relation—the right to exclude—shot through with violence. If I take food from a grocery store, drive a car off a dealer's lot, or move into your spare bedroom, and I do it without permission, without paying, and, most importantly, without punishment or fear of punishment, then we cannot say food and cars and spare bedrooms are private property. Without the enforcement of an exclusive claim there is no private property. Private property is therefore always based on force, which is to say that there is no private property without violence.[18]

The punitive organizations of the state—laws, police, prisons—protect private property in objects, land, and people for the benefit of capital accumulation, and create their own forms of confinement with devastating consequences.

We can already see how the regime of private property might lead to various forms of state-sanctioned confinement when enforced by the penal apparatus of the state. But private property is a technology of confinement in several more ways. Chief among these is the confinement of land. Since human beings rely on land and its products for survival, access to land is tightly controlled and regulated under capitalism. Whether this confinement comes with a physical barrier like a hedge, fence, wall, or barbed wire, or whether land is confined through invisible legal regulations and penalties, makes little difference. Ultimately, land becomes

16 Bensaïd, *The Dispossessed*, 28.
17 Macpherson, "The Meaning of Property," 3.
18 David Correia and Tyler Wall, *Police: A Field Guide* (Verso, 2018), 71.

encircled with the messages "do not enter," "no trespassing," and "keep out," with real penalties for ignoring these directives.

Private Property and Proletarian Dispossession

As in the Pyrenees Mountains and the forests of the Rhine, before the rise of capitalism, peasants largely had access to common lands as a means of subsistence: they used common lands to gather wood, graze domesticated animals, collect plants for food and medicine, hunt for wild fowl and game, and collect water. Despite the obvious unfreedom of the hierarchical system of feudalism, the extensive use of the commons as a means to live and survive produced a certain kind of security, one that capitalism's enclosures demolished as it spread across the world. Enclosure is the process of creating new private property on previously communal land. In many places, enclosure required the physical act of erecting a barrier (like a hedge or a fence) but that has not always been true. As the Midnight Notes Collective wrote in 1990:

> Enclosure is one process that unifies proletarians throughout capital's history, for despite our differences we all have entered capitalism through the same door: the loss of our land and of the rights attached to it, whether this loss has taken place in Front Mill, England, in Southern Italy, in the Andes, on the Niger Delta, or in the Lower East Side of New York City.[19]

Even right-wing economists like Garrett Hardin, of "Tragedy of the Commons" fame, recognized that "every new enclosure of the commons involves the infringement of somebody's personal liberty."[20]

Capitalism pursues enclosure primarily to separate proletarians from their means of survival, forcing them to sell their labor for money to access what had once been freely available. Once these common resources are turned into private property, the means of survival become either totally inaccessible or accessible only for a fee. Whatever peasants had previously taken from the commons, proletarians must purchase as commodities. Land confinement thus pushes people into what Ellen Meiksins Wood calls "market dependency," in which survival depends

19 Midnight Notes Collective, "Introduction," 1.

20 Garrett Hardin, "The Tragedy of the Commons," *Science* 162, no. 3859 (1968): 1248.

on purchasing goods on the market, whether from farmers markets or Amazon.[21] Market dependency complements the compulsion to sell one's labor, incorporating many people as both workers and consumers at one and the same time.

In Europe, the process of enclosure began before the rise of capitalism, as its historical precondition. In England, this began in earnest in the thirteenth century, and the backlash was swift and widespread. The thirteenth and fourteenth centuries saw waves of peasant resistance to these changes (beginning roughly with the Peasant's Revolt of 1381 and continuing apace beyond the Midland Rising of 1607 and then reappearing with successive waves of enclosure). At the dawn of the seventeenth century, over half of England's land was still held in common.[22] Enclosures continued in successive waves, first in England and then across Europe for centuries, until the European peasantry had been nearly fully transformed into a proletarian workforce.

For this to be possible, land regulations were completely rewritten. Enclosure empowered individual owners to dispose of land and its products for exclusive, private benefit. No matter the needs of the broader community, private owners may turn communal land into glitzy golf courses for the ultrarich or into the means of production, or they may simply take land *out* of the market, driving up the cost of real estate. The rule of private property precludes collective determination about how land is best used, enshrining the private despotism of individual owners. The human consequences are obviously immense, as most people lack any power over one of the most consequential areas of human life. But there are also direct consequences for the land itself. As Jason Moore has noted, capitalism both gives a price to that which had been free (making nature expensive) *and* constructs nature as one of the central "cheaps" for exploitation and surplus value accumulation.[23] Private property sets the stage for the world-historical degradation of the environment, polluting air, waterways, and soil when profitable. This approach to land continues to propel us toward a "sixth extinction," with incalculable costs on nonhuman life.[24] Communities the world over face devastating

21 Ellen Meiksins Wood, *The Origin of Capitalism: A Longer View* (Verso, 2002).

22 J. R. Wordie, "The Chronology of English Enclosure, 1500–1914," *Economic History Review*, no. 37 (1983); M. E. Turner, *English Parliamentary Enclosure: Its Historical Geography and Economic History* (William Dawson and Sons, 1980).

23 Jason W. Moore, *Capitalism in the Web of Life: Ecology and the Accumulation of Capital* (Verso, 2015).

24 Elizabeth Kolbert, *The Sixth Extinction: An Unnatural History* (Henry Holt & Company, 2014).

consequences to their health and livelihoods as the owning class pursues profit no matter the cost.

In another sense, capitalism confines not only physical land but the *meaning* of land. Capitalist enclosures instituted a hegemonic "land/money equivalency," stripping land of the wider set of social, cultural, religious, and communal meanings across the world.[25] Capitalism thus confines not only *access* to land but also our social imaginary about what land can do, be, and mean, subordinating its social value to the rapacious logic of accumulation. This confining capitalist imaginary wreaks devastation, both socially and ecologically; the more land seems to be a mere source of accumulation, the more the exploitation of nature drives the destruction of the planet and those who inhabit it, human and nonhuman alike. Land confinement is part of what is literally killing us all.

Property and Indigenous Dispossession

Along with disease, germs, heteropatriarchy, and racism, Europeans brought capitalist private property to the lands they colonized. Capitalism developed historically through the colonial imposition of private property, generating the social relations of colonial capitalism that remain today. As Marx writes in *Capital*:

> The discovery of gold and silver in America, the extirpation, enslavement and entombment in mines of the aboriginal population, the beginning of the conquest and looting of the East Indies, the turning of Africa into a ward for the commercial hunting of black-skins, signalized the rosy dawn of the era of capitalist production.[26]

Dene theorist Glen Sean Coulthard explains that the theft of Indigenous land and its enclosure into private property is central to understanding capitalism because "the history and experience of dispossession, not proletarianization, has been the dominant" experience of capitalism for Indigenous peoples in settler colonial states.[27] Following Robert Nichols, I

---

25 Allan Greer, *Property and Dispossession: Natives, Empires, and Land in Early Modern North America* (Cambridge University Press, 2018), 414.

26 Marx, *Capital*, volume 1, 915.

27 Glen Sean Coulthard, *Red Skin, White Masks: Rejecting the Colonial Politics of Recognition* (University of Minnesota Press, 2014), 13. We should however qualify, following Sai Englert, that this does not mean that exploitation is an irrelevant part of the settler colonial project. He shows, convincingly, that settler colonialism in general

understand *dispossession* as a recursive process in which "new proprietary relations are generated but under structural conditions that demand their simultaneous negation"; property is created and stolen at one and the same time.[28] Paradoxically, in dispossession, theft creates property (rather than the other way around). Before colonial dispossession, Indigenous peoples did not relate to land as private property; they had multiple social, cultural, legal, spiritual, and communal ways of relating to land. The vibrant diversity of these modes of understanding the relationship of human to land and water was brutally and violently suppressed through the process of colonization.[29]

Colonial land enclosures took on distinctly racialized dynamics, grounding a capitalist world order suffused with colonialism and white supremacy. Colonialism stole land and resources that produced dizzying wealth for the Global North, a dynamic reproduced by contemporary geopolitics. While legal acts of enclosure characterized European experience of land confinement, the process of colonial property-making generally took three main pathways.

First, and perhaps the most obvious, was naked conquest. European powers arrived and simply declared that the land (and, importantly, people) they had "discovered" *belonged* to them. They justified the violence of conquest in many ways: divine providence, crown charter, natural right, technological mastery, and civilizational superiority. Each European power had its own protocol for legalizing these seizures, but the British Empire saw erecting a fence or enclosing a piece of property constituted sovereignty in the Western Hemisphere, New Zealand, Africa, and India.[30]

has this bipolar structure, tending sometimes toward genocidal/eliminative logics based in land dispossession, and sometimes toward the incorporation of Indigenous peoples into relations of exploitation. Sai Englert, *Settler Colonialism: An Introduction* (Pluto Press, 2022).

28 Robert Nichols, *Theft Is Property!: Dispossession and Critical Theory* (Duke University Press, 2020), 8.

29 Scholars debate whether primitive accumulation is a historical or ongoing process. For more on this debate, see Coulthard, *Red Skin, White Masks*; Rosa Luxemburg, *The Accumulation of Capital*, 2nd edition (Routledge, 2003); Maria Mies, *Patriarchy and Accumulation on a World Scale: Women in the International Division of Labour*, 2nd edition (Zed Books, 1999); Nichols, *Theft Is Property!*; Aaron Jaffe, "The History and Afterlife of Marx's 'Primitive Accumulation,'" *Historical Materialism* 32, no. 3 (2024): 188–215.

30 Patricia Seed, *Ceremonies of Possession in Europe's Conquest of the New World, 1492–1640* (Cambridge University Press, 1995), 20; E. P. Thompson, "Customs, Law, and Common Right," in *Customs in Common* (The New Press, 1991); Ranajit Guha, *A Rule of Property for Bengal: An Essay on the Idea of Permanent Settlement* (Duke University Press, 1996).

In the French Empire, capitalist private property was imposed in phases, with Indigenous land first taken by the Crown and only subsequently turned into private parcels.[31] In some other cases, notably in part of the Spanish Empire, conquest proceeded by capturing preexisting tribute systems, which temporarily kept Indigenous peoples on their lands *to facilitate European accumulation*; ultimately, however, private property also cannibalized these lands, deploying a colonial legal structure of deeds and titles to clear land for large, profitable haciendas owned by settlers.[32]

Second, colonial enclosure was also imposed through treaty or sale, often under conditions of duress, violence, or blatant fabrication. Colonizers assumed and enforced landownership as private property, even when Indigenous communities agreed to grant use rights. We know which worldview was enforced; namely, the one that was backed with guns, cannons, and cavalry. Whatever the mode of initial enclosure, the deed and treaty system rose to prominence in the colonial capitalist world. Indeed, as Robert Williams explains, the right of Indigenous people to sell land (rather than steward it) was one of the only rights that colonizers vociferously defended: "Even the most hardened land-market capitalist assumed the mantle of zealous advocate of the Indians' natural-law right to engage in unregulated real estate transactions."[33] Just as *dispossession* recognizes property only as it is stolen, capitalist colonizers often recognized Indigenous rights and humanity only in the process of capturing land.

Third, enclosure declared land empty and ownerless. The conquest and treaty/sale methods recognized the prior existence of Indigenous peoples, even if that recognition occurred only through brutal violence: forced conversion, enslavement, theft, and war. By declaring territory *terra nullius* or other related terms, colonizing powers attempted to erase Indigenous peoples' existence altogether, declaring land "empty," and hence "naturally" open to appropriation.[34] Lest we imagine this discourse as long since passed, the Zionist schools, synagogues, and summer camps of my youth continued to repeat the colonial falsehood that before

31 Greer, *Property and Dispossession*, 174.

32 For more on this, see Daniel Nemser, *Infrastructures of Race: Concentration and Biopolitics in Colonial Mexico* (University of Texas Press, 2017).

33 Robert A. Williams, *The American Indian in Western Legal Thought: The Discourses of Conquest* (Oxford University Press, 1992), 292.

34 For more on the development of the term *terra nullius* and its relation to other, related terms, see Andrew Fitzmaurice, "The Genealogy of Terra Nullius," *Australian Historical Studies* 129 (2007): 1–15; Michael Connor, *The Invention of Terra Nullius: Historical and Legal Fictions on the Foundation of Australia* (Macleay Press, 2005).

the creation of the State of Israel in 1948, Palestine was "a land without a people," empty, just waiting to be appropriated by Jews, who were "a people without a land."[35] Perhaps counterintuitively, the deployment of the terra nullius strategy only increased as time went on, rapidly expanding through the nineteenth century.[36]

The idea that what belongs to no one is potential property waiting to be seized can be traced to the Roman legal concept of *ferae bestiae* (literally, "wild beasts"). According to *ferae bestiae*, a log in the wood or a fish swimming in a stream becomes rightful property of the one of who takes it, as long as it did not previously belong to another. This principle remained true in the European commons; once a peasant felled a tree or collected an herb or trapped a pheasant, they became personal property. In this sense, while philosopher John Locke is often credited with the idea that property is created through "mixing one's labor" with the natural world, it is much more accurate to say that Locke reflected long-held social ideas about property and radicalized them to new heights.[37] Despite its roots in much older history, the rise of capitalism transformed this idea in significant ways, moving away from concepts of personal property to the violent social relation of private property in the means of production.

Curiously, sometimes colonizers recognized that people lived on these supposedly "empty" lands. Colonizing powers might declare a land "empty" if they did not believe its residents worked the land in "productive" ways. Of course, the criteria used to assess work, productivity, and improvement reflected the worldview of European colonizers—and rising capitalism. Because Europeans had culturally specific notions of what cultivated land looked like—enclosed gardens, agricultural fields, and domesticated animals—they dismissed many forms of Indigenous

35 Interestingly, this phrase has deep roots in Christian rather than Jewish Zionism. The earliest known use of the phrase comes from the Restorationist Reverand Alexander Keith, who coined it in the 1840s in a book about his travels to Palestine. Restorationism is a particular form of religious Christian Zionism with a deep entanglement with both Islamophobia and antisemitism. Scholarly research shows that the phrase mostly circulated among Christian Zionists and was not adopted by Jewish Zionists until the twentieth century. See Alexander Keith, *The Land of Israel According to the Covenant with Abraham, with Isaac, and with Jacob* (William Whyte and Co., 1843); Diana Muir, "A Land Without a People for a People Without a Land," *Middle Eastern Quarterly* 15, no. 2 (2008): 55–62; Adam M. Garfinkle, "On the Origin, Meaning, Use and Abuse of a Phrase," *Middle Eastern Studies* 27, no. 4 (1991): 539–50.

36 Fitzmaurice, "The Genealogy of Terra Nullius."

37 John Locke, *Two Treatises of Government*, 3rd edition, ed. Peter Laslett (Cambridge University Press, 1988), 288.

stewardship as qualifying labor or improvement. As Andrew Fitzmaurice notes, Europeans often said that Indigenous lands were "inhabited in such a way that no sovereignty and very little property" existed.[38] "Proper" occupation meant capitalist use: domestication, extraction, and private property. The imposition of capitalist definitions and standards of adjudication was a central mechanism of the colonial relation. While the concept of *ferae bestiae* predates the rise of capitalism, social relations of private property radicalized the idea, defining all of nature as property-in-waiting (and therefore, later, commodities-in-waiting).

Whatever the method of colonial appropriation, the imposition of private property in land had significant consequences for Indigenous peoples. Colonial enclosures brought exogenous rule, a new form of sovereignty and the imposition of an entirely new order predicated on violence and group subordination. When British landowners encircled the Windsor commons with hedges, displaced British peasants faced new forms of dispossession internal to their own society. When British settlers arrived at Jamestown, they brought with them British law, culture, society, and the narrative of the natural inferiority of the peoples they encountered. Consolidating the system of private property in the colonies imposed an entire order of racialized subjection. Thus, colonial enclosure, while deeply connected to European enclosures, uniquely entailed the subordination of colonized society to a settler and colonial *mode of life*. In this sense, enclosures *both* were the anchor of *private* property and capitalism's highly individualizing culture, *and*, as a colonial imposition, were aimed at subordinating Indigenous peoples *collectively* under the power of European domination. I discuss the collective enclosures of land more in the next chapter.

Colonial enclosures undergirded the entire apparatus of colonial—and especially settler colonial—society, which buttressed capitalism in myriad, world-altering ways. Colonial enclosures were not "just another" imposition of capitalism; they were part of concreting the colonial-capitalist world order we still inhabit. Without colonial enclosure, in other words, capitalism may well have remained a strange and somewhat contained economic practice of a relatively peripheral set of societies in the far North rather than the world system that we see today. As Coulthard continues, the capture of land was central to the rise of capitalism in the Western Hemisphere:

38 Fitzmaurice, "The Genealogy of Terra Nullius," 4.

> These formative acts of violent dispossession set the stage for the emergence of capitalist accumulation and the reproduction of capitalist relations of production by tearing Indigenous societies, peasants, and other small-scale, self-sufficient agricultural producers from the source of their livelihood—the land.[39]

It is in this sense that J. Kēhaulani Kauanui declares that, for Indigenous peoples, "property is a form of war."[40]

The dispossession of Native land made way for other forms of confinement to develop on this land. In the Western Hemisphere, Indigenous peoples were often placed on reservations, confined to small areas of their ancestral homelands and subjected to many forms of violence, both direct and structural. Colonial enclosures and Indigenous removal undergirded the rise of capitalist plantations and the racialized chattel slavery instituted on them, forming a proliferating web of confinement. As Gary Fields describes the interconnection of Native removal and chattel slavery:

> In the end, the landscape that confined black slaves comprised a dual type of incarceration. In the first place, native groups were removed from their homelands and confined by the U.S. government in a system of reserves to make way for the onslaught of settlers seeking fortunes from cotton growing. As the indigenous were cleared from the lands and interned, a landscape of prison-like spaces associated with slave plantations emerged on the lands of evicted Native Americans and spread throughout the American South, immobilizing black slaves by chaining them to the property of their masters. In this way, American Indian reservations of removed indigenous Americans and the cotton plantations worked by slave labor were complementary elements of *a landscape where two groups of people were confined* and kept in bondage. With the native people forced into reservations, and blacks held on plantations, the landscape was cleared of color and essentially made white.[41]

The colonial project thus entailed many forms of confinement: the obvious land confinement of all enclosures and the specific confinements of the

39 Coulthard, *Red Skin, White Masks*, 7.

40 J. Kēhaulani Kauanui, *Paradoxes of Hawaiian Sovereignty: Land, Sex, and the Colonial Politics of State Nationalism* (Duke University Press, 2018), 105.

41 Fields, "Lockdown: Gaza Through a Camera Lens and Historical Mirror," 47. Emphasis added.

colonial project. The confinement of land was intertwined with land dispossession, Indigenous removal, and racialized chattel slavery.

At the same time, the conquest of Indigenous lands significantly altered the character of land confinement within Europe itself. European relations of private property did not emerge fully formed entirely within the boundaries of the continent to be imposed, unchanged, on the rest of the world. The process of colonization was rather a long process of "property formation" in which colonization shaped capitalist property relations. Jean-Paul Sartre understands this process as a "boomerang effect" of colonization on the internal dynamics of European society.[42]

Let us take land registration as just one example of this boomerang. The British began experimenting with systems of title registration in colonized Scotland in the seventeenth century, but it was first imposed on a grand scale in the mid-nineteenth century in South Australia as well as in Bengal, as Ranajit Guha detailed so painstakingly.[43] The British subsequently imposed title registration to devastating consequences in Palestine, and the Americans followed suit in the colonization of Hawaii. Only after several decades of colonial experimentation did land registration return to mainland England, where it was completed mostly in the 1920s.

Critical legal theorist Brenna Bhandar explains that the system of title registration "reflect[ed] the commodity vision of land that British land reformers carried with them to the colony" and constituted "a key means of diminishing Indigenous systems of land tenure that did not conform to an economic and legal system based on an ideology of the possessive individual."[44] She explains that the relatively late formalization of land registration in the English metropole reflected the endurance of aristocratic privilege; the landed gentry had a material and pecuniary interest in opposing forms of land control that might lessen the hold of customary privilege (as did those in the legal profession, whose expertise was needed in order to navigate the complicated conveyance system). In this sense, the class interest of the aristocracy in maintaining feudal power placed them in opposition to bourgeois reforms that made land more easily alienable in the capitalist sense. This history tells us something important about capitalism and colonization. It is not only that capitalist techniques like

---

42 Greer, *Property and Dispossession*; Jean-Paul Sartre, "Preface," in Frantz Fanon, *The Wretched of the Earth*, trans. Richard Philcox (Grove Press, 2005).

43 Guha, *A Rule of Property for Bengal.*

44 Brenna Bhandar, *Colonial Lives of Property: Law, Land, and Racial Regimes of Ownership* (Duke University Press, 2018), 29.

title registration were innovated in the colonies and only later imposed in England; it is that, in a certain sense, the colonies were more thoroughly under the control of capitalist logic than the colonial metropole.

This is just one illustrative example of a more general dynamic: techniques of capitalist confinement—whether of land, labor, or life—were often pioneered in the colonies before returning to Europe. Colonization was a central aspect of the rise of capitalism, and colonized peoples were the test subjects for so many forms of capitalist discipline that would come to enclose us all. Understanding the full historical weight of colonization to the rise and reproduction of capitalism requires a dialectical and diachronic approach: We must say at once that private property was an imposition of rising capitalism on Indigenous peoples around the world *and* that the development of capitalist property relations is partially an effect of that imposition.

Property in Personhood

Capitalism also inaugurated a new realm of private property: personhood. Throughout capital's ascendant centuries, philosophy and law alike began to construct human beings as *owners* of themselves and their labor. This new understanding introduced a complicated coextension of humanity and property that anchored both waged work and many racial forms of confinement in settler colonization and chattel slavery.

Of all the thinkers of the early modern period, perhaps none is more central to this story than John Locke.[45] Locke understands private property to encompass not only physical objects or land, but human beings' "lives, liberties and estates."[46] Throughout the *Second Treatise on Government*, Locke argues for a definition of property that even includes the relationship of human beings to their personhood: "By property I must be understood here, as in other places, to mean that property which men have in their persons as well as goods."[47]

45 To be clear, the fact that an individual philosopher, no matter how famous, argued for such a conception is less important than how those ideas are taken up by the societies they influence. No one knows more than a contemporary philosopher how marginal our ideas sometimes turn out to be! My interest in Locke's writings here is less scholastic and more political; it is rather because Locke crystallizes nascent capitalist society's overall perspective on property that I attend to the particularities of this thought.

46 Locke, *Two Treatises of Government*, 350.

47 Ibid., 401.

Bringing personhood under the sign of property constituted a foundational shift in the rise of capitalism. It inscribed the elements of private property—exclusivity in use, enjoyment, possession, transfer—*into the heart of what it means to be a person*. In a society based in profit, redefining personhood as property facilitated the use of *people*—including oneself—as a means of accumulating capital. And it implies that if you don't relate to yourself primarily as a vehicle for capital accumulation, you aren't *really* a person—or at least, you aren't *making good* on your personhood. You are *wasting* your personhood, or even, you might be *failing at being a full person*, or at least, *a good person*. This idea ties a very particular kind of productivity (as capital accumulation) to not only moral value but one's very status *as human*. The reduction of personhood to a kind of property is also a confinement of life.

Property in personhood undergirds many forms of contract, especially the waged-labor contract necessary for capitalist bosses to exploit paid workers. To be able to sell (alienate) your labor for a wage, it must be yours to sell. The entire social practice of commodity production thus hinges not only on the private property in the means of production (the machines, inputs, and products) but on a private property conception of labor and personhood.

But Locke goes even farther, recognizing private property rights not only in *one's own labor and personhood* but also in the fruits of nature and other people's labor. He continues, "The Grass my Horse has bit; the Turfs my Servant has cut; and the Ore I have digg'd in any place where I have a right to them in common with others become my *Property*."[48] Capitalism depends on this *transitive property interest in others' labor*. In Locke's initial exposition of how common property becomes individual, he argues one must "mix their labor" directly in order to appropriate it. But if the actual laborer retained property rights in it, workers—not employers—would own the products they create. If workers owned the products of their labor, the entire capitalist system of production would evaporate without exploitation and surplus value creation. So capitalist production requires private property interests in the labor not just of oneself but of *others*.

For Locke, this means that the labor of myself and my servant must be completely equivalent. For capitalism to function, it must *make no difference* whether I have done the labor myself or whether that labor has been done by employees. In Ellen Meiksins Wood's words:

48 Ibid., 289.

> This means not only that I, the master, have appropriated the labour of my servant, but also that this appropriation is in principle no different from the servant's labouring activity itself. My own digging is, for all intents and purposes, the same as my appropriating the fruits of my servant's cutting. But Locke is not interested in simply *passive* appropriation. The point is rather that the landlord who puts his land to productive use, who improves it, even if it is by means of someone else's labour, is being *industrious*, no less—and perhaps more—than the labouring servant.[49]

This last piece is crucial. If the "proper" way of relating to oneself is as a proprietor interested in a return on self-investment, then the capitalist is the vision of "proper" humanity, the one who makes the best use of private property in labor. Paradoxically, the most industrious worker, and hence the best person, is the one who labors not at all, but who is able to command and control the property interest in *other people's labor, as many other people's labor as possible.*

There are a few threads to pull out of Locke's philosophy and the liberal notion of property it represents. First, the appropriation of others' labor represents not only an admissible but a laudable innovation for capitalism, one that undergirds moral or social value. The one who best appropriates and exploits the labor of others not only accumulates more but embodies the model of humanity the most. Science, philosophy, and law will all instantiate this new definition of the human being as owner and exploiter.

Second, the idea that accumulation-oriented proprietorship defines proper personhood lays the foundation for seeing social forms based on other values (community, ecological awareness, social harmony, and so on) as not fully human. In conjunction with the culturally specific ideas of productivity explored above, we can see how liberalism would cast non-European societies as subhuman. Locke certainly said as much about Indigenous peoples in the Americas. His philosophy thus specifically secures European colonization and Indigenous dispossession.

Third, the extension of property rights to persons, both oneself and others, paves the way for thinking about others not only as workers (whose labor can be bought) but as chattel (whose personhood can be bought). Lodged deep in the heart of the liberal concept of private property is the idea that one can buy and sell people, and that one *should* do so in order to make a profit. Because liberal private property and capitalism depend on the idea of property in personhood, enslavement is a consequence not

49 Wood, *The Origin of Capitalism*, 112.

a violation of liberal philosophy.[50] Locke himself came to this conclusion quite readily (he was a remarkably consistent if deplorable thinker). When he authored the *Fundamental Constitutions of Carolina* (1669), he included the following provision: "Every freeman of Carolina shall have absolute power and authority over his negro slaves, of what opinion or religion soever."[51]

Lastly, Locke argued that the entire edifice of liberal government existed to protect these private property rights—in oneself, in lands, in objects, and in people. He writes, "The great and chief end, therefore, of men's uniting into commonwealths, and putting themselves under government, is the preservation of their property," a formulation repeated in many variations throughout the *Second Treatise*.[52]

Taken together, Locke's ideas expose the co-constitution of private property rights, capitalist exploitation, liberal government, Native dispossession, and African enslavement. The coincidence of these elements was not a historical anomaly that would be washed away in a more mature stage of capitalist development; rather, this coincidence inheres in the notion of private property that undergirds capitalist accumulation to the present day.

Private property subtends capitalist society in a wide variety of ways, entailing several forms of confinement across land, labor and life. Aileen Moreton-Robinson (Koenpul, Quandamooka First Nation) argues that Western capitalist society produces "possessive logics" that have a triadic structure: Owning Property, Becoming Propertyless, and Being Property.[53] The imbrication of ownership (of oneself, of others, of land), dispossession, and commodification is another way to name the triadic

50 As Cheryl Harris writes, "Slavery produced a peculiar, mixed category of property and humanity—a hybrid possessing inherent instabilities that were reflected in its treatment and ratification by the law. The dual and contradictory character of slaves as property and persons" thus potentially anchors the complicated notion of property in personhood, rather than follows as a consequence. Harris, "Whiteness as Property," 1718. Locke's *Two Treatises on Government* was first published in 1689; the first slave codes in the Anglo world date to 1661 in Barbados and 1680 in North America, and these built upon even earlier slave codes passed by the Spanish (Provisión del Virrey Diego Colon in 1522 and Las Ordenanzas para la Sujeción de los Esclavos Negros in 1528) and French (Code Noir 1685). Indigenous dispossession predated Locke's publication by nearly two hundred years.

51 John Locke, "Fundamental Constitutions of Carolina," The Avalon Project, March 1, 1669, Yale Law School Lillian Goldman Law Library, avalon.law.yale.edu.

52 Locke, *Two Treatises of Government*, 351. See also: 329, 351, 256, 360, 412, and other places.

53 Aileen Moreton-Robinson, *The White Possessive: Property, Power, and Indigenous Sovereignty* (University of Minnesota Press, 2015).

structure of settler colonization that involves white supremacy, Native dispossession, and the legacies of chattel slavery.

The racial dynamics of property are thus obvious. As Harris explains, the world-historical invention of race in the modern sense depended on ideas of private property that were imposed through Indigenous dispossession and enslavement (Becoming Propertyless and Being Property in Moreton-Robinson's terms): "It was not the concept of race alone that operated to oppress Blacks and Indians; rather, it was the *interaction* between conceptions of race and property that played a critical role in establishing and maintaining racial and economic subordination."[54] This aligned whiteness with the ability to own property (whether in goods or only in one's own labor and personhood), meaning that whiteness is "experienced and deployed as a resource" in the accumulation of capital.[55] Harris shows, at a minimum, that whiteness was protection from *becoming* chattel property, that, for a time, whiteness was a prerequisite for holding property, and that the meaning of private property derived from a specifically European cultural context.[56] Because whiteness "was a prerequisite for access to property in land or slaves," Vicky Osterweil contends that "whiteness became the meta-property from which all other private property flows and is derived."[57]

It is perhaps more accurate to say that because white people were recognized as having property in their personhood, they were able to control those who did not. Constructing Black and Indigenous peoples as non-owners of themselves and their lands meant that whiteness became invested with social power beyond direct ownership; a white person did not need to own Native land or Black people to exercise control over them. Because white people were assumed to have property in their personhood, they entered into a class of owners (even if, in the case of proletarians, they owned only themselves and had to lease out their labor to make ends meet) that had power over non-owners as a class.

---

54 Harris, "Whiteness as Property," 1716.

55 Ibid., 1734.

56 She also shows that at some points, the US court system has affirmed a property interest in being seen and treated as white. I am not sure that, strictly speaking, these things taken together mean that whiteness is best conceived *as property* itself, which is her overall argument. For reasons discussed below, notions of property become very tricky when they are used to describe entities rather than social relations. It is unclear to me from my read of Harris's article the extent to which she conceives of race and property as social relations all the way down, hence my hesitation in thinking about whiteness *as* a form of property.

57 Vicky Osterweil, *In Defense of Looting: A Riotous History of Uncivil Action* (Bold Type Books, 2020), 36.

The entire idea of property in person thus takes on a unique blend of class and racial dimensions. The Marxist discourse of alienation reveals how, even for the fully recognized subject of liberalism, a proprietary relationship to self has damaging effects. In the words of Georg Lukács:

> [It] stamps its imprint upon the whole consciousness of man; his qualities and abilities are no longer an organic part of his personality, they are things which he can "own" or "dispose of" like the various objects of the external world. And there is no natural form in which human relations can be cast, no way in which man can bring his physical and psychic "qualities" into play without their being subjected increasingly to this reifying process.[58]

The result of this process is a dehumanized quality of the relation to oneself and to others; thus, in the words of Theodor Adorno, the possessive relation, even for the "owners" (perhaps especially for them), constitutes "damaged life."[59]

Even though this is true for all laborers who are alienated under capitalism, as Rinaldo Walcott contends, *having once been treated as property*, the stakes of property, in both objects and personhood, hold particular meaning for Black people. For Walcott, the racial politics of capitalism's rise depended on turning human beings *into* property, as "goods" traded on a commodities market, but also *as means of production directly*; if then, Black human beings were commodified into property, then the abolition of property holds high stakes for Black liberation.[60] Another way of explaining the abolitionist project is the elimination of the property-notion of human beings, something that continues to structure the "afterlife" of capitalist slavery.

Returning to Moreton-Robinson's schema, we can see that the property-in-personhood cornerstone of liberal law and political thought bequeaths yet another differential set of possibilities: one might be the (alienated) owner of oneself, but one might also be dispossessed of one's selfhood; the self may be stolen in the same moment of its recognition, something abolitionist Mariame Kaba traced in her project exploring the denial of Black women's rights of self-defense and Saidiya Hartman highlighted

58 Georg Lukács, *History and Class Consciousness: Studies in Marxist Dialectics*, trans. Rodney Livingstone (MIT Press, 1972), 100.

59 Theodor W. Adorno, *Minima Moralia: Reflections from Damaged Life* (Verso, 2020).

60 Walcott, *On Property*.

in her analysis of how enslaved Black people's humanity was recognized in courts of law *only* as a basis for punishment.[61] It is also what Ward Churchill described in *Kill the Indian, Save the Man*, where the settler colonial genocide-by-assimilation of Indigenous peoples recognized the humanity and selfhood of Indigenous people only in opposition to their indigeneity.[62]

What does it mean to own oneself when one's personhood has been denied? Or when one's selfhood is recognized only in so far as it can be punished (Hartman), dispossessed (Nichols), or destroyed (Churchill)? The kind of imposed alienation from oneself and one's labor, oneself and community, from oneself and the structures of life in common, is necessarily much different from that described by Marx, Lukács, or Adorno, and the kind of damage incurred takes a different trajectory. It creates not only reification but, in Du Bois's words, "double consciousness." It also, as Patricia Hill Collins describes, generates a powerful "standpoint" of revolutionary critique, one that, like other forms of working-class resistance (for example, strikes, union drives, and mass protest) is heavily surveilled and policed under capitalism.

These elements, taken together, speak to the structure of a capitalist society in which ownership dictates economic, political, and social power. Capitalist power relations have thus been deeply imbricated with racialization since capitalism's inception, and they continue to undergird contemporary relations of racial domination. These dynamics—the reduction of personhood to property, the establishment of property rights in people, and the dispossession of personhood—are all elements of what I am calling the confinement of life. Rather than the promised open possibilities of movement and freedom, the property/personhood conjuncture instantiates new forms of closure and fixity. However more mobile people become in pursuit of survival, private property acts as a limiting point of friction—on where we can go, but also who and what we can become. Of all the vibrant possibilities of humanity, to be reduced to property is to be confined to a very narrow future indeed.

---

61 Mariame Kaba and Ashley J. Bohrer, "No Selves to Defend: An Interview with Mariame Kaba," *Red Wedge Magazine* (Chicago), August 19, 2014, redwedge magazine.com; Hartman, *Scenes of Subjection*.

62 Ward Churchill, *Kill the Indian, Save the Man: The Genocidal Impact of American Indian Residential Schools* (City Lights Publishers, 2004).

Private Property and the Neoliberal Turn

The idea of enclosure often evokes the historical past, but unfortunately, capitalism's rapacious desire for new forms of private property continues apace. Whether one refers to them as "new enclosures," "ongoing primitive accumulation," or "dispossession," land continues to be ever more confined as the ravenous growth of capitalism engulfs the globe. Across the world, we see continuous appropriation of collectively held lands, not confined to the "rosy dawn" of capitalism's emergence; enclosures are also the sign of high noon.

For many, neoliberalism names this "high noon"—the contemporary, brutal form of capitalism on steroids we are living through. David Harvey defines neoliberalism as "a theory of political economic practices . . . characterized by strong private property rights, free markets, and free trade" and, perhaps more importantly, an embedded system of daily practices that "values market exchange as an ethic in itself."[63] "Neoliberalism has meant, in short," Harvey tells us, "the financialization of everything."[64] Fixing the historical moment of neoliberalism's emergence in the years 1978–1980, Harvey argues that the simultaneous reorientation of the global economic priorities by Deng Xiaoping, Margaret Thatcher, and Ronald Reagan amounts to nothing less than the complete reorganization of the material reality of the entire global population. Neoliberalism has become "hegemonic as a mode of discourse," "incorporated into the common-sense way many of us interpret, live in, and understand the world."[65]

As neoliberalism became the primary economic philosophy in governments, monetary agencies, and international institutions, private property extended to even more new lands, creating "new enclosures" the world over. These new enclosures look much like the old enclosures. Land held in common or thought to be un-ownable are privatized at a rapid pace, echoing the trajectory of colonial powers in the sixteenth through nineteenth centuries: where communal land tenure is not officially protected by law (including precise surveys and registers of its boundaries), individuals lay direct claim to land and follow the bureaucratic steps for title recognition. More often, though, contemporary "land grabs" are facilitated by government intermediaries rather than directly seized

63 David Harvey, *A Brief History of Neoliberalism* (Oxford University Press, 2007), 2, 3.

64 Ibid., 33.

65 Ibid., 3.

by individuals.[66] In these cases, the government will declare a tract of communally owned land as "state land" and then use it to accumulate by extracting natural resources (oil, minerals, metals, wood, and so on) for profit, selling it to foreign developers for cash infusions, or creating a wildlife preserve (often as a basis for lucrative ecotourism).

In addition to continued enclosure of land, neoliberal capitalism seeks ever-new frontiers for expansion and profit extraction by extending the logic of private property. Neoliberalism cannibalizes previously uncommodified terrains of collective social life, imposing the norms of private property on an ever-widening sphere of social existence. In Harvey's estimation,

> the reversion of common rights won through years of hard class struggle (the right to a state pension, to welfare, to national healthcare) into the private domain has been one of the most egregious of all policies of dispossession pursued in the name of neoliberal orthodoxy.[67]

David Lloyd, Patrick Wolfe, and others call this trend the "second enclosure":

> This new mode of accumulation is effectively a renewed movement of enclosure, this time of a "second commons"—that is, of those public goods historically wrested by social movements in compensation for the original loss of commons: social security, public utilities, education and, in the form of both urban and national parklands, even the remnants of public space. These public patrimonies of the modern liberal state that emerged from an earlier moment of enclosure and dispossession represent vast storehouses of capital, resources, services and infrastructure. Held in common for generations, these are now targeted for expropriation and exploitation.[68]

Silvia Federici and George Caffentzis argue that neoliberalism has brought even "the enclosure of knowledge," as access to ideas, education, and media becomes ever-more subsumed into the neoliberal fold, and James Boyle sees intellectual property law as facilitating another "new

---

66 Fred Pearce, *The Land Grabbers: The New Fight over Who Owns the Earth* (Beacon Press, 2012).

67 David Harvey, *Spaces of Global Capitalism* (Verso, 2006), 45.

68 David Lloyd and Patrick Wolfe, "Settler Colonial Logics and the Neoliberal Regime," *Settler Colonial Studies* 6, no. 2 (2016): 109.

enclosure."[69] Others have focused on the patenting of seeds, plants, biological materials, and chemicals as capitalist appropriations of what had once been common; these all have particularly devastating effects on Indigenous communities that have stewarded biodiversity *against* previous rounds of enclosure, only to now have these materials stolen from them for profit.[70] As Bensaïd notes, the neoliberal turn has been buoyed by the coercive apparatus of the state, which supports these new enclosures through

> the destruction of existing social rights and the criminalization of popular resistance (under the pretext of "anti-terrorist" legislation). Thus we see a whole range of provisions that constitute a new kind of "poor law," aimed at strengthening social control and imposing a new discipline of flexible work through generalized precariousness.[71]

It is not only these collective resources that are subject to privatization under neoliberalism. In a very real sense, the right-wing architects of neoliberal philosophy are also enclosing the very meaning of being human in the insidious concept of "human capital." Rooted in discourses of property in personhood, the idea of human capital radicalizes the imperative to act as proprietors of capitalist property in relating to our own selves. Education, social connections, public esteem, partners—all of these should be subjected to precise cost-benefit calculation, oriented toward the return of quantifiable advantages and accolades. Proponents of this idea recommend we treat all aspects of our lives—where we live, whom we love, whether or not we have children, what we study, what we wear, how we talk—as potential sources of accumulation. It is no longer simply that one has a property stake in one's *labor*, one made potentially more lucrative through education or training—that was already explored by Adam Smith.[72] The extension of the concept of human capital attempts

69 Silvia Federici and George Caffentzis, "Notes on the Edu-Factory and Cognitive Capitalism," in *Toward a Global Autonomous University*, ed. Edu-factory Collective (Autonomedia, 2009), 65; James Boyle, "The Second Enclosure Movement and the Public Domain," *Law and Contemporary Problems* 66 (2003): 33–74.

70 Nathalia Hernández Vidal and Laura Gutiérrez Escobar, "Resistencias Epistémico-Políticas Frente a La Privatización de Las Semillas y Los Saberes Colectivos," *Revista Colombiana de Antropología* 55, no. 2 (2019): 39–63; Nathalia Hernández Vidal et al., "Defending the Commons: New Frontiers in Latin American Perspectives on Environmental Justice," *Sociological Inquiry* 93, no. 2 (2023): 370–91.

71 Bensaïd, *The Dispossessed*, 48.

72 As Adam Smith wrote in *The Wealth of Nations*, we can consider as a kind of capital all "the acquired and useful abilities of all the inhabitants or members of the

to subsume *all aspects of human existence and social life* under the rubric and rule of capital. An enclosure if ever there was one. Gary Becker won a Nobel Prize in Economics for this philosophy.

As these enclosures continue, nothing is safe from being turned into property. Capital's endless expansion, its continued movement into new domains, suggests the structural centrality of new forms of confinement to capital's ability to reproduce itself across time and space. But it also means that if this process is ongoing; the battle is far from lost.

Conclusion: Capitalism, Confinement, and the Abolition of Private Property

Private property, the unwieldy social relation at the heart of capitalism, encloses the globe as it continues to enclose us. When Marx and Engels penned *The Communist Manifesto*, they pointed to the possibility of a world that would reject exploitation and dispossession. They were clear, as we should be, that this new society would be incompatible with private property. As they wrote, infamously, "The theory of the Communists may be summed up in the single sentence: Abolition of private property."[73] There are ten basic demands in the *Manifesto*; seven relate directly to the abolition of private property.

Eliminating private property is an abolitionist demand because it takes aim at several forms of confinement at the heart of capitalist social relations. Private property in land, in the means of production, and in personhood undergird capitalist society in all its forms. From wage labor to commodity production to Indigenous dispossession to chattel slavery, private property forms the core of capitalism's history and its ability to reproduce itself in the present. No liberated society can coexist with the confinements concreted in private property.

The abolition of private property and the call for communism have long been identified as demands for class liberation but are also

society. The acquisition of such talents, by the maintenance of the acquirer during his education, study, or apprenticeship, always costs a real expense, which is a capital fixed and realized, as it were, in his person. Those talents, as they make a part of his fortune, so do they likewise that of the society to which he belongs. The improved dexterity of a workman may be considered in the same light as a machine or instrument of trade which facilitates and abridges labor, and which, though it costs a certain expense, repays that expense with a profit." Adam Smith, *On the Wealth of Nations*, ed. P. J. O'Rourke (Atlantic Monthly Press, 2007), 389–90.

73 Karl Marx and Friedrich Engels, "Manifesto of the Communist Party," in *The Marx-Engels Reader*, ed. Robert C. Tucker (W. W. Norton & Company, 1978), 484.

key to projects of racial justice and abolition. As Vicky Osterweil contends:

> Racial settler colonialism is . . . at the core of all modern notions of property. All our beliefs about the righteousness of property, ownership, and commodity production are built on the history of anti-Black violence and settler-colonial extraction. The right to property is innately, structurally white supremacist: support for white supremacy involves a commitment to property and the commodity form.[74]

Thus, just as private property must be abolished in order to achieve communism, Walcott argues property must be abolished in the fight against white supremacy, prisons, and policing. In his estimation, "the question of property" must be rethought "as a central conundrum of abolition."[75] He explains:

> This brings us to the heart of the matter, and the problem of property. At the heart of Black people's calls for abolition is the desire to bring to a close the racial terror that we are subjected to and have been subjected to on a continuous basis since Columbus's initial voyages to the Americas. It is out of those epochal crossings, which led to the colonization of the Americas and to the large-scale, forced movement of Africans to its colonies, that many of our current attitudes, prejudices, ideas, and practices of property, contract law, insurance, banking, government, city planning, travel, customer service; indeed all the networked elements of modern society arose. Foundational to all of it is property—private and public. It is property and our liberation from it that sets abolition apart as a philosophy capable of transforming our understanding of how to live differently together and how to reimagine what life and living can and should mean for all humans. Abolition as both an idea and a practice, then, is as epochal for the future as Columbus's voyages were for our collective past.[76]

Private property anchors capital's process of accumulation; it also grounds a wide range of social relations of domination, oppression, and exploitation. Whatever movement—of goods, of lives, or of money—capitalism stimulates, private property operates to fix, enclose, and confine land,

74 Osterweil, *In Defense of Looting*, 16.
75 Walcott, *On Property*, 17.
76 Ibid., 86–7.

labor, and life. For this reason, the abolition of private property forms one of the most basic conditions of liberation. The abolition of private property surely means something different for those positioned as property owners than it does for those who have become propertyless and those who have been treated as property; but despite these differences, the abolition of private property is the condition of liberation for us all.

In this context, we can see clearly how much the narrative of capitalism as movement leaves out. Proletarians certainly move more, but they do so *because* of a prior set of confinements: the enclosed common lands and the private property that keeps their labor's products just out of reach, as well as the confinements of the settler colony and the plantation. All proletarians find themselves now defined through their relationship to this property, whether they own it or not, and the entire coordinates of social, political, and economic life are defined through proximity to private property. Capitalism creates an entire alienated culture where enclosure sets the model for humanity, with devastating and different consequences for multiple groups of people. And as they move through life, proletarians encounter confinement at every turn. Private property thus anchors a multidimensional matrix of capitalist confinement over labor, land, and life that needs to be abolished if we are ever to be truly free.

The abolition of private property can seem to some as if it heralds the elimination of individuality, but nothing could be further from the case. Marx and Engels explain their vision for a communist society: "an association, in which the free development of each is the condition for the free development of all."[77] Despite the individualistic posture of private property, Marx and Engels suggest that collective visioning of our future and collective control over the possibilities of life is the prerequisite for the development of real individuality. In Bensaïd's words, "Individualization in Marx is not the same as privatization."[78]

Privatization produces horrifying outcomes because of how it disrupts collectives, to be sure. But the logic of capitalist private property also reduces the possibilities of individuality to the mere balance sheet of a property relationship. The transformation of the world into relations of liberation rather than domination surely entails the reorganization of the society we share in common—economic, political, social, and intimate. But it just as much will anchor a new mode of being an individual in the elimination of property as the foundation of personhood. The abolition of private property demands the divestment from the anemic and confined

77 Marx and Engels, "Manifesto of the Communist Party," 491.
78 Bensaïd, *The Dispossessed*, 50.

version of individuality that combines property with domination, including of the self. In other words, the abolition of private property may be the condition of the only individuality worth the name, the only individuality that makes selfhood something more than a confined life.

In the attempt to overcome the confinement of private property, many turn to the world that capitalism eliminated in feudal Europe: the commons. The commons seem an attractive model to restore what capitalism has so cruelly stolen from us: access to land, to community, to survival, to a version of humanity beyond property. The contemporary call to re-common the earth is not the first; many before our time have seen the commons as the remedy to the violences of capitalist private property. But as we shall see, appeals to the commons may be more problematic than they appear at first glance, extending rather than eliminating capitalism's regime of confinement. I turn now to the promise of the commons and the surprising history of confinement that lurks within it.

4

Collective Enclosure and the Capitalist Commons

Enclosure is the history, antonym, and nemesis of the commons.

—Peter Linebaugh[1]

Against the specter of the hedge, the glimmering hope of the commons looms large. In so much of the popular and academic understanding of the rise of private property, a seemingly obvious solution emerges: return land to the common. The commons emerge as the antidote to capitalist private property, as the condition of the possibility of communal control over the means of production and subsistence, and hence, of communism.

For Peter Linebaugh, for example, the commons represent a counter-possibility to the violence of enclosure, to the confinement that permeates capitalist relations to land and its resources (and more generally, as a grammar of anti-privatization and anti-capitalist politics).[2] Indeed, on

1 Linebaugh, *Stop, Thief!*, 1.

2 Ibid. Silvia Federici, "Feminism and the Politics of the Common in an Era of Primitive Accumulation," in *Revolution at Point Zero: Housework, Reproduction, and Feminist Struggle* (PM Press, 2012); Jason Read, "The Production of Subjectivity: From Transindividuality to the Commons," *New Formations: A Journal of Culture/Theory/Politics* 70 (2010): 113–31; Cesare Casarino and Antonio Negri, *In Praise of the Common: A Conversation on Philosophy and Politics* (University of Minnesota Press, 2008); Michael Hardt and Antonio Negri, *Commonwealth* (Belknap Press, 2008); Peter Linebaugh, *The Magna Carta Manifesto: Liberties and Commons for All* (University of California Press, 2009); Silvia Federici, *Re-Enchanting the World: Feminism and the Politics of the Commons* (PM Press, 2019); Pierre Dardot and Christian Laval, *Common: On Revolution in the 21st Century*, trans. Matthew Maclellan (Bloomsbury, 2019).

the radical left, it is near ubiquitous to treat "the idea of the commons as an unambiguous good."[3]

But there may be more ambiguity than initially appears. Are commons always anti-capitalist, and do they always gesture toward a horizon of resistance? In addition to the transformation of land into *private* property, does capitalism depend also on some forms of *collective* property? If enclosure is one form of confinement under capitalism, might the commons, at least sometimes, constitute another?

Since the "rosy dawn" of capitalism, private property has been accompanied by several forms of communal and collective property that further dispossession and confinement. If we shift our frame of reference to the colonies rather than Europe, the dark history of the commons as a technology of confinement begins to emerge.

Colonial powers often instituted racially exclusive collective property as a means of capitalist expropriation. In what I call the "settler commons," colonizers recreated the commons for themselves on stolen land—*but only for themselves.* Just as enclosures confined land beyond the reach of proletarians, the settler commons erected barriers—physical, legal, and social—between Indigenous people and colonized land. Collective enclosures also took the form of "state land" administered on behalf of the so-called common good, which of course, meant the enrichment of the crown and metropole. This "common" of this so-called common good excluded Indigenous people and communities, reflecting a white supremacist closure of land, its governance, and its beneficiaries. While collective enclosures often produce similar forms of confinement to private property—racialization, dispossession, displacement, proletarianization—the mobilization of common good creates collective power in importantly different ways.

This is not a mere artifact of capitalism's historical transition. The Israeli kibbutz movement, which emerged in the mid-twentieth century, replayed this settler colonial dynamic. And at the turn of the twenty-first century, the dizzying speed of land grabs in the name of environmental protection has created a spate of "conservation commons" that double down on dispossession. The continuity of land confinement in the name of the commons suggests that collective enclosures constitute a consistent pathway of capitalism's combined and uneven development.

Through an investigation of several forms of collective land tenure under capitalism, this chapter shows that capitalism's confinement of land

3 Ben Maddison, "Radical Commons Discourse and the Challenges of Colonialism," *Radical History Review*, no. 108 (2010): 30.

has two faces: it is *both* an individualizing, alienating social form *and* one that produces several devastating forms of collective power. Especially, though not exclusively, in the case of settler societies, the collective (but not universal) control over land has been one central axis for concreting the power of the capitalist class over and above other forms of community.

While the previous chapter charted how capitalism depends on private land confinement, this chapter complicates the tendency to uncritically celebrate the commons as the political orientation against this confinement. I argue that we often figure the commons *against* capitalism rather too easily. While capitalism surely relies on private property, it has also depended on a variety of what I call *capitalist commons*. By exploring this often-overlooked aspect of capitalist confinement, I show that capitalism is not always or exclusively invested in eliminating the common, but sometimes makes use of exclusionary, dominating forms of collective power as part of the process of accumulation. Using land confinement as an entry point, I demonstrate how capitalism relies both on "possessive individualism" and on perverse forms of capitalist collectivity.[4] The capitalist commons, I show, often expand, double, or deepen the very modes of confinement seen in the last chapter.

By focusing on confinement, I argue, we begin to see new elements of capitalist social relations that remain otherwise obscured. In bringing these elements into view, a confinement lens on capitalist collectives can reorient our theories and activism to truly abolish capitalism. From early proletarian settlers to twentieth-century kibbutzniks, the collective commons demonstrate the dangers of working-class and even putatively anti-capitalist politics that fail to see the connection between capitalism and confinement. By centering an anti-confinement, abolitionist ethos, we may be able to avoid supposedly anti-capitalist solutions that end up only replicating capitalist social relations.

The Settler Commons

When European colonizers arrived on distant lands, they not only built "fences and hedges, the markers of enclosure and private property," but also attempted to build new commons. Across the Spanish, French, and British Empires in the Western Hemisphere, settlers designated colonized lands for common provisioning in addition to individual

4 C. B. Macpherson, *The Political Theory of Possessive Individualism: Hobbes to Locke*, 6th impression edition (Oxford University Press, 1975).

lots.[5] In New England, "common pastures were close to universal" and some lasted until the American Revolution.[6] French settlers in North America implemented the *vaine pâture* system of common grazing.[7] As historian Allan Greer explains, "Over wide areas of New Spain, the intrusion of a new colonial commons into, alongside, and over the preexisting Indigenous commons was central to the dispossession of Indian peoples in the sixteenth, seventeenth, and eighteenth centuries"; several forms of common land—*montes, ejidos, estancias, agostaderos, tierras baldías*, and others—designated a significant amount of colonized land as available for common planting, hunting, and especially, as historian William Taylor has shown, for grazing.[8]

This was true beyond North America as well. The Dutch pursued this strategy in South Africa as did the British in Australia.[9] As historian Ben Maddison explains the process in Australia:

> During the nineteenth century millions of acres of crown land in Australia were officially classified as commons by the respective colonial governments of the east coast colonies, Queensland, New South Wales, and Victoria. Contradicting accepted narrative of commons decline during the nineteenth century, the tempo of Australian commons creation increased after 1860, and by the 1880s a common was considered a standard public amenity of Australian country towns, goldfields, and farming districts.[10]

Across Australia, settlers appealed to the colonial government to create new commons, based on the idea that they, as settlers, had a "rightful popular inheritance" to use of land.[11]

Settlers' pursuit of new commons shouldn't be too surprising. Most were working class and had learned enclosure's cruel lesson: only access

5 Peter Linebaugh and Marcus Rediker, *The Many-Headed Hydra: Sailors, Slaves, Commoners, and the Hidden History of the Revolutionary Atlantic* (Beacon Press, 2013), 44; Allan Greer, "Commons and Enclosure in the Colonization of North America," *American Historical Review* 117, no. 2 (2012): 380.

6 Greer, "Commons and Enclosure in the Colonization of North America," 374; Brian Donahue, *The Great Meadow: Farmers and the Land in Colonial Concord* (Yale University Press, 2004).

7 Greer, "Commons and Enclosure in the Colonization of North America," 374.

8 Ibid., 376; William B. Taylor, *Landlord and Peasant in Colonial Oaxaca* (Stanford University Press, 1972), 117.

9 Greer, "Commons and Enclosure in the Colonization of North America," 384.

10 Maddison, "Radical Commons Discourse and the Challenges of Colonialism," 38.

11 Ibid., 40.

to land offered a refuge from the market's insecurity. This security constituted a siren song so compelling that many risked the dangers of transatlantic travel, the dislocation from natal community, and even abdicating one's liberty under an indenture contract with a 40–50 percent mortality rate.[12]

The European working classes' interest in colonization was thus partially a response to the misery capitalism unleashed. It was a conservative kind of anti-capitalism, designed to save new proletarians from the worst effects that enclosure had wrought. In other words, settler interest in colonization reflected how unlivable rising capitalism had made their lives in Europe. But attempts to recreate the past are hardly ever carbon copies; they are rather, in philosopher Jacques Derrida's terms, "iterative," replications with distinct differences.[13] When settlers imposed the commons in the colonies, they would introduce a world-historical difference, one that would shape them as much as the landscape around them. That difference was race.

However Europe's working classes arrived in colonies, they would soon *become* settlers. The story of proletarians-turned-settlers in the Western Hemisphere is one in which the victims of capital become its emissaries, and in which their resistance against its violence becomes the agent of violence against others. Unbeknownst to them, their attempted flight from capital would constitute one of the main elements of its expansion, not only over the settlers themselves but over the entire world. People make their own history, but not always, indeed perhaps not ever, as they choose.

The settler commons were not only built on stolen Indigenous land but also excluded Indigenous people from their use, often by threats, intimidation, and violence. Indigenous peoples fought the capitalist confinement of land on two fronts at once: as they organized against the theft of land for private use, they also fought "an unequal struggle to preserve their Indigenous commons against the aggressive expansion of the colonial commons."[14] These commons were far from "common" in the usual sense; they were specifically *not* designed for the free and open use of all human beings that inhabited their environs. As we will see, this set a pattern on which capitalism repeatedly depends: the mobilization of the idea of the common, collective, or communal as a smokescreen for domination and confinement. The colonial commons were a central,

12 Christopher Tomlins, "Reconsidering Indentured Servitude: European Migration and the Early American Labor Force, 1600–1775," *Labor History* 42, no. 1 (2001): 38.

13 Jacques Derrida, *Limited Inc* (Northwestern University Press, 1988), 7–10.

14 Greer, "Commons and Enclosure in the Colonization of North America," 379.

spatialized mechanism for bringing into existence a settler sphere and a settler class defined by what would be shortly concreted, over time, as whiteness. The colonial commons were an important mechanism in establishing the confinement of land, labor, and life.

Though settlers' rhetoric often mobilized ideas of "egalitarianism and notions of economic independence and freedom" in their demands for commons on stolen land, they figured these values in decisively racist ways. In Australia, "Indigenous people were not allowed to be commoners. The process of colonization in Australia, organized around the concept of terra nullius, stripped away any sense of Indigenous entitlement to land and replaced it with 'Crown Land.'"[15] In other words, claims to the "commons" by settlers relied on the negating of Indigenous sovereignty, a pattern that would recur the world over. Despite the cries of liberty, the right to subsistence, and in some cases, the putatively "anti-capitalist" timbre of their demands, in quite another way, the colonial commons was a central instrument of capitalism because it "had the general effect of solidifying European occupation."[16] It was, in many cases, only after colonizers had been able to collectively seize Indigenous land that they turned to privatizing it.[17] Both the direct control over land for multiple forms of extraction *and* the rise of racism were distinctively tied to the rise of capitalism. The settler commons played a role in both processes.

Indigenous dispossession was absolutely crucial to the rise of capitalism. In many ways, the world system of capitalism as we know it today would have been impossible without the widespread genocide and dispossession of Indigenous peoples around the world. So much has been written about the centrality of colonization to capitalism that we can safely conclude that the capitalism we live through and struggle against was historically contingent on it.[18] This was certainly Marx's position when he asserted that colonization was one of the key moments of "primitive" or "original" accumulation.[19] As Coulthard explains, dispossession works

15 Maddison, "Radical Commons Discourse and the Challenges of Colonialism," 43.

16 Ibid., 43.

17 Allan Greer's discussion of the rise of the hacienda system in New Spain is instructive here.

18 See, for example, Coulthard, *Red Skin, White Masks*; Alexander Anievas and Kerem Nisancioglu, *How the West Came to Rule: The Geopolitical Origins of Capitalism* (Pluto Press, 2015); Césaire, *Discourse on Colonialism*; Ashley Bohrer, "Just Wars of Accumulation: The Salamanca School, Race, and Colonial Capitalism," *Race & Class* 59, no. 3 (2018): 20–37; Englert, *Settler Colonialism: An Introduction*.

19 Michael Perelman, *The Invention of Capitalism: Classical Political Economy and the Secret History of Primitive Accumulation* (Duke University Press, 2000); Marx,

"in concert with axes of exploitation and domination" under capitalism.[20] But what has often been overlooked in narratives about the centrality of this dispossession to the rise of capitalism is the role that settler *commons* (rather than merely settler private property) played in this history.

In the hallmark texts of Marxist whiteness studies, the control of labor forms the material background of the world-historical emergence of race. For writers like Theodore Allen, David Roediger, Elizabeth Esch, and others, whiteness emerges as a way to stabilize the existence of two different labor regimes of exploitation: free wage labor (coded as white) and enslaved labor (coded as Black). Expanding Du Bois's prescient analysis about the "psychological wage," these theorists argue that race comes into being in order to break potential bonds of solidarity between laborers, who might otherwise unite to unseat capitalist domination.[21] Racism emerges in this story primarily as anti-Blackness, is generally centered on the British Empire, and concretes at the beginning of the seventeenth century, with the introduction of several statutes about labor, especially in the 1610s and 1620s. We might call this approach "the labor theory of whiteness."

Emphasizing the collective enclosures significantly deepens and expands this picture. Collective land confinement predates the events detailed in the labor theory of whiteness by over a century. Collective enclosures were also much more widespread, deployed across all the major empires of capitalism's ascendant centuries. These processes also furnished a material basis for the rise of race in the modern sense; hence, to the labor theory of whiteness, I argue we should join a *land theory of whiteness*. The collective enclosures of capitalism's early centuries were a central part of creating a collective sense of racial superiority and difference, an element that has been underemphasized in anti-capitalist analysis. In what he calls "infrastructures of race," Daniel Nemser shows that racialization can be thought of, at least partially, as a spatial process: the colonial project *made spaces* in such a way that solidified human differences in the specific register of race in the modern sense.[22] The rise of race was based in material practices of control over *both* labor *and* land. We can best understand the "racial" dimension of racial capitalism when

Capital, volume 1; Crystal Bartolovich and Neil Lazarus, eds., *Marxism, Modernity and Postcolonial Studies* (Cambridge University Press, 2002).

20 Coulthard, *Red Skin, White Masks*, 14.

21 W. E. B. Du Bois, *Black Reconstruction in America* (Harcourt Brace and Company, 1935), 700.

22 Nemser, *Infrastructures of Race*.

we integrate the control of both land and labor, when we pluralize the historical cases under consideration, and when the full breadth of colonial domination takes center stage; understanding the triangulated racial schema of settler colonialism that involves settlers, Indigenous peoples, and enslaved people deepens our analysis of how racial capitalism formed and continues to work in the present day. As Daniel Montáñez argues, a refusal to reckon with the history of collective enclosures runs the risk of "obscuring the racism that exists at the heart of commons history."[23] But it is equally true that ignoring this history runs the risk of obscuring the commons at the heart of capitalist history.

What I am tracing here are two twin processes, both facilitated by the rise of the settler commons. On the one hand, the communal land seizures (by both settlers and the state) were often preconditions of privatization. The settler commons were an important, if relatively short-lived, institution that allowed Europeans to be brought in and bought in to the colonial project; the offer of land, security, and community in a world increasingly transformed by the poverty and competitive individualism of the European capitalist market would have been seductive indeed. If both factory labor and homesteading were brutal labor, it was only the latter in which the worker remained nominally his own boss, holding on to an ever-vanishing autonomy that anyone would be loath to lose. The land, both private *and* communal, offered settlers a direct material stake in colonization, a much closer and more obvious one than their working-class families in the metropole would have experienced. On the other hand, the creation of these exclusive commons had their own unique contribution to the history of capitalism; capitalism has always been a collective project of protecting some forms of life at the expense of many others. The settler commons were not merely a historical stepping stone to privatization, but the first of many material practices of group formation that continue to permeate capitalism's class, race, gender, and sexual politics. In other words, capitalism creates certain kinds of collectives. The settler commons birthed both a material stake in dispossessed land *and* a sense of settler collectivity opposed to Indigenous society. In other words, collective land confinement was part of a multifaceted process of bringing into being an entire settler sphere, an entire settler mode of life, and perhaps even a settler identity. It would have taken significant transformation for these settlers, divided by region, language, religion, and custom, to have seen themselves as sharing anything like an identity;

23 Daniel Montáñez, "Colonial Commons and the Decolonisation of the Left," *Guerilla Translation*, November 24, 2020, guerrillatranslation.org.

their collective administration of land brought into existence a settler sphere, which bound them together and differentiated them from the Indigenous and Black people who were excluded from these lands. The collective confinement of land thus generated multiple other forms of confinement: the confinement of racialized exclusion in the settler colony, the confinement of a racialized social order, and, ultimately, the confinement of a political vision that sees the domination of some as the only possibility of the flourishing of others.

State Land, or "Common Good" Against the Commons

On a chilly October night in 2011, I sat down in a public park—an unremarkable act if ever there were one. I had walked over to Grant Park along with several thousand of my newest comrades in Occupy Chicago from our political home base in front of the Chicago Board of Trade. That location, while steeped in political significance, had proved a challenging spot to erect the kind of permanent encampment that our New York comrades made in Zuccotti Park. After several weeks of negotiating slim sidewalks and construction scaffolding, we picked up our signs and marched over to a wider expanse of supposedly *public* property to set up what we hoped would be the permanent home of the movement.

It was not to be. As soon as we erected tents in the square, the Chicago Police Department threatened mass arrests. When the dispersal order came, many people moved to the sidewalk, continuing to make speeches, sing protest songs, and deliver blistering speeches condemning privatization, neoliberalism, and state repression. Some of us did not move to the sidewalk. A friend and I dove into the nearest nylon tent to hold our ground. Before long, that tent was cut to shreds around our heads, we were put in zip ties, and we spent a long night in the Cook County Jail with nearly 150 other protesters. We were released the next day with a court date and a citation for breaking a city ordinance limiting park hours to 11 p.m.

The tactic of holding public space has a long history; Occupy was not the first nor the last movement to assert control over public land as way of demonstrating that collective institutions like the state, police, and representative government do not actually represent the interests of the people. In fact, there is specific power that the state has at its disposal to deploy the language of "public good" against the public, of the "common good" against the common.

The case of Occupy is a particularly sticky one; the movement was roundly critiqued (often rightly) for its myriad shortcomings, not the least of which was the valorization of "occupation," a term that had poignant significance on stolen land. In a movement largely (though not exclusively) composed of settlers, "occupation" took on a complicated double meaning, one that the movement never really attempted to confront.[24] In one sense, "Occupy" is perhaps just a different manifestation of the dynamic I traced above: settlers demand access to public goods while continuing to expand (or at least failing to contest) the colonial condition on which those demands are made.[25] But perhaps equally, it dramatizes the way that the state functions as unique encloser, one that dispossesses in the name of the "common good."

In addition to enclosure for private property and the settler commons, Indigenous lands were always also seized directly by the state. Many settler commons, over time, also fell into state hands (often later becoming private property). The state is a unique encloser for several reasons.[26] On the one hand, the state is the highest legal authority in the post-Westphalian age. It is the state that often enables private enclosures and that creates a series of regulations bolstering them; but when the state itself seizes and appropriates land, there is no other (legal) recourse beyond direct confrontation with the state and its punitive mechanisms. Only the state acts simultaneously as party, judge, and enforcer of the very rules of the capitalist game. In democratic societies, the state is also uniquely positioned ideologically as the supposedly neutral arbiter of the public good; for this reason, state actions often come stamped with the added force of presumed democratic legitimacy. Thus, state lands can often

24 For more on the use of the term "occupation" in the Occupy Movement and Indigenous critiques of the term and the movement overall, see Adam J. Barker, "Already Occupied: Indigenous Peoples, Settler Colonialism and the Occupy Movements in North America," *Social Movement Studies* 11, nos. 3–4 (2012): 327–34; Miranda J. Brady and Derek Antoine, "Decolonize Wall Street!: Situating Indigenous Critiques of the Occupy Wall Street Movement," *American Communication Journal* 15, no. 1 (2013): 1–10; J. Kehaulani Kauanui, "The Politics of Indigeneity, Anarchist Praxis, and Decolonization," *Anarchist Developments in Cultural Studies*, no. 1 (2021): 9–42.

25 This is not to say that settlers, like myself, *shouldn't* make demands of settler governments; it is to say rather that the effects of doing so need to be carefully rendered in the context of their differential impact on settler, "arrivant," and Indigenous communities. The complicated political knot should not be bypassed or ignored but rather approached in the context of a decolonial horizon.

26 There is much to be said about the rise of the state in relationship to capitalism and the way that its borders have become ever-more confined since the seventeenth century, the subject of chapter 5. In this section, I look at the narrower phenomenon of state-owned land in the rise and reproduction of capitalism.

seem like they serve the common, even if activities of commoning are prohibited on them. One of the state's founding fictions is its putatively communal character, the idea that it works for or in the interest of the common good, even when we have so much evidence that it, more often than not, serves the rich at the expense of most of us. In many jurisdictions, state land is the closest thing we have to collective property, even if it falls far short of benefitting all who live there.

In general, the colonial expansion of European powers formed the backbone of nascent capitalism, and much of this occurred through the direct confiscation of land by the imperial power. Under capitalism's mercantile form, European powers attempted to gain direct control over international trade as a mode of enriching state coffers; they saw larger populations and territorial expansion as central to accumulating wealth, and for this reason, they pursued colonial capture with fervor. Empires enacted territorial accumulation directly, but they also used private instruments like corporations and joint-stock companies for the same ends (and different empires favored different strategies). For example, the French Crown tended to seize Indigenous lands for the state, while English sovereignty favored property claims by individual proprietors. While the state may sometimes conflict with the bourgeoisie and its capitalist aspirations, the state also enables the capitalist economy, providing one of its necessary background conditions.

Colonial governments in particular pioneered capitalist resource extraction. This was true of many natural resources, but perhaps none more vivid than in the gold and silver mines of the Americas. For both the Spanish and Portuguese, the search for precious metals soon became the raison d'être of the conquistador mission; from Brazil to the Bajío, gold and silver fever spurred the Conquest at a dizzying pace. Throughout the sixteenth century, mines were established across the continent, most notoriously at Potosí, Guanajuato, and Zacatecas. Much of this precious ore repaid loans European Crowns owed to Asian governments. Because this linked Latin America, Europe, and Asia together in integrated economic exchange for the first time, scholars like John Tutino suggest that the global nature of capitalism was first forged in these mines, the product of Crown land theft and enslaved Indigenous labor.[27] It was, to paraphrase Eduardo Galeano, state rather than private industry that initially opened the veins of Latin America to a colonial bloodletting that continues to the

27 John Tutino, *Making a New World: Founding Capitalism in the Bajío and Spanish North America* (Duke University Press, 2011).

present day.[28] Of course, precious metals are only one example among many that could be offered here; across the globe, direct expropriation has been central to capitalism for 500 years, and this expropriation has taken place through both private *and* public means.

More generally, colonial state land enacted new forms of confinement. These violent usurpations of Indigenous sovereignty brought with them an entire apparatus of law, culture, and economy. The state's collective colonial land seizures expanded capitalist practices: commodity production, waged labor, an interest in accumulation, and the legal and social structures necessary for the capitalist world. Though capitalism sometimes appears as a collection of individual fiefdoms, the state plays a central role in facilitating the possibility for private capitalist accumulation. Even when the state does not engage directly in extractive industry, it secures the expansion of the legal, political, and social apparatus necessary to maintain capitalist relations; it is thus a crucial intermediary in the process of global land enclosure. The capitalist ruling class remains the condition of the possibility of the capitalist individual.

The state continues to accumulate land even today. Despite generations-long struggles to maintain collective and communal control over land, neoliberalism facilitates the new enclosures daily—and these enclosures often make direct use of the state in the process.[29] Bringing collective land into the regime of private property often requires the coercive authority of the state, mobilizing one (putatively) collective institution against other, more local forms of collectivity. Despite legal protections for collective land tenure (including in international law), it often remains informal. Communities may not hold title or deeds to their lands, and their collective wisdom about the boundaries of their homeland may not be legible to those who think about land in right angles and GIS maps.

The World Resource Institute estimates that in practice about 65 percent of the world's land was under some form of communal control in 2020; however, only about 8–10 percent of land is legally protected as such. We should remember that part of what these numbers reflect is the fact that land directly under the control of the state is counted as "communal land" and hence do not necessarily reflect *actual* community, collective, or

---

28 Eduardo Galeano, *Open Veins of Latin America: Five Centuries of the Pillage of a Continent* (Monthly Review Press, 1997).

29 See Rights and Resources Initiative, *Who Owns the World's Land?: A Global Baseline of Formally Recognized Indigenous and Community Land Rights* (Washington, DC, 2015), rightsandresources.org; Rights and Resources, *Who Owns the World's Land?: Global State of Indigenous, Afro-Descendant, and Local Community Land Rights Recognition from 2015–2020*, 2nd edition (2023), 1–78.

democratic access. Collectively held land often seems uniquely valuable to capitalist eyes. It often contains the highest amount of biodiversity and has been spared some of the most devastating industrial effects (pesticides, toxic waste, chemical spills, deforestation, and so on). Where people see their land, life, history, and kin, multinational corporations and international development firms see only the possibility for profit. For this collective property to be enclosed, the state often serves as intermediary. Indeed, as Alice Kelly and Nancy Peluso argue,

> Today's frontiers of capitalism . . . are new commodity forms within the confines of already formalized state lands. Some of these lands were set aside in reaction to the most rapacious forms of capital, and some were a product of capital's working through the state to dispossess competing land claimants.[30]

The twenty-first century has seen a spate of International Investment Agreements (IIAs) to enclose communal land through highly lucrative public-private deals between foreign companies and central governments. Despite local differences, state-facilitated enclosure often follows a common pattern: states declare collectively held land as ownerless and therefore state land, and then the state either sells the land outright to private corporations (often foreign) or leases it out to those companies at extremely cheap rents and with lease terms of decades or centuries. States often offer tax breaks, publicly financed improvement projects, and exceptions to national labor and environmental regulations to sweeten the deal. These processes nearly always lack meaningful consultation with the communities that live on the land. Where legal protections for communal tenure exist, states often maneuver around the law. Crucially, the state leverages the "common good," figured as access to capital and development, as the justification for continued expropriation in neocolonial and postcolonial states alike. Often, these partnerships produce extractive plantations that bring no benefit to the expropriated community and generate large profits for investors (and kickbacks for governments). In many of these stories, from Ethiopia to the Philippines, Brazil to Papua New Guinea, states facilitate the spread of foreign capital through reorganizing land tenure. Sometimes, this transfer happens at the behest of international regulatory agencies in the course of the euphemistically

30 Alice B. Kelly and Nancy Lee Peluso, "Frontiers of Commodification: State Lands and Their Formalization," *Society & Natural Resources* 28, no. 5 (2015): 475.

named "structural adjustment," but often it is not. Enclosures displace resident communities, often to refugee camps or urban slums or into land held by other Indigenous communities, when any provisioning for the dispossessed is made at all.

In all these cases, the state's role in land confinement over the last five hundred years is notable. The state is a particular agent in land confinement, whether it uses confined land for its immediate enrichment or acts as the facilitator of private accumulation. The state and capital sometimes confront each other as rivals; but in the case of the collective confinement of land, the state has unique power as the presumed representation of the common or collective good. It also constitutes the highest power in the land, constraining many pathways of appeal or resistance.

Leisure and the Conservation Commons

In 2003, thousands of people converged in South Africa to discuss a topic that most would find relatively innocuous if not an unimpeachable good: national parks. Indigenous delegates to the Fifth World Parks Congress shattered this illusion. In their closing statement, Indigenous delegates declared, "First we were dispossessed in the name of kings and emperors, later in the name of State development and now in the name of conservation."[31]

Yosemite was the first national park in the world, enclosed in 1864.[32] As someone who grew up in California, Yosemite held an almost mystical appeal, one only solidified by a week-long camping trip my family took when I was five or six years old. We weren't a particularly outdoorsy family, though my father, uncle, sister, and grandfather loved fishing (and were, I think, disappointed when I turned out to have violent seasickness and a disinclination to killing animals for sport). For a working-class white family trying to make ends meet (and to procure a "better life" for the children), the national parks were, for much of my childhood, the only way that "vacation" was a financial reality.

What was needed to allow my working-class family this form of leisure? When Yosemite was first enclosed, Indigenous Miwok people

31 Quoted in Fergus Mackay and Emily Caruso, "Indigenous Lands or National Parks?," *Cultural Survival Quarterly* 28, no. 1 (2004), culturalsurvival.org.

32 In Britain, the story begins a bit earlier, with the General Inclosure Act of 1845. This did set aside some spaces for parks and recreation areas, but they were not quite yet the "national parks" of Teddy Roosevelt's dreams.

were initially allowed to remain inside, though the state continually reminded them that this was a privilege, not a right. From the state's perspective, they held no claim or title to the land that their people had used for thousands of years. In 1929,

> employment was required of all residents. From then on, the Miwok became cheap labor for the Park Service, which gradually lowered their population by evicting [supposed] miscreants and the unemployed, prohibiting new Miwok settlers to replace those who died or left, and allowing the Indian village infrastructure to deteriorate . . . In 1969, the last of the settled Miwoks were ushered from the park and their village was set on fire as a firefighting drill.[33]

The enclosure of Yosemite created a model for many that would follow: Royal National Park in Australia (1879), Banff in Canada (1887), and Tongariro in Aoteroa/New Zealand (1894); as colonization continued in Asia and Africa, European powers "applied the Yosemite model in the Transvaal and Serengeti where parks like Kruger, Singwisti, Ambolseli, Garamba, the Maasai Mara, and Parc Albert sprung up."[34] In all of these cases, Indigenous peoples were evicted to make way for colonial tourism and trophy hunting.

This trend continues today—the scale of contemporary enclosures for conservation is enormous:

> In the past 150 years, more than 12 percent of the world's surface has been set aside through the establishment of some 100,000 protected areas. Many of these areas have been established since 1992, when the international conservation community committed itself to a target of at least 10 percent of the world by 2002. By some estimates, around 50 percent of these protected areas encompass lands and territories traditionally occupied and used by Indigenous peoples. In the Americas, this number rises to over 80 percent.[35]

For a geospatial reference, the amount of land currently under conservation management comes to nearly 12 million square miles (31 million square kilometers), a landmass larger than Africa.

---

33 Mark Dowie, *Conservation Refugees: The Hundred-Year Conflict Between Global Conservation and Native Peoples* (MIT Press, 2009), 10.

34 Dowie, *Conservation Refugees*, 11.

35 Mackay and Caruso, "Indigenous Lands or National Parks?"

These conservation projects routinely entail displacement. Mark Dowie explains that "world estimates range wildly from five million to tens of millions of refugees created since Yosemite Valley was gazetted for protection in 1864."[36] Unsurprisingly, nearly all of these "conservation refugees" are people of color.[37] Displacement usually follows one of two patterns: either the state formally evicts Indigenous peoples from their homes, or they are more slowly (but no less violently) pushed out in "what Indigenous people have come to call 'soft eviction', a limiting of local resource use that is tantamount to displacement."[38] The creation of nearly every national park created conservation refugees: the Maasai in Tanzania, the Miwok in Yosemite, the Batwa in Uganda, the Baka in Congo, the Adivasi in India, the Basarwa in Botswana, the !Khomani and Malas in South Africa, the Penan in Malaysia, the San in Namibia, the Ogiek in Kenya, and many more.

The eviction of all communities from their homelands is devastating. Often, the state and conservation groups deny that any evictions have happened at all, alleging that mobile and semi-mobile groups were not *really* residents because they do not settle land in a normatively capitalistic way. This is a constant refrain in ongoing conservation land enclosure: mobile and semi-mobile peoples are constructed as "not really" belonging on or to their land and are then displaced in conservation projects. When they attempt to return home, they are called criminals, poachers, and encroachers, and they are often criminalized. This is what happened, for example, to the Baka; when Nouabalé-Ndoki National Park (NNNP) was created in 1993, the Congolese government and the large multinational conservation organizations

> claim[ed] there never were any permanent residents in what is now the NNNP: yes, the Baka and other ethnic groups would take extended hunting forays into the area, but they were nomadics so they never settled. It is therefore inaccurate, in the BINGO [Big International NGO] perspective, to claim they were evicted or displaced since they have been routinely and voluntarily displacing themselves for thousands of years. It was a page right out of the Yosemite playbook where similar claims were made about the semi-nomadic Miwok who would move out of the valley during its harsh winters and return every spring to replant their gardens.[39]

36 Dowie, *Conservation Refugees*, xxi.
37 Ibid., xi.
38 Ibid., 229.
39 Ibid., 74.

This same narrative continues to be used to displace Palestinians in Israel, especially Bedouin families. My friend Awdah, whose story opens the Introduction of this book, is one of the 40,000 Bedouins in the West Bank whose mobile form of life is continually deployed to deny the history of Palestinian settlement and to thus deny them the rights of Indigenous peoples.

These contemporary dispossessions, though undertaken for the "common good" rather than private accumulation, continue centuries-old patterns of capitalist displacement. Embedded in the racist and colonial worldview of conservationists like John Muir and Teddy Roosevelt, the dominant global approach to protecting planetary biodiversity has been what Dan Brockington has called "fortress conservation."[40] Under the fortress conservation paradigm, nature and wilderness become enclosed spaces designed to keep Indigenous inhabitants out of their ancestral homelands. These enclosures only sometimes bear the literal fences of more traditional enclosure; more often they include a system of private security, rangers, and police who enforce this exclusion, sometimes with lethal violence. At the same time, extractive industries, bio-prospectors, tourists, scientists, and foreign employees of transnational NGOs participate in a dense web of monetary exchanges. The movement of money and people for the benefit of business, academia, tourism, nonprofit management, science, and the state (which often facilitates these processes) depends on the confinement (and often militarization) of these lands. Capitalist industry mushrooms around these leisure commons: ecotourism (the fastest growing sector of one of the fastest growing industries in the world), hotels, tour groups, and safaris follow wherever land is enclosed for "public use"—the use of the *paying* "public" of course.

It's hardly news that conservation is itself big business. The budgets of the largest BINGOs sometimes dwarf the GDPs of the countries where they operate. Conservation NGOs often collaborate directly with intensely extractive industries (oil, pharmaceutical, logging, mining, and so on) who "are directly involved in pillaging and destroying forest areas owned by Indigenous peoples."[41] States often have huge financial incentives to participate in this process. Sometimes they are offered debt-for-nature swaps, in which countries can eliminate some portion of debilitating

---

40 Dan Brockington, *Fortress Conservation: The Preservation of the Mkomazi Game Reserve, Tanzania* (Indiana University Press, 2002).

41 Mac Chapin, "A Challenge to Conservationists," *World Watch*, December 2004, 18.

national debt (often imposed through neocolonial policies like structural adjustment) by participating in this process.

The effects of these conservation enclosures are eerily similar to the primitive accumulation of capitalism's early centuries. Where land confinement comes, so too does proletarianization; in the present, proletarianization is often coded as "development," vaunted as a pathway out of the very poverty and insecurity capitalism creates. Dowie explains this process:

> In almost every case, Indigenous people are moved into the lowest end of the money economy, where they tend to be permanently indentured as park rangers (never wardens), porters, waiters, harvesters, or, if they manage to learn a European language, ecotour guides. Under this model, "conservation" becomes "development," and native communities are assimilated into national cultures. Assimilation invariably means taking a permanent place in society at the bottom of the ladder. Whole societies . . . are transformed from independent and self-sustaining to deeply dependent and poor communities.[42]

Separation from land means more than losing access to the means of subsistence; it means separation from religion, history, ancestors, and an entire place-based system of meaning. Land cannot be reduced only to a means of survival, to a brute material fact on which life unfolds; land is itself a whole way of life, suffused into every part of what it means to live, to die, to survive, to remain. In that sense, what is taken when land is confined is not only food, water, and medicine, but something much deeper—identity, community, intergenerational connection, spiritualty, cosmology, and epistemology can often be rooted in place. In this sense, collective enclosures represent a capture of land and place it under a different world order. Capitalism is sustained and reproduced not only by imposing a series of constraints on labor and land but also by enclosing the vision of what is possible in this world, in creating the material, social, and ideological conditions under which people are forced to reckon with (if not accept) a vision of the world as balance sheet. Crude materialism would tell us that the ideological comes neatly as an aftereffect of changes to labor conditions; historical materialism illuminates the dialectical process through which the world is made and remade through constrained human agency. In other words, enclosure into property, even state or common property, is still a part of sustaining capitalism, facilitating the spread of capitalist ideas, expectations, ideologies, and forms of life.

42 Dowie, *Conservation Refugees*, xxvi.

We can see this dynamic play out in relationship to leisure. On the one hand, capital constantly increases the amount of time we are at work, what Marx identified as the tendency for capital to increase "absolute surplus value," which can take a variety of forms: expanding the number of hours we are at the office or expected to check our email or be on call, demanding we monetize hobbies into side hustles, or squeezing workers so hard we sell our blood, sperm, and plasma for extra cash. Capitalism erodes the possibilities of nonwork time. On the other, leisure time, when and where it is accessible, is also a monetized source of profit. Our leisure spaces are nearly always someone else's workplace. Where we go to blow off steam or recuperate or engage in community, someone must cook, clean, or curate.

Some attempt to regenerate in nature, in wild landscapes that *seem* far from capitalist drudgery. In response to capitalism's alienating industrialization, mechanization, and individualization, nature seems more and more like a respite, giving rise not only to the camping vacations of my youth, but also preindustrial cosplay and "back to the land" movements alike, a tendency Iyko Day calls "romantic anti-capitalism."[43] All too often, these movements and desires enact racialized practices of rejuvenation that compound rather than contest Native erasure. Day shows that capitalism explains *both* how and why workers might experience capitalism as alienating *and* how their avenues of dealing with this alienation might reinforce rather than dismantle racist, colonial, and capitalist confinement. None of these forms of reaction truly contest capitalism, because they do not uproot the view of land as a commodity, to be bought, sold, and exploited for the purpose of accumulation. In other words, the motivation for these longings for nature can be understood as a protest against capitalism's confinement of life, even if the pursued solution ultimately doubles down on it.

Socialists must demand access to leisure and green space as part of any liberatory future. But there are dangers in positioning these demands as if capitalism is *always* or *uniquely* opposed to their creation; these spaces have been, rather, created through capitalist processes of expropriation, subordinated to logics of accumulation, and deployed as a form of social reproduction for exploited workers to renew themselves and return to their workplaces after a long weekend. These spaces, further, insofar as they facilitate and regulate access, form the contemporary equivalent of the settler commons of old: they continue to maintain a settler sphere of

43 Iyko Day, *Alien Capital: Asian Racialization and the Logic of Settler Colonial Capitalism* (Duke University Press, 2016).

leisure from which Indigenous peoples are constitutively locked out. Now as then, access to the vital resources of time, leisure, rest, and regeneration in nature contributes to the reproduction of settler and working-class buy-in to Indigenous dispossession, strengthening rather than uprooting capitalism's confinement of life. If we start from the premise of capitalism's interest in confinement, we see more clearly the insufficiency of demands for more equitable access to Indigenous dispossession.

Kibbutzim and the "Socialist" Colonial Commons

Perhaps no case makes this clearer than the Israeli kibbutz movement. For centuries, Jews faced harrowing conditions in Europe: discrimination, pogroms, ethnic violence, and second-class citizenship. As an oppressed minority in a grueling capitalist society, leftist politics like socialism and anarchism more deeply penetrated their ranks than the dominant ethnoclass, and some decided to leave Europe to build a new kind of liberated future: a community without private property, social hierarchy, the nuclear family, or class distinctions. Rather than rely on a state and its repressive apparatus, their communities would operate beyond legal sanction, with the bonds of community accountability preempting any need for force. They attempted to build this utopian socialist society, like so many other colonial commons, on the stolen land of British-occupied Palestine. These new socialist-anarchist commons were called kibbutzim (singular: kibbutz).

I am the daughter of a kibbutznik. Though I am fuzzy on many of the details, I know that my mother worked on a kibbutz near Haifa sometime during the 1970s. She never spoke much about that time, with the exception of how her primary job was picking bananas. It was a detail that always stood out to me; it was hard to imagine my blond-haired, blue-eyed suburban mom doing anything like agricultural labor in her youth.

For some readers, calling the kibbutz a capitalist commons might seem strange. After all, kibbutzim were often founded directly on socialist and anarchist principles by open and avowed leftists. They were inspired by Gustav Landauer, Peter Kropotkin, and others who argued that liberation could only be achieved through community, self-management, and equality among peers.[44] They repeated Marx's dictum "from each according to their ability, to each according to their need" as the central

44 Kropotkin's *Mutual Aid* was one of the first books translated into Modern Hebrew.

organizing principle. Work was managed in common, life structured beyond capitalist norms of possessive individualism and endless accumulation; children were reared in common, gender equality was a professed (if not always practiced) operating assumption, and collective decisions were made through general assemblies, sometimes democratically, often through consensus.

If we read the kibbutzim through a lens of movement, they might seem almost dreamlike: oppressed and exploited proletarians shook off their domination, moving across the world to set up anti-capitalist communities, many of which have endured for over a century. This certainly is the dominant position in the scholarship.[45] But if we instead apply the confinement heuristic—asking, "Who or what is confined by this practice?"—a very different picture emerges. Rather than seeing socialism in the kibbutz, I find a very particular kind of capitalist commons, one in which, for the settler class, the evils of capitalism can be mitigated in a playtime version of socialism. Because kibbutzim furthered the confinement of Palestinians, it could never make good on the socialist dream of a truly liberated anti-capitalist society.

Historically, kibbutzim were vanguard institutions in the Zionist colonization of Palestine. While now they constitute a much smaller contingent of settler population, through the mid-twentieth century, kibbutzim were central parts of nascent Israeli society, important economically and to the project of building a new national consciousness and, indeed, the model of "a new man." The kibbutzniks, steeped in the ideas of people like A. D. Gordon, Franz Oppenheimer, and Chaim Arlosoroff, saw their project as "building a completely new kind of society from scratch," and this necessitated "the creation of a new kind of human being."[46] Settlers do indeed create "a new kind of human being" as they *become* settlers.

Though the early kibbutzim were significantly influenced by radical leftist ideas, Zionism always grounded the project. Despite many early kibbutzim holding distinctly anarchist, socialist, or communist ideas, the combination of ethnic homogeneity, Jewish nationalism, and anti-Palestinian hostility with a distinct communal ethos laid the foundation

---

45 In researching this chapter, I read nearly a dozen scholarly books on the history of the kibbutz, and not a single one mentioned Palestinians or Arabs in anything more than a passing fashion; several ignored them completely. None believed that the colonial condition called the utopian or emancipatory potential of the kibbutz into doubt.

46 James Horrox, *Living Revolution: Anarchism in the Kibbutz Movement* (AK Press, 2009), 25.

for their incorporation into a state-building project and for the transmutation of the "new kind of human being" they hoped to become into defenders of ethnonationalist expropriation.

While some believe Zionist state-building coopted the kibbutz project (with Jewish settlers in general functioning as "pawns in Western states' foreign policies"), Palestinians recount hostility from the early days of the first kibbutz (Degania, built on the Palestinian village of Umm Juni) in the 1910s.[47] In fact, the first baby born on a kibbutz was none other than Moshe Dayan, the Jerusalem-front commander during the 1948 Nakba and Israel's Minister of Defense during the 1967 Six-Day War. While some early kibbutzniks denounced the exploitation of Palestinian workers by Jewish settlers, seemingly none questioned their presence on Palestinian land or attempted to integrate as immigrants into Palestinian society.[48] From the outset, kibbutzim were European and Jewish and conceived of community from within those confines. To this day, most of the 270 kibbutzim are leased on land owned by the Jewish National Fund, an organization deeply complicit if not directly responsible for the expropriation of Palestinians.[49]

By 1936, over twenty years before the Nakba, kibbutzim were producing "Jewish Settlement Police," many of whom were members of the Palmach and the Haganah, the military arm of the embryonic Zionist state. Though some kibbutzim professed pacifism, the general consensus was that "the rifle is as essential to our working tools—perhaps more so."[50] The kibbutzim formed a large part of the material determination of settler colonial sovereignty:

> When the United Nations voted in 1947 to partition Palestine . . . it was largely the geographical positions of various kibbutzim that determined the borders of the Jewish state, and the settlements played a notable part in defending those borders when the war broke out.[51]

Certainly, kibbutz members played a decisive military role in the Nakba, taking up arms on the side of Israeli colonization. This military history of

47 Ibid., 95.

48 Ibid., 15.

49 Walter Lehn, "The Jewish National Fund," *Journal of Palestine Studies* 3, no. 4 (1974): 74–96; Kenneth W. Stein, "The Jewish National Fund: Land Purchase Methods and Priorities, 1924–1939," *Middle Eastern Studies* 20, no. 2 (1984): 190–205; Fayez Sayegh, "Zionist Colonialism in Palestine," *Settler Colonial Studies* 2, no. 1 (2012): 206–25.

50 Daniel Gavron, *The Kibbutz: Awakening from Utopia* (Rowman & Littlefield, 2000), 56.

51 Ibid., 5.

the kibbutz is sewn into the DNA of the movement; today, the movement is still well-known in Israel for producing a disproportionate number of government leaders and soldiers in "elite" units.

Rather than seeing the state's absorption of the kibbutzim as a fundamental perversion of their policies, we can rather see the kibbutzim in a longer historical arc of settler colonization: victims of capitalism flee their countries of origin, band together to create resources for themselves, and create settler forms of life that operate outside, over, and against preexisting Indigenous social formations. No matter how emancipatory these formations might seem or how radical their professed politics, the combination of ethno-nationalism and Indigenous dispossession concretes into a settler sphere.[52] "The kibbutz was a vital tool in the implementation of the Zionist dream," writes Daniel Gavron (approvingly).[53] He continues:

> With its tight communal framework, the kibbutz was ideal for establishing settlements. The kibbutz movement embarked on a period of establishing "tower and stockade" settlements. The new kibbutzim were subject to determined Arab attacks. They were therefore secretly mobilized and established in a single day, during which a perimeter fence and a watchtower with a search light were constructed. The Arab attacks usually came at nighttime during the first few weeks and in most cases were successfully repulsed. In the late 1930s, the ambivalent relationship between the kibbutzim and the Arabs of Palestine, which had always existed, became more extreme. On the one hand, the kibbutznik pioneers were socialists, devoted to the ideals of human fellowship and equality, who saw the Arabs as fellow workers. At the same time, they were the vanguard of Zionist colonization, settling on lands where Arabs had been living.[54]

---

52 Israeli society is less homogenous than it pretends. The majority of current Jewish settlers in Palestine are not Ashkenazi Jews, but are Sephardi, Mizrahi, Black, and Arab Jews. These groups face significant racial discrimination within Israeli society, as they have since the country's foundation. This white supremacist domination of Euro-descendent Jews is often called "ashkenormativity" and is part of how the Israeli state operates: it claims a certain kind of ethnic homogeneity, based in the (false) assumption that all Jews have the same ethnicity, contributing simultaneously to the settler-colonial displacement of Palestinians and the internal oppression of non-white Jews. For more on this dynamic, see Ella Shohat, *On the Arab-Jew, Palestine, and Other Displacements* (Pluto Press, 2017).

53 Gavron, *The Kibbutz*, 4.

54 Ibid., 4. Note that many Zionists say "Arab" rather than "Palestinian" in order to erase the specificity of Palestinian people, a subtle but consequential linguistic choice that participates in the ethnic cleansing to which Zionism is fundamentally committed.

This dual commitment is precisely the complicated knot I have been tracing since the first European settlers demanded their own commons on Indigenous lands in the Americas.

Beginning in the 1980s, neoliberalism hit the kibbutzim as much as the rest of the world. Much of the political commitment to socialism, Marxism, and anarchism is now a passé throwback on the kibbutzim, and the sense of creating a novel communal society free of markets, property, money, or inequality has been largely displaced by a more "moderate" set of principles. In the discussion of the "modernization"—broadly, the turn to private accounts, personal property, nuclear-family housing, pay-as-you-go services, and professional, full-time bureaucracy—the role of the kibbutzim in Palestinian confinement is nearly universally ignored. But perhaps this was predictable if not inevitable: socialist projects on stolen land, that entrench rather than contest capitalist confinement, that double down on the differential valuation of human life, might be uniquely susceptible to capitalist co-optation. If capitalism relies on a confinement that these "socialist" projects do not uproot, how anti-capitalist were they ever?

As far as the kibbutzim attempted to forge a new society and create a new human, they were indeed successful; they created settlers who saw themselves as equals and progressives, but who saw their own equality and freedom as bound up in Palestinian confinement. They created a world that meshed their sense of self and community so deeply with an exclusionary form of life and freedom that they would create a repressive, militarist state and an apartheid legal system in order to maintain it—one that entails so many forms of social, legal, political, and economic confinement. In many ways, the contradictions of the kibbutzim reflect larger patterns of liberal Zionism, which itself replays larger arcs of settler justice that seeks socialism and stolen land. If it is true that "in no [other] state have communes played such a central role in national life," collective enclosures like the kibbutzim should ring the alarm bells about capitalism's confining forms of communal life.[55]

Though these socialist, anarchist, utopian settlements in Palestine were unique in their integration into the state-building project of settler colonization, the kibbutzim are, like all other elements of Israeli settler colonialism, reflections of larger trends in European colonial capitalism. Zionism is, as I have argued elsewhere, not so much a unique aberration of Jewish exceptionalism than a reflection of the European colonial societies

55 Horrox, *Living Revolution*, 1.

from which the Jewish settlers came.[56] Kibbutzim were hardly the only such attempt to found socialist societies through settlement. Owenite communities popped up across the United States and Canada, as did other socialist formations like the Ruskin Colonies, the Washington Equality Colony, the Llano del Rio Cooperative Colony, the Cecilia Colony (Brazil), and the colony of New Australia (Paraguay).[57] European powers routinely encouraged the migration of leftists to their colonies to stabilize capitalism.[58] If they could not placate, repress, or contain all working-class organizing for socialism, much better to encourage emigration before these radical ideas infected the broader proletarian consciousness; moreover, European settlers demonstrated closer allegiance to the empires from which they came than to the Indigenous peoples on whose land they settled, ultimately expanding the power of Crown and capital. In addition, the kibbutzim uniquely facilitated European disavowal of the endemic antisemitism they produced; the Zionist project, especially in its socialist variants, thus served European colonial capitalism particularly well, as it continues to.

Kibbutzim thus fulfilled rather than challenged capitalism, even as they quoted Marx and Kropotkin. They stabilized capitalist accumulation and all its attendant confinements on the European continent, and they inaugurated new, brutal forms of confinement on the Indigenous peoples of Palestine. As did many collective enclosures, they deployed confinement with leftist words in their mouths and in their books. Without the analytic of confinement, they expanded rather than rejected capitalism, and similarly without this analytic, even contemporary "leftist" scholars have missed the collective enclosures they imposed. For the kibbutz as well as for many other collective enclosures, the confinement heuristic allows us to see more clearly the dangers of an anti-capitalism that hasn't digested the necessity of abolition.

---

56 Ashley J. Bohrer, "To Oppose Zionism, We Have to Deal with Christian Zionism," *Midnight Sun*, February 23, 2024, midnightsunmag.ca.

57 W. Fitzhugh Brundage, *A Socialist Utopia in the New South: The Ruskin Colonies in Tennessee and Georgia, 1894–1901* (University of Illinois Press, 1996); Julie Gauthier, "The Land of the Free," *Country Roads Magazine*, September 23, 2019, countryroads magazine.com. As Freg Stokes shows in a forthcoming article, the socialist settlement of New Australia was temporally and spatially quite close to a settlement project with a very different political orientation: the fascist colony of Nueva Germania, co-founded by Elisabeth Förster-Nietzsche, sister of the renowned philosopher. In his article "Socialist Settlers on the Capitalist Frontier," Stokes explores how the New Australia colony operated through this double displacement for capital, acting alongside rather than against the White Australia Policy ascendant at the same time.

58 Lorenzo Veracini, *The World Turned Inside Out: Settler Colonialism as a Political Idea* (Verso, 2021), 9.

Conclusion: Capitalism and the Collective

As we have seen, colonial capitalism relies on the concretion of collective power in the forms of whiteness and the settler sphere; often these forms of collectivity go unnoticed or at least underthematized in anti-capitalist analyses that figure capitalism as a purely individualistic ideology hell-bent on dissolving any collectivity it encounters. As much as capitalism creates an ideology of individual possessiveness, it also creates collective entitlement; this creation partially depends on various forms of land confinement held in common, where the "common" and the "public" emerge as silently circumscribed categories. The collective is thus a crucially important terrain for anti-capitalist theorizing and organizing. Surely, capitalism individualizes, separates, and singularizes. It relies on an ideology of individual responsibility. In its campaign of commodification, capitalism often severs ties between people and communities; it often denies the existence of collective interests altogether. But at the same time, capitalism also creates several forms of collectivity, even as it may deny or hide them. The general class character of capitalism is only the most prominent example. Just as individual capitalists may not see themselves as part of a unified class, anti-capitalist critique has shown how they not only *are* part of this class, but that the general interests *of the class* are world-making forces. The bourgeoisie wields class power not only as individuals, but indeed, as a collective entity with united interests across the economic, political, and social realms of society. So much of capitalist society remains hidden if we only attend to capitalism's individualizing valences.

Placing the collective in view of anti-capitalist critique highlights how the ideal capitalist individual itself has group membership and is formed by a particular worldview. Capitalism may be based on the ideological, economic, and juridical fiction of the hermetically sealed individual, but that individual is *in fact* embedded in enabling collectivities of bourgeois class power, racism, coloniality, heteropatriarchy, and ableism; these are, just as the enclosure of land, conditions of the possibility of the emergence of the capitalist individual.

The collective confinement of land is another terrain in which capitalism's perverse collectivism emerges. Whether in the form of settler commons, state land, leisure spaces, or settler colonial experiments, whole collectivities emerge out of capitalist land confinement. These are not random, idealist identities that emerge willy-nilly out of social discourse; land confinement is one of the material bases for collective power under capitalist societies. These collectives may be defined primarily by class, race, religion, or nationality, and these categories intersect with each other in complicated ways. These collectives work to constrain the life possibilities for all those who encounter them, shutting off many other avenues of living, being, and working together. They enact capitalism's confinement of life.

The development of capitalism—materially and ideologically—depended as much on the gendered, sexualized, ableist, and racialized content of the capitalist subject as on its capacity for individuation. In other words, the capitalist individual is based in large part on its group membership, on the creation of the very groups to which it belongs. As generations of anti-capitalist feminist, anti-racist, disabled, queer, and anticolonial scholars have highlighted, the capitalist individual was far from a neutral subject, instead shot through with Euro-whiteness, heteronormativity, patriarchy, and ableism; the creation of capitalism itself inaugurated many of the contemporary concepts of these categories themselves. Land confinement forms part of the material counterpart of capitalism's anchoring collectives. Identity and group formation are material processes under capitalism that significantly shape the trajectory and possibilities of capitalist accumulation and reproduction.

For this reason, simple claims to recover the collective or the common cannot be sufficient to uproot the malignant form of communality that capitalism creates and requires. Not all forms of collectivity mirror or prefigure comradeship or instantiate anti-capitalist values. The unified class interest of the bourgeoisie is collective and binding, but the complete opposite of anti-capitalist emancipation. The heart of the matter is rather *what kind of collective, what kind of common* will be possible. We will never be able to confront this question seriously without a direct engagement with the forms of collective violence that capitalism engenders in conjunction with its individualizing, alienating forms of violence.

In order for socialism to birth a liberating collectivity, we must first understand and critique the lurking forms of collective power and confinement that undergird capitalism. This means exposing the dialectical intertwining of the individualizing, alienating forms of violence with the violences that bind collectivities together. These, too, must be abolished if we are to really overcome capitalism.

5
The Borders of Capitalism

The state has always seemed to be the enemy of people who move around.

—James Scott[1]

The border crisis . . . is more accurately described as crises of displacement and immobility, preventing both the freedom to stay and the freedom to move.

—Harsha Walia[2]

I told them: don't build fences around your settlements. If you put up a fence, you put a limit to your expansion. We should place the fences around the Palestinians and not around our places.

—Ariel Sharon[3]

In the summer of 2019, I was back in Palestine. Along with 125 or so other activists, I was moving rocks and shoveling dirt on an uneven road in the West Bank in a mutual aid project. The small path was the lifeblood of many communities in Masafer Yatta, connecting villages like Bir al Eid, Jinba, and Al Mirkez to hospitals, schools, food, and water. The path was in bad shape, with huge potholes and sharp rocks jutting from the ground that made the multi-kilometer journey from the villages to the

1 James C. Scott, *Seeing Like a State: How Certain Schemes to Improve the Human Condition Have Failed* (Yale University Press, 1998).

2 Harsha Walia, *Border and Rule: Global Migration, Capitalism, and the Rise of Racist Nationalism* (Haymarket Books, 2021), 3.

3 Quoted in Neve Gordon, "Civilian Control," in *Israel's Occupation* (University of California Press, 2008), 116.

next paved road dangerous, especially for children on their way to school. The road could not be filled with concrete or asphalt, since the Israeli Civil Administration prevents Palestinians from building anything, including roads and homes, without an impossible-to-obtain permit in any part of Area C, which covers over 60 percent of the entire West Bank. Israeli settlements and even outposts all have running water, electricity, and paved roads, and they build seemingly whatever and whenever they want, encroaching on Palestinian land and stealing Palestinian resources as they do, dislocating Palestinians onto ever-smaller slivers of their ancestral homelands. We could not solve the despicable control of movement in one day, but perhaps we could make the road a little easier to traverse. So Palestinian and Jewish activists came together—hoes, spades, shovels, and buckets in hand—to try to remove the road hazards to make it just a little bit easier for local Palestinians to manage their daily survival.

It did not take long for the Israeli Army to appear, seemingly out of nowhere. Even though the dirt road to Bir al Eid is about as rural as you can get, the surveillance apparatus of the Israeli State clocked us in mere minutes. The uneven roads posed no problem to the armored Humvees that descended over the hills. About forty soldiers emerged from the vehicles and told us to stop. They declared the area a closed military zone (CMZ), a tactic commonly used to displace Palestinians, disrupt protests, and prevent mutual aid projects like ours. We were given ten minutes to leave.

The Israeli State uses this kind of closure as just one of many controls over movement. Border security, roadblocks, segregated roads, the infamous Separation Wall, omnipresent surveillance, and functional pass laws complement arbitrary CMZ declarations to control the mobility of Palestinians and activists in the West Bank. Israeli control over movement is constant and life-constraining, everywhere between the river and the sea. A CMZ order fabricates a border out of nothing. It creates a new zone with new rules out of the coercive capacity of the state, by fiat. As I hope to show, this apparently aberrant state capacity is actually central to its more generalized ability to create and control borders, both within and beyond the external boundaries of the nation.

The nation-state is an organizer of (im)mobilities. It is a coercive container that regulates movement, both within and without. In the current world, it has also enclosed the globe—nearly everywhere is a nation-state (or administered by one), and it is the primary form of political organization, despite its foundational and structural violences. At any point in time, we are enclosed not just within a particular nation-state, but within a system that makes the nation-state seem to be the only available option for organizing institutional collective life. While it has become a frequent refrain on the left that "it is easier to imagine the end of the world than the end of capitalism," in my own life as a teacher, I have found that students struggle more to imagine the demise of the nation-state than capitalism. The state has become so entrenched in the global understanding of what political communities *are* that our imaginations have been confined to its contours, its borders, both physical and ideological.

We often forget that this consensus is, in the grand scheme of things, quite new. The nation-state is a young political formation, a newcomer to the panoply of ways human beings have organized questions of authority, membership, and distribution over history. Younger still is the idea that these nations have enclosed physical borders that require special permission to traverse; a mere century ago, international jurists found that even nations themselves disagreed about whether sovereignty included the power to exclude foreigners from entering their territories.[4] For many centuries, state power was primarily about who made and enforced the laws within a territory, not about controlling who could be subjected to it. For a very long time, states measured their power by how many people they controlled, so they generally sought to increase their populations by whatever means they could. If foreigners chose to come and amass wealth for the imperial state, so much the better.

A new consensus emerged in the twentieth century, brought on by wars, political decolonization, and the securitization of the capitalist world order: state power includes the ability to erect barriers, regulating the flow of citizens and foreigners at will. Despite the much freer movement of capital around the world, borders began to harden for people. As this trend continues into the present, capital has become more mobile, but this mobility has come at the expense of deepening violent controls on movement for people. Where people are allowed (or forced) to move, states often deploy specific forms of confinement and social immobilization.

While I use the term "the state" for brevity, throughout this book I am referring to the modern state form that concreted alongside capitalism in the seventeenth through nineteenth centuries and that continues to dominate our contemporary international political institutions (including international law) and our political imagination. This chapter—alongside the next two—illuminates the state's function as a regulator of confinement and mobility under capitalism. Taken together, these chapters form

4 John Torpey, *The Invention of the Passport: Surveillance, Citizenship, and the State* (Cambridge University Press, 2000), 159.

an extended mediation on the state's role under capitalism as one of the key institutional regulators of confinement. By looking at the border (this chapter), the police (chapter 6) and prisons (chapter 7), these chapters look at the state as an apparatus of confinement on several levels, each of which is interarticulated with the logic of capital. The state simultaneously buttresses the forms of capitalist confinement explored in previous chapters and enacts its own logics of confinement. States pursue several forms of physical confinement: the nation-state border as regulator of inside/outside; the police as regulators of generalized social mobility; prisons (including immigration detention facilities) as violent forms of containment that stabilize the law and accumulation. Moreover, the state also captures political possibility, subjecting us all to what Gérard Noiriel calls "the tyranny of the national," narrowing the vision of political form to a violent and specifically *imperial* world order based in inequality, vulnerability, and violence.[5]

The State, Capital, and Confinement

The state-capital relationship is complicated: at one and the same time, capital depends on the state, and the capitalist class often denounces the state unjustly intruding into the "free market." The state sometimes regulates capital and occasionally mitigates some of capitalism's most devastating effects through social welfare, labor laws, environmental regulations, and taxes, to name just a few. The state's management of capital is both demanded and contested, leading to an uneasy but foundational partnership. At the same time, the state pursues its own ends of power accumulation beyond directly economic concerns and spheres of life.

Nancy Fraser explains that helpful theories of capital's relationship to putatively noneconomic formations, including the state, must encompass three simultaneous truths:

> First, capitalism's "non-economic" realms serve as enabling background conditions for its economy; the latter depends for its very existence on values and inputs from the former. Second, however, capitalism's "non-economic" realms have a weight and character of their own, which can under certain circumstances provide resources for anti-capitalist struggle.

5 Gérard Noiriel, *La tyrannie du national. Le droit d'asile en Europe, 1793–1993* (Calmann-Levy, 1991).

> Nevertheless—and this is the third point—these realms are part and parcel of capitalist society, historically co-constituted in tandem with its economy, and marked by their symbiosis with it.[6]

Thinking about the state as one of these key "non-economic" realms allows us to see several elements of the state/capital relation. The state provides necessary infrastructure for the accumulation of capital and, hence, is a central part of how capital accumulates, expands, and reproduces itself over time. For example, capital relies on the state for printing money and preventing its devaluation, enforcing contracts, legalizing exploitation and private property, and mediating conflicts between members of the capitalist class. It also, crucially, functions as one of the key mechanisms of political repression, creating order and stability in the face of potential social and labor unrest. In Althusser's words, a key function of the state under capitalism is "to guarantee the conditions for the exploitation of the exploited classes by the dominant classes."[7] The state thus sets in motion and continually reconfirms, through its deployment of force and violence, the basic rules of capitalist accumulation. For this reason, the capitalist class is also the *ruling class*: the domination of capital economically is intertwined with capitalists' power throughout political and social life. At times, the state has also, especially in colonial contexts, functioned directly as a capitalist exploiter, something Walter Rodney explored extensively.[8]

Beyond this, the state pursues the concretion of its own power through what John Torpey calls "the accumulation of infrastructural capacity."[9] That capacity includes all kinds of things—documentation, bureaucracy, agencies, enforcement mechanisms, political administration, public works, transportation, communication technologies, and much more. The state apparatus combines both repressive and productive force to achieve these ends. The repressive elements of state power are often the most obvious, encompassing all the "negative" deployments of power that we see so clearly: imprisonment, physical force, fines, legal sanctions, the disruption of social movements, and so on. Additionally, the state often constructs its power in a variety of "positive" terms—as protector, as defender, as securer of the very people it dominates. The entire gamble of liberal political theory depends on the nation-state providing, at a

6 Fraser, *Cannibal Capitalism* (Verso, 2022), 36.

7 Louis Althusser, *On the Reproduction of Capitalism: Ideology and Ideological State Apparatuses*, trans. G. M. Goshgarian (Verso, 2014), 93.

8 Walter Rodney, *How Europe Underdeveloped Africa* (Verso, 2018), 196.

9 Torpey, *The Invention of the Passport*, 11.

minimum, security, the ostensible justification for relinquishing natural liberty to the artificial authority of the state. Even if the state does violence, so the liberals tell us, they do it *in the interest of us all, for our own good.* In liberal democracies, discourses of common interest carry powerful ideological force, constructing those who most directly experience state violence (migrants, criminalized and unhoused people, and so on) as *threats* not only to the national character but to the rule of law and social order that the state supposedly protects. State power thus requires what Étienne Balibar calls the "reciprocal appropriation of individuals by the state, and of the state by individuals."[10] The state lays claim to the people under its rule as *its* people, but it also attempts to get its citizens to *lay claim to the state*, to their inclusion into it, to their inclusion into its violences.

In this sense, the state is a deeply ambivalent institution, embedded simultaneously in the production of violence and discourses of care. In order for the state to deploy its violence, to achieve its unique combination of raw power and supposed legitimacy, it must, in Torpey's words, "embrace" its people, creating a dynamic that is "at once sheltering and dominating."[11] Enfolding people into the iron grasp of the state depends on the creation of, in Polly Pallister-Wilkin's words, the "dialectics of care and control" or what David Theo Goldberg calls the duality of "comfort and control."[12]

The state appropriates individuals partially through the creation of hierarchies and inequalities, what I call the confinement of life. Most noticeably, the state differentiates between *its* people and *others*. States also enact internal distinctions, creating internal hierarchies, classifying groups of people within its bounds, and according different treatment (whether only de facto or also de jure). Historically, race, class, gender, sexuality, ability, language, citizenship, and incarceration status have all been determinants in this system of classification. The protection, entitlements, or benefits of being appropriated by state power are much more compelling if they can be denied or revoked; the possibility of state abandonment often prompts people to lay more vociferous claim to their inclusion. The state is thus produced by the maintenance of two

10 Étienne Balibar, "What Is a Border," in *Politics and the Other Scene*, trans. Christine Jones et al. (Verso, 2022), 77.

11 Torpey, *The Invention of the Passport: Surveillance, Citizenship, and the State*, 7.

12 Polly Pallister-Wilkins, *Humanitarian Borders: Unequal Mobility and Saving Lives* (Verso, 2022), ch. 3; David Theo Goldberg, *The Racial State* (Blackwell Publishing, 2002), 240.

fundamental kinds of hierarchies: between citizens/subjects and foreigners, and between/among differentially protected groups of citizens/subjects.

All these aspects of state power—its use of repression, its mobilization of rhetorics of care and protection, its investment in the hierarchical differentiation of people—come together in territorial control and the regulation of movement.[13] Recalling Max Weber's foundational definition of the state as the institution with a monopoly on the legitimate means of violence, Torpey suggests that states continually attempt to secure "a monopoly of the legitimate means of movement" over both its domestic citizen/subjects and foreigners who attempt to enter its territory.[14] Who gets to move and who is allowed to remain in place constitutes a central element of the state's power to capture people, land, resources, money, and infrastructural capacity. States regulate and control movement of both its citizens/subjects *and* foreigners in a wide variety of ways. Of course, the state does not always succeed in its monopolization of movement, but its attempt to do so is "an essential aspect of the 'state-ness' of states."[15]

Thus, the state emerges as an institution directly invested in confinement. The state secures private and collective forms of property, stabilizing these forms of confinement. It enacts the legal bases of exploitation, and sometimes, of enslavement, securing the capitalist confinements that follow these social relations. It contributes to a hierarchical valuation of human life, marking out the differential possibilities of the confinement of life. It also concretes legitimated forms of state repression and violence, creating directly carceral institutions of police, prisons, and detention facilities, all of which stabilize the accumulation of capital. It is for this reason that so many authors emphasize language of confinement when thinking about the state. Michael Mann, for example, argues that states "cage" social activity.[16] Goldberg understands the process of political concretion as "carceralities of state formation," and he argues that "the

13 Disputed boundaries notwithstanding, space is a fundamental element of how the state constitutes and projects its power. The state is not *solely* a territorial concept, nor is state power always delimited by its territorial boundaries (think, for example, of colonial empires or overseas "operations" or the 800 military bases the United States maintains in other countries). The state does not always *end* at its borders in an uncomplicated way, but it is constituted through the rule of territory and property.

14 Torpey, *The Invention of the Passport*, 1–2.

15 Ibid., 3.

16 Michael Mann, *The Sources of Social Power*, vol. 2, *The Rise of Classes and Nation-States, 1760–1914* (Cambridge University Press, 1993), 61.

modern state may be conceived accordingly as a container."[17] For Adi Ophir, "the state is but a powerful means of closure."[18]

Capital, the State, and Confinement at the Border

During the first decades of so-called globalization, in which production lines, finance, debt, and so much else became more transnational than ever before, many foretold the death of the nation-state. Pundits promised more movement than ever before, the melting away of restrictions on human beings, goods, capital, and ideas that were hindering global "progress." For some, this heralded the good fortune of a world without extra-market restrictions; others saw only the rise of terrifying transnational bureaucracy and the loss of local autonomy. In some ways, this prophecy has become true: global supply chains are longer than ever, production of even single commodities often span dozens of countries, and new arrangements among states have in some ways softened the hard edges of national boundaries, at least as far as capital is concerned. The last few decades have seen the rise of numerous regional free trade agreements (like NAFTA) and political arrangements (like the EU), as well as the establishment of over 4,000 Special Economic Zones, in which states suspend domestic regulations (taxes, labor laws, environmental regulations, import duties, and so on) for foreign companies. At least for capital and for commodities, the nation-state and its attendant borders are increasingly becoming obsolete. People are also moving more than ever. About 5 percent of the world population are migrant workers, and nearly 2 percent are displaced people. The World Bank estimates that the number of people crossing international borders for tourism has more than doubled since 1995 overall, and is increasing across low-, middle-, and high-income countries (though not at the same rate).[19]

And yet, simultaneously, we see new mobility limitations: increasingly militarized border policing, proliferating restrictions on movement, and new forms of surveillance and control to limit the movement of people both within and across state borders. As Thomas Nail shows, "there are more types of borders today than ever before in history."[20] At the current

17 Goldberg, *The Racial State*, 168, 121.

18 Adi Ophir, "State," *Mafte'akh*, no. 1 (2010): 93.

19 World Bank Group, "International Tourism, Number of Departures," Yearbook of Tourism Statistics, UN Tourism, n.d., data.worldbank.org.

20 Thomas Nail, *Theory of the Border* (Oxford University Press, 2016), 1.

moment, nearly eighty border walls separate nations from one other, most of them constructed since the new millennium; over a dozen more are in some stage of planning or development. At the same time that some borders—for example, those within the European Union—are seemingly dissolving, Europe deploys harsher and more violent policing of its now sacrosanct external borders, literally allowing migrants to drown in the sea. The Global Detention Center Project details over 2,000 facilities worldwide used to confine migrants, ranging from formal facilities like prisons and camps, to ad hoc facilities like schools and shipping containers, constituting an "inexorable expansion" of global migrant detention.[21] As Tanya Golash-Boza explains, "Globalization, enhanced by neoliberal reforms, facilitates the movement of capital across borders while restricting the mobility of workers."[22] Harsha Walia concurs, explaining that "contrary to common analysis, bordering being simultaneously monetized and militarized—open to capital but closed to people—are not contradictory juxtapositions. The free flow of capital *requires* precarious labor, which is shaped by borders through immobility."[23] How should we understand the co-occurrence of these phenomena? What does it mean for capital and commodities to move ever more freely while the movement of human beings becomes confined and controlled in new ways?

We cannot begin to answer this question without rooting our answer in the long history of racialized, colonial, carceral migration that has shaped capitalism for 500 years. Capitalism invented many forms of confined human migration: Indigenous dispossession for imperial expansion, penal transportation, transatlantic chattel slavery, and proletarian displacement from the feudal countryside. These policies of compelled movement were always pursued alongside attempts to confine populations in more easily controlled patterns of settlement: eroding traditional forms of nomadism, concentrating Indigenous peoples into new villages and reservations, transferring peasants to cities, erecting ghettos from which racialized populations were not free to leave. Whether oriented toward forced movement or forced settlement, capital and the state have often colluded to move or fix human populations to accumulate power, resources, labor, and control; they have often pursued both simultaneously, by first displacing people and then confining them to new forced

21 Global Detention Project, *Annual Report* (Geneva, 2024), 1–30, globaldetentionproject.org.

22 Tanya Golash-Boza, *Deported: Immigrant Policing, Disposable Labor, and Global Capitalism* (New York University Press, 2015), 4.

23 Walia, *Border and Rule*, 6.

"homes." In other words, whether people will be forced to move or forced to stay depends on the needs of the market, on the whims of capital. Both strategies confine the life chances and opportunities of the people they affect, enacting structural constraints and limits on their ability to enact the lives they desire, what I have been calling "the confinement of life." As discussed throughout the book, movement and confinement are not polar opposites or mutually exclusive but intertwined dynamics.

The dynamic interpenetration of forced movement and confinement structures the recent changes in borders over the last several decades. Chief among these changes has been the chilling expansion of the border far beyond the territorial limits of the state. We normally think of the border as a specific space at the boundary of nation, but in reality, the border is everywhere. Instead of encountering the border at a country's edge, migrants are now often captured and held in processing facilities in so-called third countries, functionally moving the border and its confinements hundreds or thousands of miles from where it would appear on a map. Under Australia's Pacific Solution, migrants captured at sea by Australian border security might never get anywhere close to the island itself and may be shipped off to detention facilities in Nauru or Papua New Guinea. The EU similarly operates (and is looking to expand) transit-processing centers across Africa, just as the US does across Latin America. These migrant-processing centers implant the militant policing of "destination countries" far beyond their own borders, through collusion with law enforcement in "transit countries." The latter accept these neocolonial agreements because of threats to withhold other forms of "aid"—aid that global capitalism's worldwide apartheid make necessary in the first place. The EU has used its power across several policies and "aid" packages—the Khartoum Process, Valletta Summit, the Migration Partnership Framework, the Emergency Trust Fund for Africa, and the African Peace Facility Program, to name only a few—in order to deputize African countries into serving as "Europe's new border guards."[24] In Balibar's words, "*Some borders are no longer situated at the borders at all*."[25]

The border is moving not only outward but inward as well. Border policing and domestic policing increasingly intertwine, moving the border to anywhere police are. In the United States, there are fewer privacy protections and increased immigration enforcement authority everywhere

24 Mark Akkerman, *Expanding the Fortress: The Policies, Profiteers, and the People Shaped by the EU's Border Externalization Programme* (The Transnational Institute, 2018), 2, tni.org.

25 Balibar, "What Is a Border," 84. Emphasis in original.

within 100 miles of the physical border (including maritime borders), which encompasses whole cities like Los Angeles and New York. In De Genova's words, "Migrants and refugees are made, in effect, to carry borders on their very bodies as border enforcement and the prospect of deportation come to permeate the full spectrum of racialized everyday life activities and spaces."[26] The border is also moving deeper into the body itself. While health checks have been an ableist dimension of immigrant policy for a very long time, new technologies are constantly emerging that intensify the control and surveillance of migrant bodies, functionally transposing the border to wherever they move. We can see this in the expansion of invasive health examinations and medical documentation, as well as the increasing collection of biometric data on migrants and tourists alike. Whether through fingerprints, facial recognition scans, compulsory medical exams, or DNA collection, Tamara Vukov explains,

> regimes of mobility control are increasingly inscribing themselves into the flesh and deeper, becoming increasingly invasive down to the sublevels of retinas and genetic material. With the intensifying use of biometrics in border enforcement, borders are increasingly inscribed and enacted at the subcellular level of DNA in a regime that channels and inhibits embodies movements according the indices of skin, flesh, genes.[27]

These changes transform the very concept of the border and expand the state's reach into the body as a new frontier of accumulated infrastructural capacity.

The border is on the move, expanding outward and inward at nearly every turn, increasing the reach of state confinement. Each transformation both expands the state's power and opens new pathways for capital accumulation. The confining contours of migration are themselves a massive source of capital accumulation *as an industry*, and migrants' increasing precarity tracks neatly onto rising profits for capital. At every turn, capitalist firms are capitalizing on border confinement by selling surveillance technology, biometric data collection/processing/storage, weapons for state security or private contractors, food, medical supplies, uniforms, computers, communications technology, construction materials, and much more. Capital has a direct monetary interest in the

26 De Genova, "A Racial Theory of Labour," 245.

27 Tamara Vukov, "Strange Moves: Speculations and Propositions on Mobility Justice," in *The Politics and Erotics of Mobility Justice*, eds. Liz Montegary and Melissa Autumn White (Palgrave Macmillan, 2015), 111.

expansion of these spaces of confinement and is thus embedded in their adoption, expansion, and intensification.

Moreover, immigration itself is an industry, a large transnational sector of the global economy that itself employs people and generates staggering profits. In his study of the global industry of so-called body shops, Jeffrey Kaye explains that "human export centers" constitute significant links in the global migration chain:

> On the spectrum of respectability and legality, recruitment and transportation networks range from publicly traded global companies on the one end to clandestine smuggling organizations on the other. But whether they are licensed "headhunters," recruiters, staffing agencies, placement services, or clandestine middlemen and smugglers, the business is essentially the same: to procure and deliver migrants. With as many as fifteen thousand [legal] firms, global recruitment enterprises comprise a multibillion-dollar-a-year-industry.[28]

As borders become more heavily militarized and fortified, as crossings become more dangerous to encounter without an apparatus of support, black market businesses become even more lucrative, able to extract more money and higher profits from migrants who become increasingly desperate to evade the violent clutches of state confinement.

The forces of confinement do not end once migrants cross the border. In some cases, this is only the beginning of a complex system of confinement at the behest of both capital and the state. Whether they come with or without proper documentation, migrants often experience labor as uniquely confining. In some places, Walia explains,

> migrant worker programs are carceral regimes, where many workers have their identification confiscated, are held captive in their place of employment, and are traded between employers like goods. Thus, like those of undocumented and irregular migrants and refugees, the experiences of legally authorized migrant workers are foundationally organized through immobility.[29]

This is as true of migrant-worker programs as it is of undocumented workers.

28 Jeffrey Kaye, *Moving Millions: How Coyote Capitalism Fuels Global Immigration* (John Wiley & Sons, 2010), 79.
29 Walia, *Border and Rule*, 7.

Businesses also profit from undocumented migrants' increased vulnerability in the labor market. Employers target undocumented workers to make sky-high profits through paying below-minimum wages, refusing to offer benefits, lengthening the working day/week, flouting safety regulations, preventing collective bargaining, and so on. These employers then use the threat of deportation to discourage agitation or organizing. In this context, deportability "plays a distinctly disciplinary role" under contemporary capitalism.[30] Multinational corporations target deported workers for recruitment, especially for overseas call centers and other outsourced customer-facing operations.[31] As corporations and capital hopscotch over borders, looking for favorable conditions (like low wages and tax breaks), they often "rely on migrants [they employ] to overcome cultural, linguistic, and legal barriers at the same time they stimulate migration."[32] In this sense, multinational corporations consider migration as relevant job experience in their pursuit of human capital, a set of skills and competencies that can be exploited to accumulate capital under the globalized conditions of the contemporary world.

Migration and Social Reproduction

State borders are closing down all around us, and yet people continue to cross these barriers. Capitalism makes life so unsustainable for so many that, despite the brutality and danger of border crossing, they continue to move.

Migration continues to be a central strategy of social reproduction for exploited and expropriated populations, a way that people can continue to survive against the onslaught of capital accumulation. According to the World Bank, wage remittances constitute a significant mechanism of social reproduction across borders; remittances reached $857 billion in 2022 alone.[33] Remittances constitute more than 10 percent of GDP in over thirty countries. In human terms, this means that millions of people worldwide rely on money sent home by emigrant relatives to survive. In many of these cases, remittances have been the only way families have been able to avoid starvation and death amid neocolonial pushes for

30 De Genova, "A Racial Theory of Labour," 245.

31 Golash-Boza, *Deported*.

32 Kaye, *Moving Millions*, 52.

33 World Bank, *World Development Report 2023: Migrants, Refugees, and Societies* (International Bank for Reconstruction and Development / The World Bank, 2023), 129.

greater austerity and the erosion of social safety nets. Immigration is hence, globally, a significant component to the reproduction of the global working class; it is precisely through family separation that those very same families continue to live.

But migration and social reproduction also dovetail in the gendered experiences of work upon arrival in destination counties. The gendered expectations of social reproduction labor mean that migrant women are pushed into domestic work, childcare, or elder care.[34] In an age where affluent women can buy their freedom from these responsibilities, they most often do so by employing working-class, racialized, and immigrant women to fulfill these tasks.[35] This work, because it is broadly undervalued in society, often receives meager wages, no benefits, long hours, and little legal protection.[36] Moreover, immigrant domestic workers face high levels of sexual violence and harassment, including employer pressure to use birth control or terminate wanted pregnancies. Many documented immigrant domestic workers arrive on visas that directly link them to a particular employer, meaning that they cannot leave their jobs and remain in the country. Migrants who engage in sex work or other criminalized industries face similar vulnerability and precarity in the face of the law.[37] All these transformations of the border, steeped in the logics of state violence and capital accumulation, are best rendered as technologies of confinement.

The border constitutes a particular space in which the control over mobility is directly at issue, in which agents of the state make direct determinations on the (in)ability of people to move (though increasingly, private entities like airline agents, private security firms, and other non-state entities take on these tasks). The border often presents itself as

34 Eleonore Kofman and Parvati Raghuram, "Gender and Global Labour Migrations: Incorporating Skilled Workers," *Antipode* 38, no. 2 (2006): 282–303.

35 Grace Kyungwon Hong, *The Ruptures of American Capital: Women of Color Feminism and the Immigrant Culture of Labor* (University of Minnesota Press, 2006); Sandro Mezzadra and Brett Neilson, *Border as Method, or, the Multiplication of Labor* (Duke University Press Books, 2013), ch. 4; Sara Farris, *In the Name of Women's Rights: The Rise of Femonationalism* (Duke University Press, 2017).

36 Grace Chang, *Disposable Domestics: Immigrant Women Workers in the Global Economy* (South End Press, 2000).

37 Sealing Cheng and Eunjung Kim, "The Paradoxes of Neoliberalism: Migrant Korean Sex Workers in the United States and 'Sex Trafficking,'" *Social Politics: International Studies in Gender, State, and Society* 21, no. 3 (2014): 355–81; Juno Mac and Molly Smith, *Revolting Prostitutes: The Fight for Sex Workers' Rights* (Verso, 2018); Fabian Luiz Fernandez, "Hands Up: A Systematized Review of Policing Sex Workers in the U.S." (Public Health Thesis, Yale University, 2016).

a barrier to movement, even if that barrier can be overcome or circumvented in some circumstances, and even if it allows some people to pass through it with few problems.

Comfort and Confinement

The border depends on the state and capital's differential ordering of various kinds of human life. In regulating movement, the border creates new distinctions among people based on their permission to move (or not). "Tourist," "migrant," "immigrant," "migrant worker," "deportee," and "undocumented" are not mere descriptions of people's status as they move or are prevented from doing so; these designations reflect the rule of hierarchies within and among states that constrain opportunities and life chances. Each designation involves restrictions on when, where, and how people may or may not have the ability to move, and the kinds of evasive maneuvers that might be necessary to circumvent confining restrictions. As Stephen Castles describes it, we live in a "global class hierarchy in which people with high human capital from rich countries have almost unlimited rights of mobility, while others are differentiated, controlled, and excluded in a variety of ways."[38] In Golash-Boza's estimation, "a system where mostly white and affluent citizens of the world are free to travel to where they like whereas the poor are forced to make do in places where there are less resources" can only be called "global apartheid."[39] This system, shot through with racial and (neo)colonial dynamics, is deeply intertwined with capitalism, marking a difference "between those who 'circulate capital' and those 'whom capital circulates.'"[40]

For this reason, Thomas Nail explains that the border should be thought of not as a physical object or discrete space but as "a process of social division."[41] The production of these differences is crucial to the accumulation of capital. In Walia's words, "Border controls manufacture spatialized difference not to completely exclude all people but to capitalize on them."[42] Mimi Sheller continues, "In each case, domination is achieved through control over the mobility and immobility of subalterns, advantaging some while impairing others, and leaving our common

38 Stephen Castles, "Migration, Crisis, and the Global Labour Market," *Globalizations* 8, no. 3 (2011): 312.

39 Golash-Boza, *Deported*, 3.

40 Balibar, "What Is a Border," 83.

41 Nail, *Theory of the Border*, 2.

42 Walia, *Border and Rule*, 132.

humanity under erasure."[43] It is this "common humanity" that the state and the border, and all of its attendant practices, imperil.

Difference depends on the creation not only of the uniquely vulnerable but also of the uniquely secure. As borders become more dangerous for many, some move across borders nearly carefree. Without flattening the life-defining differences between these groups, those who can move easily might have more to fear than they realize. By emphasizing *only* the relative ease with which some (white, documented, from the Global North, affluent, and so on) move across borders, we might overlook some of the more universal confinement strategies. States increasingly impose requirements of added documentation, surveillance, facial recognition, biometric monitoring, and other forms of control from which no one is exempt. These, too, are strategies of domination, power, and confinement, no matter how "comfortable" or "unobtrusive" they might initially seem.

Migrants are uniquely surveilled, policed, detained, scrutinized, brutalized, and confined by the border regime. But like so many other strategies of confinement, border technologies proceed on a "boomerang" path, deployed first toward the "outside" or "others" and then coming home to roost. Even the highly mobile among us encounter more friction than we would have a century ago; through greater surveillance, the repressive apparatus of the state grows and augments its own accumulation of infrastructural capacity. There is *no equivalence* between a required facial recognition scan at airport security and detention in border prison. But these practices *are related* to each other. As citizens empower greater security apparatuses at the border, and as the border creeps further and further inland and outward, as the control of movement becomes sewn into our very bodies, state and capital become more deeply entrenched for everyone. Peter Adey explains the boomerang effect: "[The] emergence of biometrics in contemporary airports, border zones, security spaces, and everyday life sees the systematic use of biological and bodily data as a means to identify and manage risky mobile populations, focusing upon not territory but vectors."[44] This creates, in Sheller's words, a generalized "passenger responsibility to present the data-ready body . . . [built] on colonial practices of mapping, visioning, and surveying"—no matter one's citizenship status.[45] In Wendy Brown's words, "Walls built around political entities cannot block out without shutting in, cannot secure

43 Mimi Sheller, *Mobility Justice: The Politics of Movement in an Age of Extremes* (Verso, 2018), 54.

44 Peter Adey, *Aerial Life: Spaces, Mobilities, Affects* (Wiley-Blackwell, 2010), 88–9.

45 Sheller, *Mobility Justice*, 133.

without making securitization a way of life, cannot define an external 'they' without producing a reactionary 'we,' even as they also undermine the basis of that distinction."[46]

Despite their relative comfort, those who move with ease across borders still do not *actually* experience the freedom of movement an anti-confinement global politics would offer. The insidious embrace of and by state power makes many of us *think* that our legibility to the state is part of our freedom, when it is really a hidden form of coercion. The state, even in its seemingly unobtrusive operations, even in its seemingly protective operations, also enacts physical, political, and ideological confinements that constrain our ability to govern collective social life in line with true principles of emancipation. Instead, it uses old divide-and-conquer tricks to manufacture consent to unlimited surveillance, securitization, and confinement, even conscripting working-class citizens into its project.[47]

The state tells us, mobilizing its dual logic of care and coercion, that it unleashes border violence in the interest of the citizens, that it places migrants in detention *for our own good.* We must reject this logic. Like so many aspects of domination under heteropatriarchal colonial racial capitalism, it is imperative not only to notice relative unfreedoms, confinements, and immobilities but *also* to recognize the limitations of the freedoms, life chances, and mobilities offered to the most privileged. The problem of capitalism is *both* the inequalities it produces *and* the anemic vision of life it offers. Our organizing and theorizing must simultaneously attend to the deep violences of those inequalities, of the differential production of life, value, opportunities, and freedom, *and* recognize that capitalism is not merely a *problem of distribution* that would finally be solved through the liberal notions of equality and inclusion. Capitalism is rotten to the core, rotten even for those whose comfort seems secured by it. This is why reformist strategies will never succeed in addressing the harms of capital, the state, and the border; all three must be abolished.

---

46 Wendy Brown, *Walled States, Waning Sovereignty* (Zone Books, 2017), 54.

47 These differences often place citizen and migrant communities into direct conflict with each other. As migration becomes ever more policed, and as social services available to migrants continue to be slashed with neoliberal precision, the state and capital exploit these differences to create anti-immigrant sentiment and anti-immigrant policies. One of the most heart-wrenching effects of these policies can be the conscription of working-class citizens into de facto border police: when access to social services is often contingent on citizenship and visas "mutates the working class—nurses, teachers, social workers—into border guards, and the reproduction of borders becomes a workplace ritual." Walia, *Border and Rule*, 84. I talk more about conscription in this sense in chapter 7.

Conclusion: The Power and Joy of Subversive Mobilities

On the day we tried to repair the road, we did not obey the Israeli Army's dispersal order. As some of us had many times before, we refused to comply with the state's closure of movement. We joined arms, sang songs, and refused to move. For a while, the road to Bir al Eid became not only a site of mutual aid, but one in which the state's demand to move was met with what Sheller calls defiant "friction": "a weapon of the weak, used to enact certain kinds of subaltern mobility or block the movement of the elite."[48]

What happened next was widely covered in the media: beatings, arrests, stun grenades. Four soldiers ran right up to a young Palestinian boy and choked him until his body went limp, slammed him into the ground, and then dragged him away. Soldiers choked several others, who had bloodshot eyes for days after. When I placed my body between soldiers and a Palestinian elder, soldiers grabbed each of my limbs and threw me headfirst into a large rock. I got up and tried to rejoin the protest, and they ripped my shirt to shreds on my body, exposing my flesh to the hot desert sun. The flash-bangs landed so close to me that I lost hearing in one ear for several days. A comrade landed in the hospital with a serious concussion that, even now, six years later, isn't fully healed. We had to put an octogenarian comrade on a donkey so he could ride away to safety, an unforgettable instance of what Jacob Shell calls "subversive mobilities": "ungovernable patterns of mobility and rebellious geographies of evasion and connection."[49] In our bid to remain on the road, in Palestinians' refusal to be displaced from Palestine, and in our "subversive movements" from all the world to Bir al Eid, we were able to, for a moment, create a rebellious and beautiful geography of connection.

Some—including two journalists waving their press credentials—were confined more directly, handcuffed, put in the back of a hot vehicle for several hours, taken to a military prison and interrogated. When they were finally released, the non-Palestinians received further movement restrictions: a ban from the southern West Bank. The Palestinian residents returned to their own set of movement restrictions, the routine, daily limitations on freedom that are the norm under colonial occupation.

We refused to move, but ultimately, the colonial state had the superior force to move us. The decision to remain, as so many Palestinians have

48 Sheller, *Mobility Justice*, 130–1.

49 Jacob Shell, *Transportation and Revolt: Pigeons, Mules, Canals, and the Vanishing Geographies of Subversive Mobility* (MIT Press, 2015), 51.

made in the face of unspeakable violence, is also important resistance to the imbrication of the colonial state and capital that uses the control of mobility as a weapon of domination. Forcing people to move from places they would prefer to stay and preventing people from moving are both forms of confinement under a state that positions itself as the regulator of (im)mobilities. They are two aspects of the "logics of border formation—displacing, immobilizing, criminalizing, exploiting, and expelling."[50]

In its particular contours, the border serves both capital and the state "as a tool of population management and racial [and gender] ordering that is at once domestic and global."[51] Beyond the border, the capitalist state enacts various other forms of confinement, including policing and prisons. Given the repressive and violent administration of life that forms the center of state power, and its constitutive commitment to the hierarchical ordering of life, the state emerges as an entity whose role in capitalist society is the confinement of so many aspects of life, in and beyond the capitalist market. While we must dismantle capital's logic of accumulation, no freedom worth the name is possible inside the institution of the state.

The subversive movements of those who stay when they are told to move and who move when they are told not to speak to an abolitionist dream, of a world without and beyond borders, of a world in which our forms of collective governance no longer stand over and against us to ensure our domination, exploitation, and subjection. In yet another moment of subversive mobility, at the end of the action in Bir al Eid, as everyone dispersed, I hid Awdah in the back of our van, holding the window shades closed the entire way back to his village. He squeezed himself onto the floor between two rows of seats, and I sat above him, ready to defend his body if, as also happens frequently, soldiers boarded the van and demanded to see everyone's papers. It was one of the longest rides of my life, though it couldn't have taken us longer than half an hour. My heart pounded so loudly in my ears I couldn't hear anything else. Every few minutes I leaned over my friend and whispered, "Ana m3ak"—I am with you. What I meant was that I was with him in that moment, and that I would not leave him no matter what transpired. But I also meant that I was *with him* in the long struggle for freedom—freedom of movement, freedom to remain, the freedom of Palestinian self-determination, and a kind of freedom neither of us has ever known. "If there were no borders, there would be no 'migration' as such—only mobility"—a mobility that

50 Walia, *Border and Rule*, 2.
51 Ibid., 37.

capitalism and the state routinely confine.[52] If we are to eliminate the rule of property, exploitation, capital, white supremacy, and other forms of domination, we must abolish the border in all its forms, physical and immaterial, administrative and carceral.

Building toward border abolition requires confronting the state and capital as partners in the contemporary regulation of (im)mobilities and the production of human life as differentially valuable. In the place of this colonial system of politico-economic violence, we must instead ask, following Vukov, "How would we *move* differently in a just world, in the kind of world that decolonial, global justice, feminist, queer, and disability justice movements long for and work to build?"[53] Only an abolitionist approach to capital, the border, and the state will provide us with tools for answering such a question and for beginning to build a world in which our mobility is joined to our liberation.

52 De Genova, "A Racial Theory of Labour," 241.
53 Vukov, "Strange Moves," 109.

6

Policing Social Order

Capital is on the move, and so are the police.

—Nevada[1]

There is no police without racism, no racism without police, and no capitalism without either.

—Ben Brucato[2]

The police, domestic caretakers of violence, are the oppressor's emissaries, charged with the task of containing us within the boundaries of our oppression.

—Angela Davis[3]

On May 28, 2020, the Minneapolis Police Department's Third Precinct Station burned to the ground, and before the embers of the station were extinguished, the word "abolition" buzzed around the United States and the world like never before, giving rise to resistance from all corners. This upsurge in political struggle did not occur at a workplace (or at least, the protesters weren't at *their* workplace). Protesters' demands centered around racial justice rather than poverty, jobs, or any explicitly "economic" considerations. Nevertheless, we should understand the demand for police abolition as an anti-capitalist demand. Policing is a

1 Nevada, *The Abolition of Law* (Friends Publishing, 2022), 73.

2 Ben Brucato, *Race and Police: The Origin of Our Peculiar Institutions* (Rutgers University Press, 2023), 26.

3 Angela Y. Davis, "Political Prisoners, Prison, and Black Liberation," in *The Angela Y. Davis Reader*, ed. Joy James (Blackwell Publishing, 1998), 46. Emphasis mine.

central institution of capitalism. Understanding policing's role in contemporary society helps us expand and revise our entire understanding of what capitalism is and how it functions.

As explored in the previous chapter, the state's central power is its ability to use violence. It dispenses violence through many institutions, police foremost among them. Police function as the armed agents of state violence, who capture, surveil, track, control, interrogate, and infiltrate. In the words of Mark Neocleous, "The ultimate truth of the police is that it deals in and dispenses violence in protection of the interests of the state."[4] For this reason David Bayley defines police as "people authorized by a group to regulate interpersonal relations within the group through the application of physical force," and explains that it is the ability to use "physical force, real or threatened, to affect behavior" that differentiates police from other institutions.[5] Carl Klockars also locates violence as the sine qua non of police, writing,

> No police anywhere has ever existed, nor is it possible to conceive of a genuine police ever existing, that does not claim a right to compel other people forcibly to do something. If it did not claim such a right, it would not be a police.[6]

Police may claim that they deploy violence to enforce the law, but policing is much more about confirming capitalism's social order of exploitation and differential domination. At times, police may appeal to the law as justification for their violence. But policing is not generally about the law at all. Police rarely know the law and, even when they do, often flout it flagrantly. They move around with near if not total impunity for even the most brazen violations of the law. Police are empowered with "the discretion to use its coercive capacity in lieu of, beyond, or contrary to the law."[7] At most, "the police directive constitutes a cop's ability to make law in the moment."[8] "The law," Peter Manning explains, mostly "serves as a mystification device or canopy to cover selectively, legitimate, and rationalize police conduct."[9]

---

4 Mark Neocleous, *The Fabrication of Social Order: A Critical Theory of Police Power* (Pluto Press, 2000), 118.

5 David H. Bayley, *Patterns of Policing* (Rutgers University Press, 1990), 7.

6 Carl Klockars, *The Idea of Police* (SAGE Publications, Inc, 1985), 9–10.

7 Brucato, *Race and Police*, 7.

8 Steve Martinot, "The Militarisation of the Police," *Social Identities* 9, no. 2 (2010): 211.

9 Peter K. Manning, *Police Work: The Social Organization of Policing* (MIT Press, 1977), 101.

Policing's true aim is securing social order consonant with capitalism, and it uses violence or its threat to do so. Police enforce social order in a wide variety of ways: surveillance, protest disruption, infiltration, harassment, arrest, entrapment, and so on. What unites these disparate acts is the ability to use violence in the name of the state to secure favorable conditions for capital. In writer Ben Brucato's words:

> Police is the institution sanctioned by the state to use coercive violence. Its purpose is articulated by the state through a mandate to fabricate a specific kind of social order, namely one that is most conducive to capital accumulation through the extraction of labor power using whatever processes are favored at the time by the capitalist class. A core component in the administration of capital accumulation, indeed to the very security of the capitalist economy, is maintaining the control of workers, the reserve army, and surplus populations. Police is an activity rooted in the state conception of proper order and is made active through the organized mobilization of state violence for the purpose of fabricating that order and maintaining it thereafter, chiefly through class formation and regulation, taking raw labor power and imposing work, and administering the class of poverty produced by systematized exploitation.[10]

The police—like the border, prisons, and other state institutions—are a technology of confinement. Rinaldo Walcott argues that police function primarily as "regulators of movement."[11] Policing oscillates between two poles of movement regulation: the "immobilizing activities" in which police attempt "to render disorderly elements harmless" and "mobilizing activities" that seek "to fashion these elements into a mobile and active workforce."[12] Understanding police as regulators of movement and confinement allows us to see two different but interlinked ways they operate: to *stop* (prevent, confine, immobilize) some people or activities and to *facilitate* (move, ease, channel) others.

What must be facilitated? The most frictionless accumulation of capital, the reproduction of a hierarchical social order in which some flourish while others flounder. What must be stopped? Anything that imperils this possibility, whether legally proscribed or not. This may take the form of defending private property or infiltrating leftist social

10 Brucato, *Race and Police*, 67.

11 Walcott, *On Property*, 44.

12 Christopher D. O'Connor and Phillip C. Shon, "Civilising the Police: Reconceptionalising the Role of the State in Theories of American Policing," *Global Crime* 20, no. 1 (2019): 51.

movements, but it may aim more broadly at punishing exploited and expropriated people, reconfirming the state's interest in abandoning some populations to death or neglect. Where police go, whom they surveil, and the intensity of their violence are ultimately directed at confirming a social order in which profits matter more than people, and in which some people matter more than others.

That social order is one deeply committed to racism and heteropatriarchy as part of the differential valuation of life under capitalism. As Brucato explains, "Police has always been fundamental to racial formation, fulfilling a mandate *to define, confine, and control* Blacks [and other groups] and ensure the security of racial capital."[13] Nevada, a participant in the 2020 demonstrations against police violence in Minneapolis, argues that the whole apparatus of policing can be understood as agents of social domination concerned with containing and managing the movement of people who are harmed by capitalism. In their words,

> The constant flows of people since the transatlantic slave trade, from massive black migrations to the North to forced marches of Native people and the constant inward flows of immigration, along with the comparatively open borders of commodities and money creates a complex and disorderly social world. The police, who were the main object of contestation in the 2020 uprising, were formed in response to the disorder *arising from this mobility and flux in order to contain and manage it.*[14]

Capitalism requires the regulation of movement and confinement to secure the conditions of accumulation, and police form a central mechanism of this regulation. As the most visibly violent arm of state violence, police constitute the enforcement mechanism for so many forms of confinement. The modern incarnation of policing arose alongside racialized and colonial capitalism, deploying violence to defend capital's interests and subdue any who resisted its capture.

The Origins of Police

When the term "police" emerged in Europe in the sixteenth century, its meaning was broader than it is today, denoting something closer to "general administration" or "organized governing." Basically anything

13 Brucato, *Race and Police*, 9.
14 Nevada, *The Abolition of Law*, 78. Emphasis mine.

we would now use the term "policy" to denote was initially thought of as a "police matter."

Adam Smith, rising capitalism's theoretical spokesman, was quite interested in the police in this larger sense. His *Lectures on Jurisprudence* speak extensively about police in nearly every aspect of life: "The objects of police are the cheapness of commodities, public security and cleanliness."[15] He explains, "Whatever regulations are made with respect to the trade, commerce, agriculture, manufactures of the country are considered as belonging to the police."[16] The term "police" encompasses nearly any action that a government might take in order to facilitate economic accumulation. Smith's definition was hardly unique; across Europe, "police" designated the general control of a society in the interests of capital, only later acquiring a narrower definition as one specific arm of state administration.

Notice that Smith's definition does not invoke the law at all; rather, policing regulated the general character of capitalist social order. In Michel Foucault's words, "In short, life is the object of the police . . . Society and men as social beings, individuals with all their social relations, are now the true object of the police."[17] Even as the term narrowed over time, the confinement of life remains the true object of the police. In and out of uniform, police intervene in the patterns of life and survival, ensuring that the possibilities of life remain confined to capital accumulation.

Police in the modern sense—a regularized, professional group of paid state employees who secure capital's interests through state-sanctioned violence—remain rooted in the broad project of policing that Smith explained. Police as institution distill and concentrate the pursuit of social order into a profession, into a way people *make their living.* Much like capitalists, cops *make their living* by controlling and confining *the lives of others.* It is no wonder that regularized police emerge historically in capitalism's ascendant centuries. Scholars debate whether the first "real" or "modern" police force was the Paris Police (1667), London's Marine Police (1797), or London's Metropolitan Police (1829), but generally agree that control of the working classes and securing potential disorder propelled their formation. Fewer scholars recognize that even before police patrolled the banks of the Seine, colonial powers instituted police forces to secure the intertwined orders of capital accumulation and colonial subjection.

15 Adam Smith, *Lectures on Jurisprudence* (Oxford University Press, 1978), 398.

16 Ibid., 5.

17 Michel Foucault, "The Political Technologies of Individuals," in *Power: Essential Works of Foucault*, vol. 3, *1954–1984*, ed. J. D. Faubion (The New Press, 2001), 412–14.

The Portuguese created the first police station in Mumbai in 1661; they promptly turned it over to the British East India Company later that year. The British expanded and reorganized the Mumbai police continuously, at least in 1780, 1793, and 1808, showing their continued interest in the institution. British colonial forces promptly established police in Sri Lanka (1806) and Ireland (1814) before London's Metropolitan Police, and subsequently established police forces in Guyana (1839) and Jamaica (1867). Where colonization proceeded by state-aligned joint-stock companies and corporations, as in many parts of Asia and Africa, these semi-sovereign corporations often established their own professional police; the British South Africa Company, the British East India Company, the Imperial British East Africa Company, and the Royal Nigeria Company, among others, all did so. In Mike Brogden's words, "Professional policing was directly linked to the commercial interests of an expanding capitalism in search of new markets and resources . . . The primary justifications for the new police were the exigencies of trade and company profit."[18] Joan Mars highlights three general characteristics of colonial policing: first, a primary objective of control and coercion over the colonized population; second, the "legitimation of police behaviour, however reprehensible, by the executive and judiciary"; and third, the "indiscriminate resort to violence or 'deadly force' as a means of 'social control and especially crowd control.'"[19] Frantz Fanon highlights the centrality of the police to the entire apparatus of colonization:

> The colonial world is a world cut in two. The dividing line, the frontiers are shown by barracks and police stations. In the colonies it is the policeman and the soldier who are the official, instituted go-betweens, the spokesmen of the settler and his rule of oppression . . . The policeman and the

18 Mike Brogden, "The Emergence of the Police: The Colonial Dimension," *The British Journal of Criminology* 27, no. 1 (1987): 12. While it may seem like this dimension of private or private-public police is a relic of rising capitalism and more formal colonial domination, William Robinson explains that there is a continuity in the way that contemporary corporations capture state capacity, especially in policing to their own ends. He explains, "It is important to state the obvious here: corporations accrue police powers and usurp the authority of states as they hire private military and security forces to do their bidding free from any restraint. Several centuries ago, in the heyday of European colonial exploits in Asia, British and Dutch chartered companies were authorized by their imperial governments to amass and deploy their own private armies for colonial expeditions in India, Indonesia, and elsewhere. This bygone era has now been resurrected under the contemporary conditions of global capitalism as the TCC [transnational capitalist class] conquers and re-colonizes the world." William I. Robinson, *The Global Police State* (Pluto Press, 2020), 83–4.

19 Joan Mars, *Deadly Force, Colonialism, and the Rule of Law* (Bloomsbury, 2002), 85.

> soldier, by their immediate presence and their frequent and direct action maintain contact with the native and advise him by means of rifle butts and napalm *not to budge*.[20]

Policing was an essential piece of the colonial empire, securing the conditions for the accumulation of capital, which meant stabilizing the confinement of land, labor, and life.

Where chattel slavery reigned, so too did police. Even before the establishment of regularized police forces, white people were given broad "police powers" over enslaved and colonized people in every aspect of life. As a defining feature of settler colonization in the Americas, especially in the British and French colonies, racialized chattel slavery was the fulcrum of economic, political, and social life. To take the United States as just one example,

> a 1686 law *permitted* any white citizen to apprehend, chastise, and send home any slaves found off their plantations without written authorization. The Act for Better Ordering of Slaves, enacted by the [South Carolina] legislature in 1691, *required* all white citizens to capture and return escaped slaves.[21]

Sally Hadden explains that this "mandated duty effectively turned the entire white population into a community police force."[22] From the first slave codes through abolition, gangs of white people, both directly deputized and more ad hoc, coalesced to enforce the subordination of enslaved people. They were empowered to arrest, detain, transport, maim, and murder those they suspected of defying the social order of slavery, both through obvious acts of rebellion and minute infractions like being unable to produce a valid pass. Policing thus emerges as yet another institution birthed by the conjunction of capitalism and slavery. Just as slavery integrated exploitation and oppression, so too did the policing invented to protect and reproduce it. Policing anchored the colonial project infiltrating every aspect of social, political, and economic existence. In other words, "police" as a specific institution enacted colonial and racialized confinement in order to secure the generalized "police" policies in Adam Smith's larger sense.

---

20 Fanon, *The Wretched of the Earth*, 40, 52. Emphasis added.

21 Brucato, *Race and Police*, 69.

22 Sally E. Hadden, *Slave Patrols: Law and Violence in Virginia and the Carolinas* (Harvard University Press, 2001), 17.

These were the first police units in the United States, and the distinctly racial character of this origin has continued to define the role of policing not only in the US but around the world.[23] I have sometimes received pushback (usually from Brits and Europeans) about the US-centricity of this element of policing. While my analysis surely reflects my own social location, the chattel slavery origin of police remains of global significance for several reasons. In the first place, the US did not invent transatlantic chattel slavery, nor did the US monopolize it. This practice began before the United States even existed in the *British colonies* of Virginia and the Carolinas, a practice imported from European colonies in the Caribbean, especially in Barbados and Brazil.[24] The practice of fugitive slave policing had spread to all thirteen *British* colonies before the American Revolutionary War. The emergence of police through slave patrols is European history, even if a disavowed European history.

Decades or centuries after the colonial adoption of police, they came home to target the working classes of Europe. Initially, domestic police primarily targeted proletarian "crimes" of survival or resistance in an increasingly commodified world: theft, vagabondage, sex work, unemployment, radical organizing, and the like. To paraphrase Neocleous, the police emerge less to make sure that workers weren't breaking the laws that kept them hungry and poor and more to keep intact the system that kept them hungry and poor. In other words, rather than focus on specific laws, police were called in to control generalized "disorder," which meant anything that the ruling class found threatening to the system of economic exploitation or social deference. The royal edict establishing the Parisian police reflects this combination of economic and social concerns, describing the role of police as "ensuring the peace and quiet of the public and of private individuals, purging the city of what may cause disturbances, procuring abundance, and having each and every one live according to their station and their duties." Interestingly, the law appears nowhere in this description of police duties; it is rather maintaining social hierarchy and ensuring the smooth functioning of accumulation, or in the words of Louis XIV, "procuring abundance."[25]

---

23 Victor E. Kappeler, "A Brief History of Slavery and the Origins of American Policing," *Eastern Kentucky University Police Studies Online*, January 7, 2014, plsonline.eku.edu; Ben Brucato, "Fabricating the Color Line in a White Democracy: From Slave Catchers to Petty Sovereigns," *Theoria* 61, no. 141 (2014): 30–54.

24 Hilary Beckles, "From Land to Sea: Runaway Barbados Salves and Servants: 1630–1700," *Slavery & Abolition* 6, no. 3 (1985): 80; Stuart B. Schwartz, *Slaves, Peasants, and Rebels: Reconsidering Brazilian Slavery* (University of Illinois Press, 1996).

25 While it might seem as though the past 500 years has seen a general restriction

Colonial and European police forces are more connected than we are often led to believe. London's first police (the Marine Police) were established in 1797 to secure profits made from enslavement and colonization. Patrick Colquhoun, infamous in police studies circles, organized the Marine Police to prevent dock workers (nearly all criminals in his estimation) from stealing cargo they were unloading. Where was that cargo coming from? The Caribbean, largely carrying goods produced by enslaved labor. In fact, that first group of fifty police officers was mostly funded privately, by the London Society of West India Planters and Merchants. The model was so successful at defending colonial profits against the British working classes that a mere few years later, the Depredation on the Thames Act established the more permanent Thames Police, which merged with Robert Peel's Metropolitan Police in 1839, the force which still polices London today, and which many consider the oldest continuously operating police force in the world.

Policing continues to operate through these colonial-metropolitan circuits, controlling racialized and colonized people as well as the white working classes. Perhaps the most effective strategy of controlling the white working classes has been giving them comparative advantages over racialized and colonized peoples. The history of policing is transnational, racialized, and deeply interested in securing the order of accumulation, and since its birth, policing has always been approached as a combined and uneven enforcement of confinement.

The interpenetration of colonial and domestic policing is not a mere historical artifact but a consistent dynamic of global racialized capitalism that persists into the present moment.[26] Many methods and structures of domestic policing in the Global North were innovated in the colonies, through both police and military. Personnel was often a revolving door; leaders of colonial wars and veterans of frontier colonization were frequently tapped for leadership of urban police departments. This is yet another example of what Sartre called "the boomerang" of colonial

---

of policing so that it now *only* deals with issues of law, Neocleous argues that the reverse is in fact true: the institutions of policing have multiplied, with several agencies taking on policing functions, all directed toward the maintenance of a social order amenable to capitalist accumulation. We certainly saw the expansion of this policing function in the previous chapter on the border, which itself includes the policing of immigrants and transnational movement.

26 I would like to thank the many collaborators I have been working with on the global dimensions of policing: Andres Fabián Henao Castro, Kojo Koram, Sarah Balakrishnan, Jishnu Guha-Majumdar, and all the participants in the 2022 Capitalism and Confinement Workshop.

violence, in which techniques of state violence developed in the colonial world are subsequently unleashed on the metropole, tying together the experiences of colonized people and Euro-American working classes in a material network of inflicted misery.[27] As Julian Go explains, many techniques associated with domestic police are originally colonial innovations: "Everything from fingerprinting (which was originally created in British India in order to identify ostensibly unidentifiable Brown and Black populations) to pin mapping (initially created for colonial counterinsurgency campaigns) and beat patrols (which originated in plantation colonies)."[28]

The colonial dimension of policing is perhaps accelerating in the current neoliberal world. As international borders hardened over the last century, new border police agencies emerged over the twentieth century, simultaneously mirroring the development of "domestic" police and exceeding them in stabilizing neocolonial forms of capitalist extraction. Border cops are, at the end of the day, just cops.

Domestic police agencies are increasingly empowered to transgress state borders, a practice historically rooted in US Marshals' pursuit of escaped enslaved people in Canada and Mexico. Since their very beginning, police forces have worked together across national borders to share techniques, data, software, surveillance information, weapons, intelligence, and other material elements of police infrastructure. The Israeli military industrial complex has been particularly enterprising at this strategy, facilitating ironclad connections with police around the world. Through international policing conferences, formal police exchange programs, joint investigations, and sales of both hardware and software, the Israeli settler colonial apparatus has lodged itself deep within the global economy of state violence.[29] Though the United States has been, by far, the largest consumer of these programs, agencies in the United Kingdom, India, Turkey, and Colombia have also participated in these transnational trainings on techniques of violence and domination. Borders are no obstacle for the infrastructure of repression.

Then we have the emergence of truly *international* police. International agencies like the UN have their own police forces (even if they have more

27 Sartre, "Preface."

28 Julian Go, *Policing Empires: Militarization, Race, and the Imperial Boomerang in Britain and the US* (Oxford University Press, 2023), 18–19.

29 Ashley J. Bohrer and Andrés Fabián Henao Castro, "A People's History of Police Exchanges: Settler Colonialism, Capitalism, and the Intersectionality of Struggles," in *The War on Drugs and the Global Colour Line*, ed. Kojo Koram (Pluto Press, 2019).

limited powers than their domestic counterparts), and transnational policing agencies like Interpol only continue to grow in their power and influence, creating transnational databases with DNA, fingerprints, surveillance, intelligence, and photos. Transnational police associations like the Association of Southeast Asian Nations Chiefs of Police (ASEANAPOL), Southern African Regional Police (SARPOL), Association of Caribbean Commissioners of Police (ACCP), and European Police Office (EUROPOL) are on the rise, as are overseas posts for police and policing agencies. In just my home context of the US, the Federal Bureau of Investigations (FBI), the Drug Enforcement Agency (DEA), the Transportation Security Administration (TSA), Treasury Department, State Department Diplomatic Security Service, Alcohol, Tobacco, and Firearms (ATF), and Federal Marshals all have overseas posts. Many municipal police departments like NYPD also have foreign posts. These dynamics are rooted in colonization; the UK and France immediately implemented police liaison officers in their former colonies after national liberation movements successfully won independence.

Moreover, the US facilitates the imperial "Americanization" of policing around the world, facilitating the implementation of techniques that characterize the US system: asset forfeiture, electronic surveillance, widespread use of paid confidential informants, and undercover policing.[30] It is a cursed cycle: the US adopts techniques forged in colonial domination (either domestically or abroad), imposes those techniques on its own citizens, and then exports these techniques to other countries. In this sense, policing may less follow a boomerang path, in which violence unleashed on the colonies "comes home" to the Global North and stays there, and might more closely resemble a hellish spiral in which Western powers unleash violence abroad that return to the metropole only to be redeployed in imperial domination.

This global history reveals several important aspects of policing. First, policing is fundamentally about the creation and maintenance of a hierarchical social order in which some lives are valued and protected while others are subjected to state violence. Second, policing has always pursued the interests of capital accumulation, and it has done so in a distinctly racialized and colonial manner that continues to shape its current contemporary trajectory.

Though police undertake many activities, I want to focus on tracing three in particular: protecting private property, political repression, and

30 Ethan Nadelmann, *Cops Across Borders: The Internationalization of US Criminal Law Enforcement* (Penn State University Press, 1993).

racial subjugation; these three show clearly how confinement and capitalism are interlinked and how police form a central institution in the ability of capitalism to accumulate. As such, police abolition will emerge as a central part of anti-capitalism, to creating a world beyond capital, institutionalized hierarchies, and a dominating state form.

Policing Property

Police maintain and defend private property and the capitalist commons. They stabilize private property, just as much as they police access to "public" space, determining *which* public is allowed to access it, and in forcibly removing those who are not. As one of the cornerstone social relations of capital, property replicates a logic of confinement ultimately undergirded by the threat or implementation of police violence. As David Correia and Tyler Wall explain,

> Private property, established through force, has transformed the world we live in. And it was and is the job of police to patrol the landscapes of private property, to enforce these boundaries and barriers, walls and enclosures. Thus property might best be understood as a police category. Police arrest the trespasser, evict the squatter, and foreclose on the jobless homeowner. Encroachment on private property is a threat to capitalist order, and it is police who manage this threat.[31]

If private property is a form of confinement in the many senses already explored, police form a central link in the chain of confinement that secures capitalist conditions.

For Rinaldo Walcott, the confinement of private property and the police role in securing it are distinctly racialized and racializing features, contributing to the creation of a society structured around the differential valuation of human life:

> The very idea of what constitutes a successful society is currently organized around the private ownership of property, for which an entire apparatus has been developed to perpetuate and protect. At the center of that apparatus is policing, the legal and court systems, and prisons. If the first police were formed to manage and protect the slave-wealth of

31 Correia and Wall, *Police: A Field Guide*, 73.

> white masters by policing the actual body of the Black enslaved person, then the accumulations of modern or even postmodern life now partially transfer those policing practices to managing property and the assumed transgressions against it. What has not changed is that Black and other poor people remain the substantial focus of policing's concerns and thus lie within its dragnet. Modern policing represents a tremendous subsidy for property owners, one paid for by all citizens through our taxes, including those of us who own no property at all.[34]

Police defense of private property and capitalist commons, then, participates in confinement in two distinct ways: first, by securing the confinement that *is* property; and second, by enforcing the differential valuation of human life, what I have been calling "the confinement of life."

Repression

Repression is a central police function under capitalism. By repression I mean "any actions taken by authorities to impede mobilization, harass and intimidate activists, divide organizations, and physically assault, arrest, imprison, and/or kill movement participants."[33] Or in Charles Tilly's words, "Any action by another group which raises the contender's cost of collective action."[34] Just as police uphold the property regime, they also contain resistance to capitalism's confinement of life, often by disrupting social movements, arresting rioters, punishing resistance, and breaking strikes.[35] In so doing, police seek to materially disrupt the possibilities of creating a more just, equal, and free world. This is why Stuart Hall refers to police as capitalism's chief "means of repression."[36]

Angela Davis explains that political repression is primarily about securing the social order rather than the law. Police engage in repression against anyone who has broken the

34 Walcott, *On Property*, 88.

33 Brett Stockdill, "Multiple Oppressions and Their Influence on Collective Action: The Case of the AIDS Movement" (PhD Dissertation, Department of Sociology, Northwestern University, 1996), 146.

34 Charles Tilly, *From Mobilization to Revolution* (Addison-Wesley Publishing Company, 1978), 100.

35 Geo Maher, *A World Without Police* (Verso, 2021).

36 Stuart Hall et al., *Policing the Crisis: Mugging, the State, and Law and Order* (Macmillan Press, 1978).

> unwritten law which prohibits disturbances and upheavals in the status quo of exploitation and racism. This unwritten law has been contested by actually and explicitly breaking a law or by utilizing constitutionally protected channels to educate, agitate, and organize the masses to resist. A deep-seated ambivalence has always characterized the official response to the political prisoner. Charged and tried for a criminal act, his guilt is always political in nature.[37]

Rather than the primary object of policing, the law emerges as a weapon and a strategy, one that police will appeal to or ignore whenever convenient. When existing laws condemn radicals and racialized people, police will deploy "lawfare" to contain them; when laws protect resistors, police will find other mechanisms to secure the capitalist order. She explains, "Anyone who seeks to overthrow oppressive institutions, whether or not he has engaged in an overt illegal act, is a priori a criminal."[38]

Davis traces political repression as a central feature of American society, rooted in the policing of abolitionist organizers from the invention of transatlantic chattel slavery, but as we have seen, these features are also embedded in the long and global history of European colonialism.[39] Repression was a central feature of colonial policing the world over, embedded in the state's attempt to secure chattel slavery, settler colonialism, and racial capitalism.[40] As each new grassroots movement emerges to contest conditions of domination, the repressive apparatus of the state rises to meet it, a lesson many have learned firsthand in the global protest movements against Israel's ongoing genocide in Gaza.

At the same time, political repression functions partly by denying its own existence. Political repression remains widely tolerated even in putatively democratic societies precisely because it mobilizes supposedly apolitical discourses like legality and crime as ideological cover. Davis

---

37 Davis, "Political Prisoners, Prison, and Black Liberation," 41. She sheds further light on the idea that policing and repression are not actually about the law itself, but about the social order of capital accumulation: "In resisting we have sometimes been compelled to openly violate those laws which directly or indirectly buttress our oppression. But even when containing our resistance within the orbit of legality, we have been labeled criminals and have been methodically persecuted by a racist legal apparatus." (Davis, "Political Prisoners, Prison, and Black Liberation," 40). Legality is not a safeguard from political repression, and activists should not be lulled into a false sense of security that obeying law will protect them.

38 Davis, "Political Prisoners, Prison, and Black Liberation," 42.

39 Ibid., 42.

40 Maher, *A World Without Police*; Neocleous, *The Fabrication of Social Order*; Brucato, "Fabricating the Color Line in a White Democracy: From Slave Catchers to Petty Sovereigns."

continues, "The political act is defined as criminal in order to discredit radical and revolutionary movements."[41] In our day, politicians mobilize the discourse of terrorism in a similar way.

Political repression is not only a feature of domestic policing but increasingly forms a central part of transnational policing; since the world economy is more integrated than ever, repression *within* any specific country is directly linked to the entire process of accumulation. For this reason, it is not only the state and domestic elites that clamor for police to fulfill their role in political repression, but an entire transnational capitalist class that demands the expansion of policing against social movements that threaten to upend the global capitalist order. As William Robinson explains, the transnational capitalist class

> directly instrumentalizes states around the world and at the same time every country and the whole global economy is structurally dependent on transnational capital. States have to generate the conditions for transnational capital accumulation, and this means not only assuring a favorable climate for making profit but also repressing any threat to the rule of capital.[42]

This is why police disrupt social movements, infiltrate organizations, and surveil, harass, arrest, detain, and murder activists with such fervor. When the police fulfill their role as the armed means of repression, they produce a material foreclosure of possibilities that the world could be different, confining the very vision of possible social and material relations. The confinement of a liberatory imaginary is a central part of their charge. The material disruption of anti-systemic organizing constitutes a brutal form of "thought policing" that often flies under the radar. In eroding the material basis for new ideas of emancipation and alternative arrangements of meeting human needs, police repression constricts what we are able to see as real possibilities of social transformation. With police so deft at repression, explicitly outlawing liberatory ideas is hardly necessary; indeed, in societies that profess political pluralism, explicit censorship is roundly condemned as authoritarian overreach. Police repression performs this function instead, all while political institutions claim an open marketplace of ideas, even if that openness is confined to a very specific and calculated Overton window. Police repression confines the horizon of our freedom dreams by disrupting communities, actions, organizing,

41 Davis, "Political Prisoners, Prison, and Black Liberation," 43–4.
42 Robinson, *The Global Police State*, 12.

and projects that would show us how else we could be living, resisting, and building together.

Policing Social Order and the Differential Valuation of Life

Policing is thus predominantly about securing the social order of capitalism. The initial formation of the concept of "police" in a general order of administration continues to inform the sweeping nature of police jurisdiction, even after the term becomes restricted to one particular institution (cops). At its core, capitalism requires a stabilized hierarchy in which some prosper and some starve; it is this order of hierarchy that police are called in to solidify. In this sense, when policing takes on so-called lifestyle crimes as their target or "broken windows" as their strategy, they are stabilizing the social relations of inequality necessary to maintain the illusion of capitalism's normalcy and naturalness.

And of course, this social hierarchy generated by capitalism is not only class-based but constitutively raced, gendered, and sexualized, as well as marked by dynamics of coloniality and ableism, and thus policing stabilizes these elements of capitalist social relations as well. We can only understand the intense racial violence perpetrated by policing or the pervasiveness of gendered police violence (like sexual assault) through understanding that the *order* of "law and order" is a set of hierarchical social relations that designate some (white, straight, cis, male, able, bourgeois) life as worth protecting, and all other life as subordinate, only selectively worthy of defense.

Fred Moten explains this insight, taking police officer Darren Wilson's 2014 murder of Michael Brown in Ferguson, Missouri, as his point of departure: "I don't think he [Wilson] meant to violate the individual personhood of Michael Brown, he was shooting at *mobile Black sociality* walking down the street in a way that he understood implicitly constituted a threat to the order he represents and that he is sworn to protect."[43] If the racist, heteropatriarchal, settler colonial order of capitalism is based in confinement, then unauthorized mobility is a threat. Thus, when police infiltrate Black and brown neighborhoods as an occupying force, intent on causing harm and violence to its residents, it is part and parcel of how capitalism operates. When the police engage in extrajudicial murder, it is

43 *Do Black Lives Matter? Robin D. G. Kelley in Conversation with Fred Moten*, performed by Robin D. G. Kelley and Fred Moten (Critical Resistance, 2014), vimeo.com. Emphasis mine.

part and parcel of how capitalism operates. When the police harass and assault trans people, when they engage in "stop and frisk," when euphemistically termed school resource officers send kids to cages rather than to class—all of this is part and parcel of how capitalism operates. And when communities and activists demand an end to these policies *because they are racist*, they are also (implicitly) making an anti-capitalist demand, because the only way to counter the white supremacist confinement of life is the abolition of both capitalism and policing.

All of this taken together suggests that the differential ordering of life is central to capitalism, and that this is part of what police uphold. Police reproduce racism, heteropatriarchy, and ableism because policing reinforces a societal order in which some lives have value and others do not. It is both the differential access to the economy *and* the differential valuation of life that capitalism depends on; police stabilize both at every turn. This is why police abolition is an inherently anti-capitalist demand, even when it is not articulated as such.

Though police often target oppressed and vulnerable populations, police ultimately confine the entire working class, even if that targeting takes on slightly different social and political dynamics. For the white working classes, police have nearly always come from the very classes they are intended to control. Part of Peel's nineteenth-century vision for policing was for it to be "performed by working-class men, supervised by working-class men."[44] Shared class origins incentivizes working-class identification with police, an aim significantly easier to achieve when police come from the same communities, go to the same schools, frequent the same shops, and engage in the same recreational activities as the people they police. General identification with police undergirds the conscription of many members of the working class into deputized functionaries of capital. It is much easier to coalesce resistance against a foreign occupying power than against your kid's softball coach.

That cops tend to come from the working class, of course, doesn't prevent them from unleashing violence on those communities. They still break strikes, they still disrupt protests, they still defend private property over human life. The identification goes only one way, blunting working-class critique of capital and policing but almost never prompting police to disobey violent orders. This is why abolitionists are often skeptical of calls for "community policing": in a certain way, a large part of policing *has always been community policing*, at least for white people. This insight

44 Clive Emsley, *Crime, Police, and Penal Policy: European Experiences 1750–1940* (Oxford University Press, 2007), 109.

grounds many abolitionists' critiques of how the City of Minneapolis appropriated the concept of abolition in the aftermath of the 2020 rebellion, instituting a form of "community policing" under the name of abolition. As Nevada explains, this was a form of "abolition from above" that was, in the end, no abolition at all. They continue, "The idea of self-policing, of the community policing itself, forms the nexus in which police abolition and police enforcement fuse and become one. Unfortunately for earnest abolitionists, the city [of Minneapolis] is well ahead of us in developing this model."[45] And while community policing for some has meant that they have escaped the most severe cruelties police regularly unleash on communities of color, it has also systematically conscripted the white working classes into reproducing an order committed to our own unfreedom.

As in other realms, the relative security of white communities should not be confused with actual liberation. Though policing's damage is different and less severe in white communities, ultimately capitalism and policing harm even those with relative advantages. As Fred Moten explains, the possibility of liberation does not emerge "so that you can come help me" but rather "out of your recognition that it's fucked up for you, in the same way that we've already recognized that it's fucked up for us. I don't need your help. I just need you to recognize that this shit is killing you, too, however much more softly, you stupid motherfucker."[46] Working-class people and white people are immeasurably worse off for living under a system of legitimated state violence, in which social problems are solved with cages, and in which the rule of property and profit supersede meeting human needs.

I do not mean to suggest that the advantages of whiteness are merely illusory; they are very real. But they are, like so many temporary advantages under capitalism, double-edged. They come at the high price of empowering armed agents of the state to do whatever they please in order to protect the rule of capital that dominates, exploits, and expropriates the vast majority of all people—including the vast majority of white people. A system that thrives on institutionalized hierarchy, that devalues some human lives in favor of others, that legitimizes state violence with impunity is not a system in which anyone is actually secure—let alone free. As Nevada writes, "Only by seeing that white people have something to gain, not just to lose by betraying whiteness, can we truly understand the

45 Nevada, *The Abolition of Law*, 105.
46 Harney and Moten, *The Undercommons*, 140–1.

potential to be found in complicity."[47] If white people want *actual* freedom and *actual* security, we must disinvest from the state, capital, and their assigned deputization duties, throwing in our lot with the rebels, looters, dispossessed, and exploited of the world. That is the only pathway toward the world we all deserve.

Conclusion: Abolishing the Police and the Differential Valuation of Life

In 2020, the question of police abolition was put on the public agenda by the brave people of Minneapolis who understood the fundamental violence of policing. In their rebellion, they invited the world to imagine what would be possible in a world beyond police, in a world beyond capitalism. In the words of Correia and Wall:

> What happens when the oppressed rise up and riot in challenge to the privileges and whiteness of property? The elite fear the destruction of their property, yes, but even more they fear the destruction of the social relations that make private property possible. And so they fear a world without police.[48]

Policing is a central institution of capitalism's development and its ability to reproduce itself. In addition to the police role in securing property and repression, they also secure a hierarchical order in which some lives are valued and others are exposed to violence. Capitalism depends on this order, because it is the underlying logic that makes capitalism durable over time. Racism and colonization, as well as heteropatriarchy, ableism, and nativism, anchor social narratives that justify the massive inequalities in material resources and mobility that capitalism necessarily produces. Police are one potent element in this divide-and-conquer strategy that reproduces cleavages between exploited people; part of the social order of capitalism requires playing several groups off each other, inculcating general climate of distrust as well as a material stake in the oppression of others.

And beyond the police as a single institution, *policing social order* becomes generalized across multiple institutions of capitalist society. Civilians become conscripted into defending a system of inequality and

47 Nevada, *The Abolition of Law*, 98.
48 Correia and Wall, *Police: A Field Guide*, 74.

hierarchy, even when that is the very system that harms us and our communities; indeed, it becomes incredibly difficult to identify that harm is even occurring.

To eliminate capitalism, we must embrace police abolition. Walcott explains what this would entail: "True abolition involves *at least* three necessary components: defunding of the police, the disarming of the police, and the abolition of policing as an institution."[49] Abolishing the police is thus a central aspect of the project of anti-capitalism. We cannot abolish private property without abolishing the police. We cannot abolish collective enclosures without abolishing the police. We cannot abolish the state or its confining borders without abolishing the police. We cannot abolish exploitation or expropriation without abolishing the state institution that violently defends them. We cannot make good on the real promise of the abolition of slavery until we create a society that would not live in the permanent shadow of the afterlives of slavery, which police continue to reproduce. As Brucato writes,

> The capitalist mode of production was founded in a world economy built by slavery, and today the core of the capitalist world system is secured through the racial division of the working class, a security provided by police. The abolition of the rule of capital will entail the abolition of race and police, and so a critical theory of race and police must be abolitionist.[50]

The promise of abolition and of communism is a society no longer based in capitalism's confinement of life. In that sense, police abolition points beyond the abolition of a specific institution, toward the abolition of a society that *needs* police in order to function. Understanding capitalism as an institutionalized social order based in confinement, and seeing police as violent enforcers of this confinement, reveals the imbrication of anti-capitalism and abolition as visions for a liberated future. In Nevada's words, "We don't want a society in which the police have been formally abolished but everything else continues as it did before. We want to abolish the disparities and alienation that the police exist to enforce."[51] This is one meaning of abolition, and there is no possible communism without it.

In addition to a horizon of justice, abolition also describes an orientation to the present, what activist and author Sarah Lamble calls "everyday

49 Walcott, *On Property*, 65.
50 Brucato, *Race and Police*, 28.
51 Nevada, *The Abolition of Law*, 111.

abolition."[52] Whether they knew it or not, the abolitionist dream in Minnesota was also connected to the people of Palestine; the Minneapolis Police Department had been training with Israeli law enforcement for years. Six years earlier in another Midwestern city—Ferguson, Missouri—residents had also risen up in defiance of the racist brutality rained down on them by the local police. Two of the police agencies there had also been trained in Israel: the St. Louis County Police Department and the St. Louis Metropolitan Police Department. As tear gas filled the streets of Ferguson, Palestinians on Twitter recognized the imprint on the canisters of tear gas that littered the streets: they were the same cans, the same manufacturer, the same product that the Israeli military used to suppress Palestinian resistance. Immediately, Palestinians began tweeting advice to the people in Ferguson about how to stay as safe as possible. Information about how to properly flush eyes and avoid inhalation moved quickly across the globe, forming an emergent network of resistance and solidarity that transcended the hard barriers of borders and walls.

Moments like these, when different groups of dominated and oppressed people join together to combat the global circuits of confinement, are examples of abolition in action. Abolition is not only a name for the world we want to build in the future, but a kind of practical, embodied action we engage in *now*. There is also no communism without this element of abolition, moving in solidarity together against the forces that confine us, even when the barriers we face might appear distant and disconnected.

52 Sarah Lamble. "Everyday Abolition," in *Abolishing the Police*, ed. Koshka Duff (Dog Section Press, 2021), 147–60.

7

Cages and Capital

> *Greater discipline is required both for those expelled and made surplus and those incorporated under the new regimes of super-exploitation, which also means new methods of social control and subjugation. Savage global inequalities are politically explosive and to the extent that the system is simply unable to incorporate surplus humanity it turns to ever more violent forms of containment. The methods of control include sealing out the surplus population, through border and other containment walls, deportation regimes, systems of mass incarceration and spatial apartheid.*
>
> —William Robinson[1]

Across Palestine, the prison looms large. While the United States incarcerates more people than any regime in the history of the world, Palestinians are some of the most likely people in the world to face the inside of the literal human cage. Even before the accelerated genocide began in 2023, Gaza was an "open air prison" of over 2 million people.[2] Palestinians in the West Bank live under the constant terror of a carceral state that uses an apartheid legal system to incarcerate at dizzying proportions: 20 percent of all Palestinians (40 percent of Palestinian men) have spent some time in jail or prison. In the West Bank, the Israeli government uses "administrative detention" to incarcerate any Palestinian for six months without charge; a British Mandate–era policy allows secret evidence to extend the period of detention without trial or charge even longer. Charge and trial are little relief; Israeli military courts have a 99 percent conviction

1 Robinson, *The Global Police State*, 63.

2 Noam Chomsky, "My Visit to Gaza, the World's Largest Open-Air Prison," *Truthout*, November 9, 2012.

rate.[3] The military regime systematically targets children, with over 700 minors incarcerated every year. Occupied Palestine is nothing short of a carceral topography, overlayed with an extensive network of detention centers, prisons, military courts, and interrogation sites. I already believed in prison abolition before setting foot in the West Bank, but there is no place on earth that makes abolition feel more urgent and necessary than Palestine.

The prison is perhaps the most obvious form of confinement under contemporary capitalism. The prison is a literal human cage, the most direct form of physical confinement most of us could imagine. Contemporary interest in the prison is due not only to its extreme violence but its deep entrenchment in discourses about freedom, justice, the law, and social control.

Incarceration predates capitalism. Hostages, slaves, political opponents, debtors, and prisoners of war have been held captive in fortresses, dungeons, military garrisons, and other carceral institutions since ancient times. Under noncapitalist modes of production, captivity mostly takes hold of the body as collateral; for example, to enforce the repayment of debt or as a threat against political opponents. This never completely disappears from the institution of the prison, but the prison undergoes two rapid transformations in the hands of European/colonial modernity. Alongside the rise of capitalism in the fifteenth and sixteenth centuries, institutions of extreme confinement buttressed widespread forced labor. At the very same moment that serfs are "freed" from their forced labor obligations, the workhouse captured anyone who either failed or refused to grovel for a wage. Forced labor was not so much ended by proletarianization, even for Europeans, as transformed: what was once an obligation by birth, a mark of hereditary status, became a criminal punishment foisted on mostly the same communities. The shift from heredity to criminal punishment did not so much change the class character of forced labor as much as it shifted its narratives of justification. Since capitalism relies on discourses of freedom, the punishment of forced labor takes on ideas of moral deficiency, idleness, and criminality to justify the extraction of labor that was once secured by feudalism's naturalized hierarchies. This displacement of class warfare onto the discourse of criminalization is unique to capitalism and underlies the idea of prison as, in the words of Angela Davis, "the most influential paradigm for punishment over the past two centuries."[4]

---

3 Noam Sheizaf, "Conviction Rate for Palestinians in Israel's Military Courts: 99.74%," +972 *Magazine*, November 29, 2011, 972mag.com.

4 Angela Y. Davis and Gina Dent, "Prison as a Border: A Conversation on Gender,

The prison remains a site of punishment in contemporary capitalism, even as its specific practices have shifted. Institutions can grow and change over time, as can their relationship to capitalism. In its initial implementation, the prison's primary aim was inculcating capitalist values and work discipline on an unruly and rebellious emerging proletariat. In the colonies, prisons expanded the colonial, racial, and gendered logic of white supremacist capitalism, consolidating control over land, labor, and life through confinement of Indigenous peoples and dissidents. In both cases, the prison was an important instrument of establishing ideological control that moralized poverty and cast aspersion on resistance. As a colonial export, it facilitated Euro-American imperialism. In both the colony and the metropole, prisons captured human beings to make them useful to the process of accumulation. In the present moment, the prison predominantly serves a different function: warehousing surplus populations. As neoliberalism and automation squeeze proletarians further and further into misery and destitution, this aspect of imprisonment will only become more widespread—unless we can abolish prisons and the capitalist society that demands them.

This chapter looks at the development of prisons alongside capitalism, charting its changes over time. I analyze several historical precursors that continue to inflect the contemporary role of the prison in the current conjuncture. I bring together what historian Sarah Balakrishnan calls the "labor genealogy of the prison" with what we might call the "colonial/racial genealogy" of the prison.[5] Contemporary imprisonment reflects both its importance to capitalist modes of accumulation and its investment in the reproduction of white supremacy, heteropatriarchy, and (neo)colonialism.

The Historical Genesis of Prisons in Institutions of Forced Labor

Forced labor has been central to the development of capitalism. On the heels of enclosure, new proletarians found confinement lurking at every turn. If they resisted waged work, or if they were unable to find it, they were remanded the workhouse. If they stole to provide for themselves,

---

Globalization and Punishment," *Signs: Journal of Women in Culture and Society* 26, no. 4 (2001): 1237.

5 Sarah Balakrishnan, "Of Debt and Bondage: From Slavery to Prisons in the Gold Coast, c. 1807–1957," *Journal of African History* 61, no. 1 (2020): 6.

hunted or gathered on enclosed lands, or turned to criminalized industries like sex work for subsistence, they were branded as criminals and shipped to the colonies, as forced agents of different institutions of confinement. In a very different way, capitalism profited from the forced labor of Indigenous and enslaved people as central mechanisms of accumulation, as well as from the widespread dispossession and confinement of land. Among many of the differences between the use of forced labor across the colony-metropole divide was the discourse of crime: while racialized peoples were consigned to forced labor as a matter of *birth*, European forced labor mostly operated under the discourse of *crime or debt.*

For nearly 700 years, if a European found themselves in prison, it was likely because they could not repay a debt. Sarah Balakrishnan gives staggering figures for the prevalence of debt prison in Europe during the eighteenth century: 60 percent of English and 69 percent of Scottish prisoners were confined for debt, and

> as late as 1830 . . . three to five times as many people were imprisoned for debt as for crime in the US states of Massachusetts, Maryland, New York and Pennsylvania. In some counties, as many as one debtor prisoner stood for every ten households. In New York City, roughly 10,000 people were incarcerated for debt in 1830 out of a population of less than 150,000.[6]

Through the sixteenth and seventeenth centuries, prisons were also used as pre-trial detention facilities, as places to administer physical punishments like whippings, and for short-term sentences of hard labor.[7] In Britain, 50 percent of sentences lasted one week and two-thirds lasted two weeks; nearly half of sentences included physical punishments like whipping.[8] When authorities determined harsher penalties were required, they tended to favor executions (often after torture) rather than lengthy incarceration. The turn to penal transportation, which we will come back to, enacted major changes to this system.

As eighteenth- and nineteenth-century European reform movements began to contest the practice of public torture on the continent, longer

6 Sarah Balakrishnan, "The Jailhouse Divergence: Why Debtors' Prisons Disappeared in 19th Century Europe and Flourished in West Africa," *Punishment & Society* 24, no. 5 (2022): 4.

7 The contemporary distinction between jails (for those awaiting trial) and prisons (which house those convicted) is a later development.

8 Robert B. Shoemaker, *Prosecution and Punishment: Petty Crime and the Law in London and Rural Middlesex, c. 1660–1725* (Cambridge University Press, 1991).

prison sentences became more normalized. In lieu of focusing punishment on the body, European reformers suggested long prison sentences would, in Michel Foucault's words, take aim at the soul. A deeply moralistic social view of poverty and crime imbued the rising prison system with a patina of virtue: prisons were to be institutions that would "reform" and "change" the deficient heart of the criminal, fashioning the convict into the perfect capitalist subject. These liberal reformers saw hard labor as a vehicle for instilling the moral virtue obviously lacking among the working classes, whose crimes (and poverty) were attributed to the sin of idleness rather than the dictates of capitalist accumulation.

As Foucault chronicles across several works, targeting the "soul" rather than the body was central to the formation of capitalist society. The extreme discipline of the prison attempted, by rote repetition and further punishment for noncompliance, to shape incarcerated people into a new kind of subject, one who would be "docile" to the accumulative imperative of capitalism. To forced work the prison regime added extreme surveillance, rigid scheduling, machinic regulations, and forced prayer to inculcate an association between poverty, crime, and moral deficiency. The relationship between work and criminality thus operated in two directions. On the one hand, lacking or resisting work was criminalized; on the other, work rehabilitated criminality. This double implication sutured the prison into the social relations of rising capitalism. As Foucault argues, "If, in the final analysis, the work of the prison has an economic effect, it is by producing individuals mechanized according to the general norms of an industrial society."[9] In conjunction with other transformations of collective social life, the prison was a key institution in the creation of capitalist values, of inculcating "hard work" and time discipline into the working classes, confining the rhythms of life in new ways.

The prison's moralizing features also served an important ideological function: individualizing the failure to survive under capitalism. Through discourses of immorality, idleness, and evil, incarceration mystified the true structural causes of poverty and misery. It continues to serve that ideological function to the present, cleaving resistors away from communities and casting aspersion of moral turpitude on those who are remanded behind its walls. The workhouse was eventually phased out of the European carceral archipelago, and in the twentieth century, forced labor gradually receded in importance as well; however, many elements of the workhouse model continued to endure in colonial prisons.

9 Foucault, *Discipline and Punish*, 242.

Penal Transportation

To the workhouse was joined another carceral practice: penal transportation to the colonies. Richard Hakluyt first proposed convict transportation in 1584, suggesting that idle persons and thieves be "'condemned for certain years in the Western parts' (principally in Newfoundland) where they could be kept usefully occupied in producing various commodities."[10] In 1619, the same year that the first enslaved Africans arrived in the Jamestown colony, the London Common Council sent 100 "vagrant" children there rather than provision for them in England, a practice that became commonplace in the British Empire.[11] The British frequently deported Irish and Scottish prisoners of war, consolidating their colonial forays into those lands. The Continental Congress swiftly outlawed the practice after US independence; thereafter, Australia became the primary receiver of British transportees, with over 170,000 people sent to the penal colony of New South Wales alone. The vast majority of settler women in Australia before 1852 (when the British ended the policy) arrived either as incarcerated people (disproportionately convicted of sex work) or as their wives; the British were unique among colonial powers for transporting whole families.[12]

Several empires used penal transportation to encourage settlement in their colonies. The Spanish commuted long prison sentences to one or two years servitude in Española.[13] The French impressed criminalized people into service in the royal galley fleets or directly transported them to colonies in Guinea, Algeria, Morocco, Tunisia, French Guiana, and New Caledonia.[14] Between 1830 and 1962 when the practice was finally

---

10 Edith M. Ziegler, *Harlots, Hussies, and Poor Unfortunate Women: Crime, Transportation, and the Servitude of Female Convicts* (University of Alabama Press, 2014), 2.

11 Ibid., 2.

12 James Davie Butler, "British Convicts Shipped to American Colonies," *The American Historical Review* 2, no. 1 (1896): 12; Eleanor Conlin Casella and Clayton Fredericksen, "Legacy of the 'Fatal Shore': The Heritage and Archaeology of Confinement in Post-Colonial Australia," *Journal of Social Archeology* 4, no. 1 (2004): 99–125.

13 Daniel Castro, *Another Face of Empire: Bartolome de Las Casas, Indigenous Rights, and Ecclesiastical Imperialism* (Duke University Press, 2007), 44–5. Most Anglophone and Francophone readers will be familiar with the island as Hispaniola, but it mostly acquired that name after the time period under discussion. It is still called Española in Spanish to this day.

14 An interesting counterexample, the Portuguese largely eschewed the workhouse system altogether, relying on the Catholic Church and encouraging migration to the colonies. They did also adopt penal transportation, initially for Jews who had refused to convert to Christianity; soon, however, this expanded to a wide array of offenses, and penal transportation was not ended in Angola until the 1930s. Julia Wardhaugh, "Beyond

outlawed, "anywhere from 600,000 to 800,000 men (condemned for a disparate set of minor infractions and political offenses)" found themselves in these "forced labor camps for the building of roads, sewage systems, and ports."[15]

Penal transportation directly contributed to the expansion of colonial power. In New Caledonia (famed among leftists as the destination for transported Paris Commune revolutionaries), "each expansion of the penal colony caused further encroachments on Kanak lands."[16] The French established the first reservations on the island in 1876, on the heels of the new penal colony. This is just one example among many; all over the world, penal transportation became a significant vehicle of settler colonial expansion. Whole cities cropped up to support penal colonies and their employees' needs for food, housing, and recreation. Every expansion further displaced Indigenous peoples.

Penal transportation played a particular role in the history of capitalism. It was itself a profitable business; shippers were paid well, and "granted a property right in the convicts' labor for the term of their sentence—a right they could sell upon arrival" to private households.[17] Shippers often then used the return trip to bring back "tobacco and other commodities such as wheat, flour, lumber, and pig iron."[18] Many also returned with enslaved people. Beyond its direct profitability, penal transportation "was a relatively inexpensive means of disposing of unwanted felons, a source of colonial labor, a visible deterrent to would-be offenders, and a change of redemption to those already under sentence."[19] As Sai Englert has noted, penal transportation was extremely effective at stabilizing European class relations: "Deporting the poor (and the rebellious) to the colonies would serve a double purpose: lessen social tensions at home and strengthen settlement abroad."[20]

---

the Workhouse: Regulating Vagrancy in Goa, India," *Asian Criminology* 7 (2012): 212. For more see Paul Ocobock, "Introduction," in *Cast Out: Vagrancy and Homelessness in Global and Historical Perspective*, ed. Paul Ocobock and A. L. Beier (Ohio University Press, 2008); Jan Vansina, "Confinement in Angola's Past," in *A History of Prison and Confinement in Africa*, ed. Florence Bernault (Heinemann, 2003).

15 Ann Laura Stoler, *Duress: Imperial Durabilities in Our Times* (Duke University Press, 2016), 94.

16 Alice Bullard, *Exile to Paradise: Savagery and Civilization in Paris and the South Pacific, 1790–1900* (Stanford University Press, 2000), 168.

17 J. M. Beattie, *Crime and Courts in England, 1660–1800* (Oxford University Press, 1986), 479.

18 Ziegler, *Harlots, Hussies, and Poor Unfortunate Women*, 47–8.

19 Ibid., 2.

20 Englert, *Settler Colonialism: An Introduction*, 52.

The circuit of confinement, capitalism, and coloniality runs through the history of incarceration in capitalism's rising centuries. Far from a victorious narrative of movement, the rise of capitalism layers confinement on confinement. The confinement of enclosures generated the confinement of the wage or the workhouse; those who resisted were confined in prisons and penal colonies on confined Indigenous land. If criminalized proletarians survived their imprisonment, they became settlers themselves, benefitting from the theft of Indigenous lands on which they found themselves, often incorporating directly into the settler fabric of colonial society. Their supposed freedom was thus predicated on the continued confinement of land and life in the growing colonial order.

Imprisonment and Colonization

Prisons formed an integral part of the colonial architecture of confinement. Before the arrival of European colonizers, Indigenous peoples around their world had their own systems of settling disputes and righting infractions. None included the long-term incarceration of people as punishment.[21] Through colonization, this practice would come to nearly every continent. Prisons were not only a part of everyday administration in the colonies, but they were a significant tool of developing colonial control; they were established in garrisons, outposts, military posts, and other administrative zones at an embryonic stage of colonial development.[22] Prisons grounded the emerging repressive apparatus of the colonial state, projecting European power into areas that were not yet firmly in its grasp.

The prison was thus a central institution of empire building. Nearly all prisons across the French, British, Spanish, and Portuguese colonies

21 In Vietnam and China, flogging, indentured servitude, exile, and death were more common punishments, while imprisonment was used only for individuals awaiting trial or execution. African societies tended either to settle minor disputes through mediation and reparation or to punish more serious crimes by exile, execution, or sale into slavery.

Peter Zinoman, *The Colonial Bastille: A History of Imprisonment in Vietnam, 1862–1940* (University of California Press, 2001); Andrew Coyle, "Prison Privatisation in the African Context," *Review of African Political Economy* 35, no. 118 (2008): 660–5; Mary Gibson, "Global Perspectives on the Birth of the Prison," *American Historical Review* 116, no. 4 (2011): 1040–63.

22 Odile Goerg, "Colonial Urbanism and Prisons in Africa: Reflections on Conakry and Freetown, 1903–1960," in *A History of Prison and Confinement in Africa*, ed. Florence Bernault (Heinemann, 2003), 111.

imposed grueling work requirements; in the French colonies, this practice continued even after the supposed abolition of forced labor in 1945. Moreover, "colonizers used administrative imprisonment as an economic incentive to enforce tax collection, forced labor or cultivation, and to provide colonial companies with a constant influx of cheap labor."[23] In the Belgian-occupied Congo, up to 10 percent of the adult male population would be incarcerated every year. In effect, incarcerated colonized people were forced to literally build the machinery of empire, as prison officials lent their labor to building public infrastructure (roads, ships, quarries, bridges, and the like). In many places, colonizers leased incarcerated labor to private corporations, providing a significant boost to private industries. Similar to the convict-leasing system in the United States, the South African government regularly sent incarcerated people to labor on private white-owned farms beginning in the 1890s. The system was so widespread and profitable that the white farmers began treating prison construction as an investment in its own right:

> By 1947, the number of black convict workers on white farms had increased massively, prompting, in 1948, the establishment of farm-jails housing nonwhite prisoners sentenced to long-term sentences (over two years). White farmers financed the construction of these facilities by buying shares of the farm-jails and drawing convict labor in proportion to their contribution.[24]

Incarceration transformed entire colonial economies, increasing the rate of exploitation for all by holding wages artificially low for all colonized people. Prisons thus confined and contained resistance *and* made that resistance productive for the colony in the form of forced labor.

Colonial prisons were also highly gendered spaces, constituting one mechanism Europeans used to impose heteropatriarchy on colonized peoples. Whatever previously existing social worlds colonizers encountered, they imposed stark heteropatriarchal norms, including by "implement[ing] a gendered division of labor in the prison . . . [that] confined [women] in unpaid domestic duties . . . They [incarcerated women] cooked for the prisoners, pounded food, cleaned and swept the wards."[25]

---

23 Bernault, "The Politics of Enclosure in Colonial and Postcolonial Africa," 12.

24 Ibid.

25 Dior Konaté, "Ultimate Exclusion: Imprisoned Women in Senegal," in *A History of Prison and Confinement in Africa*, ed. Florence Bernault (Heinemann, 2003), 161.

Colonial incarceration also facilitated rampant sexual violence, as prisons continue to do today.[26]

Colonial prisons distinguished themselves from their European counterparts by their continued investment in physical violence. While in Europe, imprisonment gradually *supplanted* physical torture, in the colonies, prisons "did not replace but rather supplemented public violence."[27] Eugenic ideas of race and criminality flooded European and colonial ideologies, suggesting colonized peoples carried a natural and inborn predisposition toward lawlessness. On this basis, the British passed legislation in India declaring certain ethnic groups to be "Criminal Tribes"; members of these groups were subject to restricted movement, a Draconian pass system, and forced settlement into segregated communities. By 1947, when India shook off British domination, 13 million people across 127 groups were subjected to this treatment. This was but one pointed example of a broader racist logic that continues to permeate penal discourses to this day. Where the nineteenth- and twentieth-century prison reformers in Europe focused on a coercive, moralizing rehabilitation of their working-class inmates, race was seen as a permanent mark from which colonized people could not be rehabilitated. Colonial prisons thus did not pursue reforming their inmates, focusing rather on exploiting them and using their unique vulnerabilities to consolidate deeper control over the colonized population as a whole. In this sense, colonial prisons "aimed to reinforce the social and political separation of the races to the sole benefit of white authority by assigning the mark of illegality to the whole of the dominated population."[28] The prison was a central implement of imposing a racialized confinement of life in the colonial world.

As one of the main tools of the imperial state's repressive apparatus, the prison also attempted to contain and punish any form of resistance to colonial rule; whether Indigenous peoples resisted foreign political rule, forced labor, pass laws, or other markers of white supremacy, colonial authorities deployed the prisons. For example, in South Africa alone, over 17 million people saw the inside of a prison cell for allegedly

26 Maria da Conceição Neto, "Colonial Incarceration and Selective Memories: What Is Remembered? Who Is Forgotten? The Case of Peasant Women Deported to São Nicolau (Angola, 1969)," *The Journal of Imperial and Commonwealth History* 47, no. 2 (2019): 325–42; Beth E. Richie, *Arrested Justice: Black Women, Violence, and America's Prison Nation* (New York University Press, 2012).

27 Bernault, "The Politics of Enclosure in Colonial and Postcolonial Africa," 3.

28 Ibid., 16.

breaking these laws between 1916 and 1986.[29] As Dior Konaté explains, in the French Empire, "prisons became a tool for banishing Africans who tried to resist French hegemony."[30] The Portuguese deployed prisons as a method of colonial counterinsurgency.[31] At the same time, in the colonies as elsewhere, imprisoned radicals often found each other in its confines, and prisons sometimes emerged as a hotbed of insurgent organizing.[32]

When settlers faced incarceration in the colonies, they generally encountered a very different experience from that of Indigenous peoples, a testament to how thoroughly prisons formed a tool of racial (not only class) control. White people accused of crimes were often, first of all, transferred back to the metropole for trial and punishment. If they were incarcerated in the colonies, white people were often exempt from the forced labor demanded of other incarcerated people. They were often also housed separately, and given substantially better treatment in housing, food, and other aspects of incarcerated life. Bernault continues,

> Colonial penitentiaries did not aim at organizing standardized punishment in a neutral space, since no such equality of status and right existed outside the walls of the prison. To the contrary, prison architecture sought to reproduce colonial hierarchies, erected not only upon the race distinction, but also upon a subtler contrast between individual citizens (whites) and the collective, untitled mass of African subjects.[33]

The distinction in treatment between colonizer and colonized was part of a larger program of instantiating an entire world of colonial domination, not simply a legal, political, or economic regime, but a whole world. The colonial prison was rather

> a conscious strategy to constrain bodies rather than disciplining minds, to control crime and labor rather than initiating social engineering. In this perspective, colonial prisons never served as true penitentiaries, but as practical fortresses where the conquest of Africa could be safely pursued.[34]

---

29 Rodney Davenport and Christopher Saunders, *South Africa: A Modern History*, 5th edition (Palgrave Macmillan, 2000), 511.

30 Konaté, "Ultimate Exclusion," 156.

31 Da Conceição Neto, "Colonial Incarceration and Selective Memories."

32 Peter Zinoman, "Colonial Prisons and Anti-Colonial Resistance in French Indochina: The Thai Nguyen Rebellion, 1917," *Modern Asian Studies* 34, no. 1 (2000): 57–98.

33 Bernault, "The Politics of Enclosure in Colonial and Postcolonial Africa," 21. Bernault focuses on Africa, but the same dynamics held generally across the colonial world.

34 Ibid., 26.

We can understand the true impact of the colonial prison only when we see its connections to other modes of confinement deployed in the process of concreting colonial capitalism. As Bernault explains, colonized people

> did not simply face a new repressive system [of incarceration]; they also experienced broader mutations in the political construction of physical and spiritual space, the public and domestic spheres, the collective and the private, the invisible and the apparent. For this reason, the history of prisons must be located in the larger context of colonial and postcolonial *tactics of confinement*. Through the delimitation of borders, the sedentarization of villages, the classification of ethnic groups, and the stabilization of workers in model cities, colonizers and Africans inaugurated a series of new articulations between social identity and physical space.[35]

The colonial prison interlaced with other forms of colonial confinement as foreign rule and capitalism were imposed as interlocked structures.

The great waves of political decolonization unfortunately did not uproot the prison, constituting one element in what we might call the "afterlives of colonial domination."[36] On the contrary, prisons have only expanded. In our world, "imprisonment [is] the dominant form of worldwide punishment."[37] Gina Dent refers to prisons as "a preeminent American export," highlighting the prison's embeddedness in the wider projects of imperialism and neocolonialism.[38] The widespread uptake of the prison as a supposedly just and modern system of punishment is the effect of an imperial world order that reverberates to the present day, and as in the colonial heyday, it tends to disproportionately target poor, racialized people the world over.

The colonial and racial dynamics of the prison, in both its historical and contemporary manifestations, highlight its role in the global project of consolidating capitalist control over land, labor, and life. Despite a somewhat altered global order, the prison remains a predominant mode of capitalist confinement, one that reproduces the racial and colonial character of capitalism's rising centuries in its contemporary practices.

---

35 Bernault, "The Politics of Enclosure in Colonial and Postcolonial Africa," 4. Emphasis added.

36 Of course, we are not postcolonial everywhere, as many places remain under direct colonial domination, and any invocation of the term "postcolonial" must recognize we still inhabit a generally neocolonial world order.

37 Gibson, "Global Perspectives on the Birth of the Prison," 1057. For more on this topic in the African context, see Coyle, "Prison Privatisation in the African Context."

38 Davis and Dent, "Prison as a Border," 1239.

Contemporary Capitalism's Prisons

Prisons remain highly gendered institutions in a wide variety of ways.[39] Important queer and feminist prison work shows that the current practices of policing and imprisonment lead to higher rates of incarceration and system-contact for trans and nonbinary people overall.[40] It highlights the historical investment in incarceration as spaces of gender regulation, teaching those housed in women's prisons how to be "good" women, which of course meant performing a very specific gendered script of normative, white, middle-class femininity and subservience.[41] It further explores how dimorphic housing (based on sex assignment at birth), rampant sexual violence, refusal of adequate medical treatment (especially for pregnancy and gender-affirmative care), child separation, lack of consistent access to menstrual products, forced sterilization, and the history of medical experimentation especially in gynecology contribute to an overall gendered nature of incarceration.[42] It details how women

39 Angela Y. Davis and Cassandra Shaylor, "Race, Gender, and the Prison Industrial Complex: California and Beyond," *Meridians* 2, no. 1 (2001): 1–25; Sarah Pemberton, "Enforcing Gender: The Constitution of Sex and Gender in Prison Regimes," *Signs: Journal of Women in Culture and Society* 39, no. 1 (2013): 151–75.

40 Spade, *Normal Life*; Joey L. Mogul et al., *Queer (In)Justice: The Criminalization of LGBT People in the United States* (Beacon Press, 2011).

41 Angela Y. Davis, *Are Prisons Obsolete?* (Seven Stories Press, 2003), ch. 4; Beth Ritchie, "Queering Antiprison Work: African American Lesbians in the Juvenile Justice System," in *Global Lockdown: Race, Gender, and the Prison-Industrial Complex*, ed. Julia Sudbury (Routledge, 2005).

42 Elida Ledesma and Chandra L. Ford, "Health Implications of Housing Assignments for Incarcerated Transgender Women," *American Journal of Public Health* 110, no. 5 (2020): 650–4; Valerie Jenness et al., "Sexual Victimization Against Transgender Women in Prison: Consent and Coercion in Context," *Criminology* 57, no. 4 (2019): 603–31; Priscilla A. Ocen, "Punishing Pregnancy: Race, Incarceration, and the Shackling of Pregnant Prisoners," *California Law Review* 100, no. 5 (2012): 1239–311; Jennifer G. Clarke and Rachel E. Simon, "Shackling and Separation: Motherhood in Prison," *AMA Journal of Ethics* 15, no. 9 (2013): 779–85; Mitchell Carney, "Cycles of Punishment: The Constitutionality of Restricting Access to Menstrual Health Products in Prisons," *Boston College Law Review* 61, no. 7 (2020): 2541; Margaret E. Johnson, "Menstrual Justice," *UC Davis Law Review* 53, no. 1 (2019): 1–79; Rachel Roth and Sara L. Ainsworth, "If They Hand You a Paper, You Sign It: A Call to End the Sterilization of Women in Prison," *Hastings Women's Law Journal* 26, no. 1 (2015): 7–50; Jess Whatcott, "No Selves to Consent: Women's Prisons, Sterilization, and the Biopolitics of Informed Consent," *Signs: Journal of Women in Culture and Society* 44, no. 1 (2018): 131–53; Mark A. Largent, *Breeding Contempt: The History of Coerced Sterilization in the United States* (Rutgers University Press, 2011); Anastazia Schmid, "Crafting the Perfect Woman: How Gynecology, Obstetrics, and American Prisons Operate to Construct and Control Women," in *Abolishing Carceral Society*, ed. Abolition Collective (Common Notions, 2018); Eric A. Stanley and Nat Smith, eds., *Captive Genders: Trans Embodiment and the Prison Industrial Complex*, 2nd edition (AK Press, 2015).

of color are denied any right to self-defense, routinely criminalized for resisting patriarchal, transphobic, and homophobic violence, as well as abuse by family or intimate partners.[43] It shows how, inside the prison, repressive regulations about gendered dress abound.[44] It exposes how correctional officers in "women's" facilities often respond with heightened scrutiny and aggression toward those who read as masculine.[45] It details the gendered state violence of placing trans and nonbinary people in so-called administrative segregation (solitary confinement) in the paternalistic narrative of "protection" is a form of state violence. In this sense, it shows how "policing of sexual and gender 'deviance' is central to notions of crime, and serves both as a tool of race-based law enforcement and as an independent basis for punishment."[46]

Contemporary prisons also continue to profit from the misery of confined human beings through what Gina Dent calls "the socially destructive business of imprisonment."[47] The capitalist prison is also a workplace just like any other under capitalism; and like all industries, it operates through calculations about wage exploitation, profit maximization, and efficiency pressure. As Ruth Wilson Gilmore shows, entire towns depend on the jobs connected to the prison industry.[48] Some prisons still compel labor, and others collaborate with corporations to pay incarcerated people extremely low wages to produce profit or public infrastructure. In the absence of other work, incarcerated people continue to engage in the unwaged labor of their own reproduction through cooking, cleaning, laundry, and circulating books in underfunded libraries. The prison's daily functioning depends on the social reproduction work of incarcerated people, injecting a new and extremely direct layer to what, in the next chapter, I call the carcerality of care. Social reproduction in the prison,

---

43 Mariame Kaba, "No Selves to Defend: An Interview with Mariame Kaba," interview by Ashley Bohrer, *Red Wedge Magazine*, August 19, 2014, redwedgemagazine.com; Richie, *Arrested Justice: Black Women, Violence, and America's Prison Nation*.

44 Gabriel Arkles, "Correcting Race and Gender: Prison Regulation of Social Hierarchy Through Dress," *New York University Law Review* 87, no. 4 (2012): 859–959; Gabriel Arkles, "Safety and Solidarity Across Gender Lines: Rethinking Segregation of Transgender People in Detention," *Temple Political & Civil Rights Law Review* 18, no. 2 (2009): 515–60.

45 Julia Sudbury, "Maroon Abolitionists: Black Gender-Oppressed Activists in the Antiprison Movement in the US and Canada," *Meridians: Feminism, Race, Transnationalism* 9, no. 1 (2009): 19.

46 Mogul et al., *Queer (In)Justice*, xiii.

47 Davis and Dent, "Prison as a Border," 1235.

48 Ruth Wilson Gilmore, *Golden Gulag: Prisons, Surplus, Crisis, and Opposition in Globalizing California* (University of California Press, 2007).

like in the rest of the capitalist world, both sustains incarcerated people and is a source of their domination. Whether that labor remains directly gendered or not, the conscripted nature of care, in which the survival of oppressed and exploited people depends on work that they are not free to choose or desist from, and which sustains a vast total institution of domination, activates the central knot of capitalist carcerality.

The state and private businesses accumulate also through the dizzying array of fines and fees imposed on incarcerated people, who are often charged for everything they access: phone and video calls, personal hygiene products, food to supplement paltry (and sometimes rotting) rations. Even though these facts do not *account* for the existence of prisons, anti-capitalist analysis helps us understand why these modes of extraction are so common, patterned, and predictable under capitalism. Wherever institutions arise under capitalism, someone will always be trying to make a buck from them, and because profit dominates the social calculus, institutions that have other concerns as their raison d'être often get caught up in accumulation.

Even as most prisons in the world are government run, the prison industry involves a wide variety of private corporations. Whether they run private prisons directly or serve as prison contractors (food, transport, technology, security, and so on), many for-profit businesses make their money through the prison system. Corporations are especially prominent in the migrant detention, even where domestic prisons have largely eschewed direct privatization.

Prisons are thus big business, and one could not adequately understand the economics of imprisonment without an anti-capitalist lens. At the same time, these directly economic elements do not and cannot, on their own, account for the continued existence of prison overall. So while these analyses are helpful at illuminating aspects of the contemporary prison system, they fall short of offering a systematic account of capitalist incarceration, in part because they focus on practices (like privatization or in-prison factories) that are more the exception than the rule. To more fully understand the relationship between capitalism and carcerality, we have to move beyond these directly monetary exchanges and look deeper at how capitalism is invested in the differential production of human life and death.

Capitalism and the Confinement of Surplus Life

The largest transformation in the prison over the history of capitalism has been its move away from labor exploitation and toward the confinement of what Marx called the "reserve army" of labor. While capitalism exploits many, not everyone can find a job. Marx understood that not-currently-exploited proletarians could supplement the "regular" army of the working class when conditions were favorable (for capital). In many societies where gender, ability, and age affect labor conditions, women, children, the elderly, and disabled people have cycled in and out of the formal labor market, as employers have sought to supplement or shrink the workforce.

Thus, capitalism produces a stratum of people who need wages but cannot access them, who need to buy goods on the market to survive but cannot get the money to do so. While in many circumstances, they may rely on kin for survival, as the capitalist family has become more nuclear and as bonds of community have been frayed by individualistic and competitive ideology, and as social safety nets have been eroded or eliminated by the rise of neoliberalism, more people under capitalism find themselves both without a job and without another way to survive. In Michael Denning's words, "Under capitalism, the only thing worse than being exploited is not being exploited."[49]

Capitalist production thus produces unwaged proletarians, whose labor is not directly folded into the capitalist economy.[50] Marx explains in the *Grundrisse*:

> It is a law of capital . . . to create surplus labor, disposable time . . . It is therefore equally a tendency of capital to increase the laboring population, as well as constantly to posit a part of it as surplus population—population which is useless until such time as capital can utilize it . . . It is equally a tendency of capital to make human labor (relatively) superfluous, so as to drive it, as human labor, towards infinity.[51]

49 Michael Denning, "Wageless Life," *New Left Review*, no. 66 (2010): 79.

50 The phrase "unwaged proletarians" might initially seem counterintuitive to some Marxist readers who identify proletarians with the waged working class. Indeed, as I will return to below, the relationship between waged and unwaged parts of the class has sometimes been fraught. However, I concur with Clyde Barrow, Michael Denning, and others who see expropriation and exploitation as constituting two faces of the global proletariat. Denning for this reason proposes that the proletariat be defined more on the basis of its dispossession than the shape of its relationship to the realm of production. For a contrary perspective, see Hal Draper, "The Concept of the 'Lumpenproletariat' in Marx and Engels," *Économies et Sociétés*, no. 15 (1972): 285–312.

51 Marx, *Grundrisse*, 398–9.

The exploitation of labor and the production of surplus populations are thus two sides of the same coin. This dynamic is so central to capitalism that Marx called it "the absolute general law of capitalist accumulation."[52] He argues also that capitalism tends to produce larger surplus populations over time, and that the capital's entire "form of motion" depends on this surplus: "Modern industry's whole form of motion therefore depends on the constant transformation of the working population into unemployed or semi-employed 'hands.'"[53] Indeed, for Marx, this surplus population constitutes the very "lever" of the entire mode of production:

> If a surplus population of workers is a necessary product of accumulation or of the development of wealth on a capitalist basis, this surplus population also becomes, conversely, the lever of capitalist production, indeed it becomes a condition for the existence of the capitalist mode of production. It forms a disposable industrial reserve army, which belongs to capital just as absolutely as if the latter had bred it at its own cost. Independently of the limits of the actual increase of production, it creates a mass of human material always ready for exploitation by capital in the interest of capital's own changing valorization requirements.[54]

Marx also refers to this surplus population as the "lumpenproletariat," the part of the working class who, in Clive Barrow's words, is defined "by its *nonrelation* to economic production and by its position outside capitalist relations of production."[55] Since capitalism developed in and through gender, race, sexuality, and colonial forms of domination, oppressed peoples are often overrepresented in this immiserated group of people who must scrimp and scrounge to survive, relying on kin, community, and sometimes on criminalized activity. In this sense, capitalism produces the very crime it polices, a point I return to below.

Thus, more than enacting labor discipline, the contemporary prison acts as a way to contain the danger of this surplus population, the lumpenproletariat. With increasing automation, worker productivity rates, and industrial efficiency, we simply need fewer laborers, even as we produce

52 Marx, *Capital*, volume 1, 798.

53 Ibid., 786.

54 Ibid., 784.

55 Clyde W. Barrow, *The Dangerous Class: The Concept of the Lumpenproletariat* (University of Michigan Press, 2020), 15. Barrow argues here that despite some different resonances of the terms "reserve army," "surplus population," and "lumpenproletariat," the most consistent way to read these terms across Marx's corpus entails reading the lumpenproletariat as the overarching category, with the others as subdivisions that reflect differences in their political and cultural character. I use them here broadly as synonyms.

more goods and services. It is no coincidence that the massive explosion of contemporary prisons broadly coincides with deindustrialization in the Global North. As the ranks of the global surplus population swells, we no longer use prisons as a mechanism of breaking people into the labor discipline of the wage; capital uses these institutions of confinement instead to contain the potential unrest surplus populations might incite. Ruth Wilson Gilmore argues that the prison's primary function under contemporary capitalism is to "warehouse" these people, to create a container for them, to create an institution to control and banish them.[56] Prison is a destination for people who have been abandoned by both the state and capital, hiding this abandonment and deploying the ideology of punishment to justify locking them away in cages. As Angela Davis describes it,

> The institution of the prison serves as a place to warehouse people who represent major social problems. Just as there is a disproportionate number of Black people in US prisons, there is an equally disproportionate number of aboriginal people behind bars in Australia. Getting rid of the people, putting them in prison is a way not to have to deal with immigration in Europe. Immigration, of course, happens as a result of all the economic changes that have happened globally—global capitalism, the restructuring of economies in countries of the Global South that makes it impossible for people to live there. In many ways you can say that the prison serves as an institution that consolidates the state's inability and refusal to address the most pressing social problems of this era.[57]

The prison's transition from a tool of labor discipline to a tool of containment should not be understood as a total one; it is better to see these transitions and uses as what Stuart Hall once called "structures in dominance," where certain tendencies, while existing alongside others, take on outsized importance.[58] *Which* structures ascend to dominance always depends on local conditions, power struggles, and resistance, and cannot be determined outside of a historical analysis.

The prison as warehouse shapes capitalism's racial and gendered constitution. Capitalism's surplus population is undisputably racialized, deeply involved with the continuity of white supremacy, both domestically

56 Gilmore, *Golden Gulag*.

57 Davis, *Freedom Is a Constant Struggle*, 25.

58 Stuart Hall, "Race, Articulation, and Societies Structured in Dominance," in *Essential Essays*, vol. 1, ed. David Morley (Duke University Press, 2019).

and globally, so much so that Angela Davis draws a direct line from "the prison of slavery to the slavery of prison."[59] The "slavery" that Davis thematizes is less about unpaid labor than about the social relations of racialized capital accumulation, which, though transformed, remains deeply embedded in the production of surplus populations. Because contemporary surplus populations are so obviously embedded in racial and colonial dynamics, the concept of the lumpenproletariat became a central piece of anti-racist and anticolonial anti-capitalist theorizing in the twentieth century. Anticolonial revolutionaries like Frantz Fanon and Black Panthers like Elaine Brown, Eldridge Cleaver, and Huey Newton all put the surplus population at the center of their analyses of capitalism's intertwining with white supremacy.

Both workers and lumpenproletariats experience capitalism's violence, but the two groups may find themselves at odds. Clyde Barrow argues that while these two groups are "parts of the same class," they tend to "occupy radically different status positions within capitalist social formations."[60] Workers under capitalism have split interests, with their survival at least partially tied to the reproduction rather than the elimination of capitalism. This stake in the reproduction of capitalism has often positioned the working and surplus wings of the global proletariat in tension with one another. Bue Rübner Hansen highlights Marx's attentiveness to how the ruling class plays the lumpenproletariat and waged workers off one another; this constitutes, in Hansen's estimation, "the secret of the maintenance of power by the capitalist class. And the latter is fully aware of this."[61] This antagonism has led to wildly different assessments of the revolutionary potential of the lumpenproletariat across the history of anti-capitalist theorizing. In his historical writings, Marx emphasized that the lumpenproletariat's desperation makes them susceptible to right-wing co-optation. Amílcar Cabral noted a similar dynamic in the colonial context, where reactionary postcolonial elites exploit the lumpen precarity for political gain.

On the other hand, the working class's partial stake in the reproduction of capitalist society can also create the opposite political tendency, in which waged workers, because of their material interest in capitalism's reproduction, can constitute a reactionary force against unemployed,

59 Angela Y. Davis, "From the Prison of Slavery to the Slavery of Prison," in *The Angela Y. Davis Reader*, ed. Joy James (Blackwell Publishing, 1998), 75–6.

60 Barrow, *The Dangerous Class*, 47.

61 Bue Rübner Hansen, "Surplus Population, Social Reproduction, and the Problem of Class Formation," *Viewpoint Magazine*, October 31, 2015, viewpointmag.com.

incarcerated, unhoused, and otherwise surplus populations. Precisely *because* the lumpenproletariat is so locked out of capitalist relations of production, they might be *the most* revolutionary group in society. This was Fanon's position: "The lumpenproletariat, that horde of starving men, uprooted from their tribe and from their clan, constitutes one of the most spontaneous and the most radically revolutionary forces of a colonized people."[62] Elaine Brown, former Chair of the Black Panther Party, applies this line of thinking to racialized people in the Global North:

> The black lumpenproletariat, unlike Marx's working class, had absolutely no stake in industrial America. They existed at the bottom level of society in America, outside the capitalist system that was the basis for the oppression of black people. They were the millions of black domestics and porters, nurses' aides and maintenance men, laundresses and cooks, sharecroppers, unpropertied ghetto dwellers, welfare mothers, and street hustlers. At their lowest level, at the core, they were the gang members and the gangsters, the pimps and the prostitutes, the drug users and dealers, the common thieves and murderers.[63]

What if both sides of this assessment are true? Marx once argued that the lumpenproletariat was as capable of "the most heroic deeds and the most exalted sacrifices, as of the basest banditry and the dirtiest corruption."[64] Angela Davis argues that

> too many Marxists have been inclined to overvalue the second part of Marx's observation—that the lumpenproletariat is capable of the basest banditry and the dirtiest corruption—while minimizing or indeed totally disregarding his first remark, applauding the lumpen for their heroic deeds and exalted sacrifices.[65]

My own assessment is that while these debates helpfully clarify the internal multiplicity of the global proletariat, there is no structural position that automatically determines the source of revolutionary upheaval. Extreme deprivation can just as easily lead to co-optation as it can to political

---

62 Fanon, *The Wretched of the Earth*, 129.

63 Elaine Brown, *A Taste of Power: A Black Woman's Story* (Anchor Books, 1994), 136.

64 Karl Marx, *The Class Struggles in France (1848–1850)* (Martin Lawrence, 1895), 50.

65 Davis, "Political Prisoners, Prison, and Black Liberation," 46.

clarity; as debates about identity and politics show clearly, social position does not determine political affiliation. The search for an automatic revolutionary class, a silver bullet protagonist is less useful to revolutionary strategy than is often supposed. Nothing about resistance is automatic. Theories and analysis can offer us, at best, good guesses for where to begin agitating or where to look for opportunities to push against the ruling order. But where, in the end, resistance will flourish and where it will be prevented or contained cannot be derived theoretically. If and when our theories of resistance conflict with real conditions, when the world surprises us either by the paucity of resistance or its abundance, any worthwhile theorist revises their predictions.

The relationship between the lumpenproletariat and the rest of the class thus tends in two opposing directions:

> In this increasing immiseration of the proletariat it is possible to find both a deepening contradiction between capital and labor—and thus an increased hope of a revolutionary clash rather than an integrationist class compromise—*and* an increasing competition between workers and between workers and the unemployed, and thus a decreased hope for solidarity and collective action.[66]

It remains to be seen whether this moment of neoliberalism, increasing crisis, and accelerating speed of automation will result in Huey Newton's prediction of the becoming-lumpen of the entire proletarian class, and whether that softens the antagonism between these parts of the global proletariat.[67] However the shape of the structural conditions evolve, understanding the global proletariat as including both workers and surplus population—as well as composed internally of a wide variety of other positional differences—is necessary for effective anti-capitalist struggle. The task of organizing requires we

> respond to the problem of the contingency of proletarian reproduction, which all proletarians have in common, but deal with in many different ways. This means that class composition must start from the recognition that the modes of proletarians' struggle are extremely diverse: from the limit condition of peasants fighting against becoming proletarianized to

66 Hansen, "Surplus Population, Social Reproduction, and the Problem of Class Formation."

67 Huey P. Newton, *To Die for the People: The Writings of Huey P. Newton* (Vintage Books, 1972), 26–8.

> the classical figure of the wage-laborer on strike, lies a whole range of struggles to which feminist and anti-colonial writers are more attuned than most Marxists.[68]

Recognizing the prison as the primary institution confronting the surplus population bolsters possibilities of effective anti-capitalist analysis and struggle.

Capitalism and the Production of Crime

As noted above, when surplus populations become locked out of the formal wage sector, they must find other modes of survival, which may involve reliance on criminalized industries, black markets, and other strategies to meet basic needs. What the state calls "criminality" is often an index of material deprivation. As Davis explains:

> In the context of class exploitation and national oppression it should be clear that numerous individuals are compelled to resort to criminal acts, not as a result of conscious choice—implying other alternatives—but because society has objectively reduced their possibilities of subsistence and survival to this level. This recognition should signal the urgent need to organize the unemployed and lumpenproletariat, as indeed the Black Panther Party as well as activists in prison have already begun to do.[69]

In this sense, Sayak Valencia reads many forms of criminalized activity —including those that directly involve violence—as a form of "necroempowerment" against a racist and colonial form of capitalist domination.[70] Understanding the law as a primary instrument of protecting private property and capitalist social relations, we can see at least part of what is constituted as "crime" as the criminalization of lumpen survival in a society that leans heavily on necropolitical violence and abandonment. This is as true when targeted at the working classes of the Global North as in the Global South.

"Crime" is directly produced by the conditions of capital accumulation and the devastating misery to which increasing shares of the global proletariat is consigned. Despite positioning itself as the supposed savior

68 Hansen, "Surplus Population, Social Reproduction, and the Problem of Class Formation."

69 Davis, "Political Prisoners, Prison, and Black Liberation," 46.

70 Sayak Valencia, *Gore Capitalism*, trans. John Pluecker (Semiotext(e), 2018).

of regular working people from violence, capitalism ultimately produces them. In Gina Dent's estimation, "the prison industrial complex underwrites the social problems that it purports to solve," both domestically and transnationally.[71] Davis shows that the investment in prisons reproduces the surplus conditions that produce the crime it purports to control:

> The prison and its discursive deployment produce the kind of prisoners that in turn justify the expansion of prisons. As a matter of fact, the term *prison industry* can refer precisely to the production of prisoners even as the industry produces profits for increasing numbers of corporations and, by siphoning social wealth away from such institutions as schools and hospitals, child care and housing, plays a pivotal role in producing the conditions of poverty that create a perceived need for more prisons.[72]

In Foucault's words, prison reform demands function through "the principle of utopian duplication"—positing, miraculously, that prison expansion will somehow solve the problems they themselves create.[73] They cannot do so, so they must be abolished rather than reformed.

Prisons also serve capitalism as part of the confinement architecture of repression. They contain, discipline, and attempt to silence political dissidents and those who militate against capitalism and its injustices. Prisons thus attempt to undercut the power of social movements engaged in projects of direct resistance and building alternatives. By "resistance," we should understand not only self-proclaimed political organizing but also the whole set of "crimes" of survival. When women, transgender, and queer people are jailed for self-defense against abuse and violence, this is political repression. When pregnant people are jailed for ending unwanted pregnancies, this is political repression. When Black men are jailed for merely existing, this is political repression. When working-class people are incarcerated for stealing bread and baby formula, this is also political repression. Prison confinement thus serves multiple functions: it reconfirms the capitalist law of property as more sacrosanct than life. It further disincentivizes resistance, foreclosing possibilities of a world organized otherwise. It reconfirms the striated system of life that capitalism needs in order to function. In this moment of rising political repression in the United States and elsewhere, attention to the prison as an institution uniquely situated at the intersection of the capitalist

71 Davis and Dent, "Prison as a Border," 1238.
72 Ibid. Emphasis in original.
73 Foucault, *Discipline and Punish*, 271.

production of surplus populations and the state's interest in political repression remains of paramount political importance. In this sense, all prisoners are political prisoners.

The prison's interpenetration with state violence is also uniquely important because of the ideological construction of crime itself. Not only does "crime" offer the state and capital a putatively race- and class-neutral alibi for the violent confinement of surplus populations, but mobilizing discourses of "crime" displaces social and structural explanations for material privation, blaming the victims of capitalist development for their own misery. This ideology of crime preys on proletarian fear to heighten the antagonism between workers and lumpenproletariats. While the early modern ideological contour of confinement relied most heavily on the moral character of idleness, the contemporary construction of crime relies by contrast on constructing incarcerated people as *threatening* to their neighbors, community members, and the working class. By convincing proletarians that their incarcerated brethren pose an existential threat, capitalism can prevent exploited, oppressed, and expropriated human beings from joining together in anti-capitalist struggle.

Conclusion: Communism without Cages

The first time I came to the West Bank as an activist, I encountered the system of detention firsthand. I was meeting with some of the activists at Youth Against Settlements (YAS), the incredible grassroots organization in the middle of al-Khalil (Hebron). One feels the confinement of the military occupation perhaps most acutely in al-Khalil, a city with a Jewish settlement right in the middle of the urban fabric. There are checkpoints everywhere, soldiers armed with automatic weapons everywhere, surveillance everywhere. One of the main urban arteries, Al-Shuhada Street, is completely closed to Palestinians, even though they own homes on that street. The Israeli military has literally welded their front doors shut so that they cannot walk on their own street or their own sidewalk. I, on the other hand, a person who had never been to the city, could walk down the street freely. It is sometimes possible to access the YAS house from Al-Shuhada Street, but there is often a soldier sitting at the base of the gate, as there was that February afternoon in 2015. He directed us to the nearest checkpoint, right down the hill from the YAS property. We received a phone call that Issa, one of the key organizers at YAS, had been detained by the military, so we turned around and marched to the jail. We organized a spontaneous protest, and Issa was eventually released. We had to walk separate routes to the YAS house to have our long-awaited meeting. This was not the first time I had protested at a jail, and it would not be the last. Years later, after an action I helped coordinate and plan with the activists at YAS, several organizers were arrested and taken to the jail at the nearby settlement of Kiryat Arba. We protested there, too.

Over the course of many years and many actions, in Palestine and in the United States, I have experienced firsthand how jails and prisons have been deployed to prevent, contain, and punish resistance. These are the consequences activists face in the struggle for a better world, and so these institutions cannot be part of the world we are trying to build. The modern prison, along with some of its predecessors—the workhouse, the penal colony, and the colonial prison—are distinctly capitalist modes of confinement. Without understanding how carcerality serves capitalist interests, our vision of communism is liable to be seduced by the very ideologies we must contest. If the prison cannot be reformed, if the promise of reform is rather part of the prison's tenacious hold on us, then any anti-capitalism worth the name must be abolitionist, dispensing with the prison in particular and carcerality in general.

Seeing the prison as a specifically capitalist form of confinement should caution us away from using the repressive apparatus of the state for even supposedly revolutionary reasons. Though some revolutionaries have been optimistic about using repression for emancipatory ends, every attempt to do so only entrenched collective reliance on punishment, control, and confinement rather than liberation.[74]

I spent the spring of 2022 in several currently and formerly communist countries, including Laos, Vietnam, and Cambodia. In these places, I was struck by how deeply the supposed victories of communism relied on often brutal networks of imprisonment, torture, mass execution, and confinement, something I began considering while living in China almost a decade earlier. Walking through the infamous prison at Tuol Sleng in Cambodia immediately reveals the real human cost of believing we can

74 For a particularly stark example of this optimism, one can look at the anarchist-turned-Bolshevik Victor Serge. While the majority of his writings on state repression are extremely useful, the last chapter devolves into a defense of using prisons against supposed counterrevolutionaries, even arguing for their necessity. With the benefit of historical hindsight, we know how devastating the repressive apparatus of prisons became in the Soviet Union, and how confinement was used against the very ideals of the Bolshevik revolutionaries. Victor Serge, *What Every Radical Should Know About State Repression: A Guide for Activists* (Seven Stories Press, 2024).

appropriate capitalist tools of domination for our own ends without inheriting their violences.

Like most communists in the West, I have spent too much time (with students, belligerent internet trolls, and extended family members) responding to the "crimes of communism" argument—basically, the idea that every time people have practiced communism, it has unleashed death, forced labor, torture, and repression rather than justice, equality, and liberation. Organizing for communism in the capitalist world, at least in my experience, has meant being hammered with this argument so many times in bad faith that many communists simply roll our eyes rather than confront the question of what it means for our politics that communism has so often been linked with carcerality.

Of the over 20,000 people who arrived at Tuol Sleng, there are *seven* confirmed survivors. In February 2020, I met two of them, who are often on the grounds, selling memoirs of their experiences and talking with visitors. It is a painful place to visit. The descriptions of the torture that Cambodians endured is incredibly graphic, and it was directed at nearly everyone. No one was safe, and, it seems, no one felt safe, which is why so many people carried out the brutal orders they were given. Certain demographics were targeted with special intensity: members of the previous regime, intellectuals, anyone who spoke a foreign language, members of the Vietnamese Cham minority, city dwellers, and anyone who wore glasses. The Khmer Rouge had a policy of killing entire families, to eliminate the possibility of later revenge. In all, one in every four Cambodians was killed in under four years.

Before Tuol Sleng was a torture factory, it was one of the only secondary schools in the country. The fruit trees that stand in the center courtyard once witnessed recess and schoolyard shenanigans; they would see much more gruesome things after its conversion to a prison. Now, a list of the rules imposed by the prison guards stands in front of those trees. The rules include that you must not cry out when being beaten or electrocuted.

Inside the museum, one finds several rooms: some preserved as they were with shackles, some filled with torture instruments, with clothing taken from those incarcerated there, with maps and informational posters. But the one that was perhaps the hardest to walk through are the rooms and rooms of photographs of the victims.

Walking through Tuol Sleng, I reflected on how and why so many of our movements for justice and liberation end up replaying rather than undermining the brutality they are fighting against, an outcome surely at least partially begotten by the culture of secrecy, hierarchy, and obedience that permeated the Khmer Rouge (and many other communist movements). Too many movements divorced communism from radical democracy, rooted in paranoia about counterrevolutionaries. Anywhere the party is a hierarchy and your superiors have the power to execute you seems like a situation ripe for abuse and atrocity.

This mode of carceral organizing seems to betray the very values professed by the movements. Isn't the world we are fighting for one in which the many rule rather than the few? In which human life is treated as so important that we are willing to risk the world to provision for it? The hierarchical models so often pursued seem an obvious reflection of the capitalist system that *I wonder why we expect to be immune.* We are materialists, after all, and so we understand structures determine individual actions. If we institute the same structures as the capitalists, those based in hierarchy, secrecy, authority, and obedience, and if we use the same institutions as the capitalist (prisons, torture, forced labor), why would we expect a different outcome?

All of this suggests to me in a different way something I have known in activist circles for a long time: process determines product. *How* we organize toward revolution will impact *the kind of revolution* we are able to bring about. As I've written about elsewhere, the question isn't only "What is to be done?" but "*HOW* is it to be done?"

The answer, if we are to avoid repeating these mistakes, must lie in making sure that our methods mirror our vision of the world we want. What I see in these many carceral communisms was a theory of capitalism that ignored how centrally confinement replicates capitalist principles. A communism without abolition produces merely a different organization of despair, a form of carceral collectivity fundamentally unable to deliver on the liberation politics of communism. We cannot leave capitalist logics and institutions intact and expect them to produce something new. We need to be building the world we want to live in as we are dismantling the old. And that world cannot include prisons, torture, forced labor, and summary execution. They aren't compatible with any communism worth the name.

8

The Carcerality of Care

The world is wrong. You can't put the past behind you. It's buried in you; it's turned your flesh into its own cupboard.

—Claudia Rankine[1]

There is no thoroughly anti-capitalist politics that does not include a critique of the household as a social unit of capitalist governance. There is no critique of value that succeeds without becoming queer. Household and mode of production are never segregated: their motion grinds us between workplace and homestead . . . Capital and its mediating categories do not just direct distribution of a social surplus. They are actively productive of the ways of understanding and behaving towards which it leads us. The motions of capital link subjectivity with objectivity, form with content, abstract with concrete, universal with particular.

—Jules Joanne Gleeson and Elle O'Rourke[2]

The political reproduces itself through the personal.

—Angela Davis[3]

Many experience the home as a site of confinement, a feeling lived anew in the global coronavirus pandemic. Even those lucky enough to experience the home as a space of nurture, joy, and safety began to chafe against its walls in the face of shelter-in-place orders, the pivot to remote

1 Claudia Rankine, *Citizen: An American Lyric* (Graywolf Press, 2014), 63.

2 Jules Joanne Gleeson and Ellie O'Rourke, eds., *Transgender Marxism* (Pluto Press, 2021), 15.

3 Davis, *Freedom Is a Constant Struggle*, 106.

everything, and the threat of infection lurking seemingly everywhere beyond the front door.

As much as the stay-at-home orders of the COVID-19 pandemic renewed or generalized a sense of the home as confinement, it was equally true that, for many of us, the home felt like a unique site of protection—perhaps the only safe space we could access. When the world outside felt like a sea of infectious microbes, many of us could breathe easy only from the relative safety of our apartments.

As someone with an autoimmune condition, I felt this contradiction deeply. After years of a strange and seemingly disconnected symptoms, I was diagnosed with an incurable autoimmune condition in 2017. That diagnosis and the medication I took to manage it shaped my experience of the pandemic in lasting ways.

Every week I injected myself with immunosuppressive medications, I experienced an acute double bind. This medicine, which reduced my symptoms and chronic pain to a level of manageability, also weakened my ability to fight potential infections, making any microbe (including but not only COVID-19) a potentially life-threatening danger. My partner and I were particularly cautious about preventing infections. For the fourteen months before we were vaccinated, we saw others only a handful of times, always outside, always masked, always at a distance of six feet or more. When my dear friends Jenny and Michael got married in the county clerk's office in the summer of 2020, I baked and decorated their wedding cake, and we stood in a Chicago community garden six feet apart to take off our masks to eat it.

As the initial excitement of vaccination gradually waned and we all learned that the vaccines did not prevent infections so much as mitigate the risk of severe infection, I continued to be cautious. As the world began to "open up"—though most places were never really *that* closed—and infection rates began to spike, now with an expanding hubris from the supposed inoculation, I felt with renewed pain how much safer I was in my home—and how little most people, including people I loved, cared about the safety of disabled people like me.

The home was a contradictory terrain—after so long cooped up inside, especially through the very long Chicago winter of 2020–2021, I wanted to get out. The monotony of my one-bedroom rental felt so constraining that I began grocery shopping at a different store every week—just to feel a jolt of novelty that was so severely lacking. But there was nothing like actually going outside to make me exhale with relief at coming home. In public, every sniffle or throat clear from a passerby felt like a life-threatening danger. At least at home, I could breathe fully, even if my sanity was starting to fray.

I was lucky to weather these acute pandemic years in a supportive and safe household. So many others were not so lucky—too many lack stable housing altogether or are forced to share homes with people who disregard their safety. For so many, the pandemic forced a choice between two forms of violence—the deadly virus lurking outside or the brutalities of the home.

So little of the public pandemic messaging and public health policy was able to hold on to the fundamental contradiction that framed my life: the home is simultaneously a site of confinement and a refuge. I still wonder how differently things might have turned out if we were able to appropriately craft policy that understood the wide variety of needs, desires, and situations people experience at home.

The contradictory positioning of the home is not unique to the pandemic. The truth is that, under capitalism, *in addition* to being a site of terrorizing confinement the home is *also* a space of resilience. We experience the home as oppressive, as refuge, as the thing we can't get out of, as the thing we have been cast out of, as the site of our most ineffable desires, as the terrain of vibrant aspiration.

Confinement at Home

For some, home confinement was just as novel as the coronavirus itself. But for others, feeling encased in the domestic sphere evoked forms of confinement with much longer and more violent lineages. The bourgeois nuclear family notoriously demands unwaged social reproduction, especially from women and feminized people, creates children as inferior dependents whose relative autonomy is always subject to despotic refusal, and is one of the key sites for the imposition of hetero-compulsive, cis-normative, and monogamous norms that are oppressive in their own right. The home is too often also a site of direct violence, in which rape, physical abuse, and emotional trauma are, unfortunately, par for the course.

The home is a banner institution for capitalism, the most private, separated, and contained institution of social reproduction. In its broadest sense, social reproduction comprises all the activities that keep people alive. Cooking, cleaning, laundry, and care for children, elderly, and disabled people are all part of the work that keeps us alive, that allows us to keep going. This labor never ends and is too often erased as work at all.

While the factory or the workplace produces commodities for sale, social reproduction produces workers and, for that reason, is some of the most important work anyone does. The labor of social reproduction makes *us*—in a literal sense—but it also *makes us who we are.*

While some social reproduction is also commodified—restaurants, schools, childcare facilities, laundry and cleaning services, hospitals and doctors' offices are all waged forms of social reproduction—much of this labor happens in families and in the home, with unwaged reproductive work accounting for 45–55 percent of all labor time in most countries.[4] In some ways, the home is a workplace just like any other, one that capital depends on to reproduce itself, to valorize, to grow. But the home is also a workplace *unlike* any other, one that serves particular functions for capital by enclosing the private or domestic sphere from public intrusion. A capitalist society is defined by the subordination of life to the reproduction of capital, and thus social reproduction may be the very hinge of capitalist society.

The household is deeply important for capital. In the first place, as the primary site of social reproduction, the household creates the labor capital needs to survive and reproduce itself. No worker can continue to clock in for very long without the satisfaction of basic needs, and no class of workers would survive very long without a new generation to take their place. The labor of social reproduction thus enables both *the individual* worker and *the working class* to continue to serve as the source of accumulated value for capital. Capital needs the reproduction of workers, both individually and as a class.

In many societies, this labor became the near-exclusive provenance of feminized people. Enabled by the rise of the heterosexual nuclear family, women and girls experienced the rise of capitalism as a kind of double confinement—on the one hand, they experienced the same forms of confinement that accrued to the working class in general. Women always worked for money, though generally under more precarious conditions than men. They experienced the same forms of social immobility of capitalist waged labor, with no more power to free themselves than anyone else. On the other hand, they often found themselves confined in particular ways—sometimes to the physical perimeter of the household or more often by a set of life trajectories consonant with the gendered expectations of social reproduction work. Naturalized, this work ceased to be seen as labor at all.

---

4 Helen Hester and Nick Srnicek, *After Work: A History of the Home and the Fight for Free Time* (Verso, 2023), 8–9.

Under capitalism, this labor is privatized. Even though social reproduction serves a public purpose, it is born as a private responsibility, an insight that Michèle Barrett and Mary McIntosh name "the anti-social family."[5] As Sophie Lewis understands this importance, "the family's most fundamental feature . . . is that it privatizes care: *a process of enclosure* in which all kinds of families unintentionally participate."[6] Lewis is not the first to liken the terrain of social reproduction to the enclosures of land so important to capitalist production; Richard Burt and John Michael Archer see the early modern policing of sexuality as replaying the enclosures of land, and J. Kēhaulani Kauanui traces how the enclosure of land and the imposition of colonial heteropatriarchy on Kanaka Maoli (Indigenous Hawaiians) were intertwined projects.[7] All of these accounts point to the connection between the privatization of social reproduction, the creation of rigid social relations of hierarchy, and the subsumption of intimate life under the societal reproduction of capital. Private property, heteropatriarchy, and colonialism meet in the enclosure of social reproduction.

But not all of us live in nuclear families, and that has not spared us. Social reproduction feminisms, which have often focused on the experiences of white women in the Global North, tend to overemphasize the role of the nuclear family as the only or paradigmatic form of the capitalist household. The nuclear family is, of course, a confining institution, one that inculcates boredom and terror with equal weight. But the nuclear family is only one organization of capitalism's confinement of care.

For racialized and colonized people, capital was always just as likely to promote the nuclear family as to impose family separation. Chattel slavery entailed natal alienation, severing relationships of kin as a general condition of life. Capture on the African continent separated enslaved people from their kin, communities, and homelands, and in the Western Hemisphere, one of the most consistent terrors of the plantation was the threat of separation for profit. Beginning with initial waves of colonization and continuing to some extent today, many extractive industries like mining instituted sex-segregation in production, often sending men hundreds or thousands of miles away from their partners and children for

5 Michèle Barrett and Mary McIntosh, *The Anti-Social Family* (Verso, 2015).

6 Lewis, *Abolish the Family: A Manifesto for Care and Liberation*, 30. Emphasis added.

7 Richard Burt and John Michael Archer, eds., *Enclosure Acts: Sexuality, Property, and Culture in Early Modern England*, 1st edition (Cornell University Press, 1994); Kauanui, *Paradoxes of Hawaiian Sovereignty*.

months or years at a time. The more social reproduction labor becomes mediated by the market, the more some workers live with their employer's families as housekeepers, nannies, and au pairs, sometimes on the other side of the world from their own families. Boarding schools for Indigenous children traumatized entire communities across the settler colonial world, ripping young people from their families and indoctrinating them into white culture. Rigid nation-state borders continue to separate loved ones, and as the border regime increasingly militarizes, family reunification becomes ever more mediated by bureaucracy, walls, surveillance, police, and prisons. Governmental child welfare agencies consistently disrupt the domestic lives of people of color at highly disproportionate rates, separating children from their caregivers as a matter of course; in reality, these institutions work more like police than they do as social services, often destroying families merely for being poor and racialized.[8]

The nuclear family may be more generally losing its shine. Labor-imposed non-nuclear living arrangements are in a new era of resurgence in the contemporary world; large corporations are increasingly turning to dormitory-style housing for employees. Though China's Foxconn factory is perhaps the most well-known example, many tech companies around the world have adopted this model, including in the European Union.[9] The skyrocketing rates of surrogacy and transnational adoption create family beyond the boundaries of the nuclear family, or at least, are transforming what the nuclear family means. While in some ways queer life is being pushed into preexisting heteronormative family molds, this incorporation is at best uneasy. Over the capitalist centuries, young people's increased mobility and autonomy—including choosing to live with friends and lovers rather than biological family—in some ways fits into social norms, and in other ways does not. The contemporary world sees higher levels of adoption, wider availability of gestational technology, fewer births on average, lower rates of marriage, more frequent divorce, higher gestational age, and more state protections for queer families than

8 Dorothy Roberts, *Torn Apart: How the Child Welfare System Destroys Black Families—and How Abolition Can Build a Safer World* (Basic Books, 2022).

9 Hannah Schling, "(Re)Production: Everyday Life in the Workers' Dormitory," *Society and Space*, November 7, 2017, societyandspace.org; Charlotte Goodburn and Soumya Mishra, "Beyond the Dormitory Labour Regime: Comparing Chinese and Indian Workplace–Residence Systems as Strategies of Migrant Labour Control," *Work, Employment and Society* 38, no. 2 (2024): 505–26; Ong Khang Chuen and William Tng, "CENTURION: Homes for Workers Can't Be Built Fast Enough, so This Company Is Enjoying a Rental Boom," July 20, 2023, *Next Insight*, accessed April 20, 2025, nextinsight.net.

a generation ago.[10] Social narratives about gender, sex, and sexuality seem to be shifting alongside these practices. These social forms are certainly unevenly taken up, but in broad strokes, we can chart the rise of many non-hetero, non-normative, non-procreative ways of living and loving. Unlike some of the exuberant optimism about how much non-nuclear forms of life would tear at the existing fabric of capitalism, these latest transformations of intimate life have been weathered (or profited from) just like so many transformations before.

At the same time, gendered labor in the home is also shifting. Gendered asymmetries in household and childcare are trending down in many places, even if they remain far from equal. Overall, *how* workers meet their reproduction needs today tends to be more market-mediated (grocery delivery, take-out meals, laundry service, paid childcare) than fifty years ago. In some countries, public institutions have taken on some of the roles of social reproduction. These transformations exist also alongside the truth that in some parts of the world under capitalism, the bourgeois nuclear family was never the dominant social form, with intergenerational housing as the normative form of social reproduction. Estimates suggest that "nuclear families now tend to make up less than 60 percent of intergenerational households in the Western world."[11] It is worth noting that despite a real transformation in the shape of social reproduction over the last five hundred years, *the nuclear family may never have been the most common model in numerical terms, even if it maintained aspirational, disciplinary, and normative force.*

These changes should not be taken to mean that the ironclad grip of capital is loosening, nor that its racist and heterosexist character is diminishing; rather, it is to say that social relations of production and reproduction shift over time, *and that these changes are part and parcel of how capitalism operates*, because reproduction always entails change.

These transformations may constitute real and important developments in how we experience the world, in the conditions of our labor, and in the people that labor makes us. What these changes have not and cannot accomplish on their own, however, is delinking our own survival from the accumulation of capital. As long as we remain within capitalism—that is, as long as our reproduction remains subordinated to

10 I wrote the first draft of this sentence in March 2023. As I revise it now in March 2025, as the global right wing seems to be concreting its power faster than ever, and as a particularly regressive form of gender, sex, and sexuality politics serves as one of its primary vehicles, it remains to be seen how long the trend described in this paragraph will continue.

11 Hester and Srnicek, *After Work*, 109.

the logic of capital accumulation—we remain beholden to reproducing ourselves and the conditions of our domination at the same time. Under these conditions, we make each other in ways both beautiful and barbaric; we are the condition of each other's flourishing and each other's destruction, equally, poignantly, intensively.

Home as a Refuge

At the same time, social reproduction and the home may *feel* to us much more the space of our freedom than the coordinates of our domination. Social reproduction is care work, and care can be a supremely beautiful form of relating. Care is just as much what protects us from capital as an element of capitalist accumulation.

Feminists of color have long insisted that, in addition to their oppressive functions, the family and the home *also* act as refuges from capitalist alienation and from the violence of white supremacy.[12] In the face of organized abandonment to death, in the face of capital's retreat, communities of kin and care are often *the only* defense many people have. As Kathi Weeks explains:

> The model of the nuclear family that has served subordinated groups *as a fence* against the state, society, and capital *is the very same* white, settler, bourgeois, heterosexual, and patriarchal institution that was imposed by the state, society, and capital on the formerly enslaved, indigenous peoples, and waves of immigrants, all of whom continue to be at once in need of its meagre protections and marginalized by its legacies and prescriptions.[13]

One might say, moreover, that the family also reproduces social rather than capitalist values. For some, family is their most consistent experience of banding together to achieve a common aim, an incubator of collectivity, care, selflessness, joy, and even refuge against capitalism. Though Marx believed the Church was "the heart of the heartless world," for many, it may be the family and the home. In this sense, social reproduction might potentially reproduce *anti-capitalist value*s at least as much as directly capitalist ones.

---

12 Angela Y. Davis, "The Approaching Obsolescence of Housework: A Working-Class Perspective," in *The Angela Y. Davis Reader* (Blackwell Publishing, 1998); Collins, *Black Feminist Thought*.

13 Kathi Weeks, "Abolition of the Family: The Most Infamous Feminist Proposal," *Feminist Theory* 24, no. 3 (2023): 436.

Under capitalism, then, the home, social reproduction, and care emerge as complicated and contradictory terrains. They simultaneously are rife with violence, constraint, and abuse *and* are spaces of defense, connection, and resistance. This is the double bind of care under capitalism. Much like my own home during the pandemic, it simultaneously confines and enables survival.

Care and Captivity: The Double Bind

One thing the pandemic laid bare was the gap between the *value* of essential work and its *valuation* in broader society. I, like many people, am a pretty inessential worker. I certainly don't have a "bullshit job," but there were certainly a lot of bullshit meetings that were mercifully canceled while we all dealt with much more important upheavals.[14] While I believe intellectual enrichment, critical thinking, reading, and ideas are indispensable for any society we want to live in, I equally know that we might all have benefitted from a longer pause in labor like mine, for the sake of workers and students alike, and that we mostly did not pursue this pause because for capital's constant propulsion, immobility is death.

Differences in labor conditions were immediately visible in the split between so-called essential work and everyone else. While my work pivoted online, those who provided "essential services" were compelled to leave their homes every day, with little to no protection. They did so because without them, people would die, but more importantly for policymakers, capital would grind to a halt. Some of those people work in industries—like healthcare—that are readily recognized as socially valuable. But far and away the majority of "essential workers" faced a completely different balances of forces—agricultural workers, grocery store clerks, restaurant staff, home aides, sanitation workers, and many others were functionally sacrificed. Calling their work "essential" was little salve on the generalized conditions of precarity they were forced into, and it did not save their lives.

---

14 David Graeber, *Bullshit Jobs: A Theory* (Simon and Schuster, 2018). To my endless dismay, the interminable set of meetings have all since returned since the triumphalist "reopening" of the world, even as the WHO is reporting (as of March 2025) 11,000 COVID hospitalizations and 3,500 COVID deaths per month. The most current and comprehensive set of global data shows at least 400 million people worldwide have long COVID. The pandemic is not over. Ziyad Al-Aly et al., "Long COVID Science, Research and Policy," *Nature Medicine* 30, no. 8 (2024): 2148–64.

When New York streets reverberated with nightly clapping in support of healthcare workers, we ought to have pushed for a transformation in how we understood the relationship between work, security, risk, and value. There was a momentary opening—when city streets hummed with corpse-filled refrigeration trucks, when vaccines were being developed with public money—that could have been more effectively used to overhaul our entire social system to be more concerned with people and less concerned with profits. Alas, public displays of support were so often *not* accompanied by real action that would make the work of caring for life less dangerous or precarious. Eventually, even the performances of gratitude stopped.

This pandemic ritual revealed something that social reproduction theorists had been saying for decades: social reproduction is the most essential work, and it is chronically underappreciated and underpaid, often undertaken by the most precarious people in our society.

In this context, it makes sense that social reproduction theorists have focused on calling attention to the unfree conditions under which many do this labor, condemning the naturalization, feminization, and racialization that frames this labor. Against its denial as labor, social reproduction theory has often sought to reclaim the value of this labor. Care work is real work. Care work is important work. Care work is the most essential work there is.

I affirm this line of thinking, unequivocally. In addition to it, though, the work of social reproduction, as necessary for the reproduction of capital, also serves less liberatory ends.

Social reproduction can also inculcate capitalist values, transmitting ideas and norms that reflect and affirm societal hegemony. For many of us, our earliest memories of gender imposition are organized around our caregivers, either at home or at school. Part of the way capitalist society reproduces itself is by reproducing the social ideals that allow capitalism to continue—norms of private property, individualism, oppression, work discipline, and countless others. The labor of social reproduction includes not only the reproduction of human beings but also their reproduction *as useful for* capital, as enmeshed in and attached to the social relations of domination that sustain capitalist reproduction. Whether they intend to or not, caregivers are often responsible for inflicting violence on those they care for; care can be a most violent thing.

Stuart Hall and his coauthors understand the family primarily as an institution of social discipline:

> In the traditionalist lexicon, the sphere of the family is of course where moral-social compulsions and inner controls are generated, as well as the sphere where the primary socialisation of the young is first tellingly and intimately carried through. The first aspect has to do with the repression and regulation of sexuality—the seat of pleasure—in the family nexus; and thus with authority. The second has to do with the power which the family has, through its intimate exchanges of love and anger, punishment and reward, and the structure of patriarchy, to prepare children for a competitive existence—work and the sexual division of labour . . . Few would deny its central role in the construction of social identities, and in transmitting, at an extremely deep level, the basic ideological grid of society. Family ideology is undoubtedly also changing; and we have learned to think of the family, also, in more positive, less punitive terms. But, when we come "right down to it," the dominant image of the family—perhaps across classes—still has more to do with the duty of instilling a basic understanding of fundamental "do's and don'ts" than it does of providing a mutually sustaining and releasing framework. Love is what we hope and pray will emerge from the family, but disciplining, punishing, rewarding and controlling is what we seem actually to do in it a great deal of the time. [Wilhelm] Reich, with some justification, called it a "factory for creating submissive people."[15]

In other words, social reproduction can be violent in two completely different ways. In the first, social reproduction is violent because of the conditions that structure it—racialization, gendering and the rule of capital. We might call this the "external constraints" of social reproduction. But in another way, precisely because families are *trying to help us survive a violent world*, they also reproduce the violent norms *of* that world. In inculcating the norms and values of survival, they often teach us to internalize the violences of social relations so that we can more effectively navigate them. Families thus reproduce constraints *internally*, as a form of care. Not all the violence we experience in the home is done out of care, but some of it surely is. That we sometimes create harm in an attempt to reduce harm is a central, but underthematized, part of capitalism's simultaneous hold on social and societal reproduction, a testament to our painfully split interests.

This may, in the end, reveal the true meaning of social *reproduction*. It is not only *we* who are reproduced by it, but capital too. The question

15 Hall et al., *Policing the Crisis*, 144–5.

of reproduction is primarily a question of stability over time, through crisis, through change. "Reproduction" tends to suggest a mere copying of that which came before, an unproblematic translation of the past into the present, of the practices and ideals of the previous generation or the previous day onto the present. But of course, this isn't, strictly speaking, true. Both social and societal reproduction happen rather in iterative ways, meaning that reproduction is always the production of difference. As Donna Haraway explains, even in the case of biological reproduction, "there is never the reproduction of any individual" since a child is a "randomly assembled genetic package" of their parents; for humans, "literal reproduction is a contradiction in terms." The metaphor of reproduction is immensely helpful for understanding how capitalism works, in terms of both social and societal reproduction—precisely because of the role of this difference, not in spite of it. Reproduction does not create a carbon copy; its logic is not mimetic, it is genetic.

Care thus emerges as a site of split interest for all of us under capitalism. Social reproduction partially reproduces *us* and partially reproduces *our domination*—this is the heart of the care problem for anti-capitalism. In addition to all the important, laudable, joyful elements of caring for each other, care work also emerges as a particular site of capitalist oppression and exploitation. Especially if we bring social and societal reproduction together, we begin to see how care labor itself is often oppressive and exploitative, and also how general social relations of domination are partially reproduced through this labor, materially and ideologically. The home is often the most concreted and dense terrain in which homophobia, transphobia, racism, and class power are taught, enforced, and disciplined—often masquerading as "care." We might even say that the reproduction of these social relations, as violent as they are, is a central part of how "care" is defined in class society. Care is thus this double-edged sword, something we wield against capital to survive, but also something that molds us into subjects of capital. Workers do not emerge as empty, homogenous vessels from the labor of the social reproduction that makes us, but as human beings created in and through the social relations of domination capital requires. Through care, the fundamental contradiction of capitalism emerges: the very thing that enables our survival inhibits our flourishing.

This double bind may account for why the worse capitalism gets, the harder it seems to be to overcome. As Jules Joanne Gleeson and Elle O'Rourke explain:

> Capitalism constantly renews its social foundations. Rather than merely destructive, capitalism is simultaneously productive of affects, attachments, fierce passions, commitments, and hatreds. Each of these passions provides sources of legitimacy and social assent for the continued organization of production and exploitation . . . That capitalism does us harm is to be assumed; what must be explained is how it survives through us. And how, despite this wounding and bitterness required at each turn, it endures over generations.[16]

The fact that capital survives through us is not a trivial fact; it constrains the very possibilities of life available to pursue. It also constrains the available avenues of resistance. Understanding how we become conscripted into the capitalist project is a question far deeper than the state's repressive capacity or the wounds of domination; it is easier to fight oppression of an external power than an internalized one.

Capitalism and Autoimmunity

The experience of the pandemic made me think more about my own autoimmune condition and about how capitalism's production of split interests mirrored that autoimmunity. Autoimmunity occurs when the body's protective system attacks itself. Often, though not always, the body might start by attacking a real threat or invader, and then it might turn on itself. An autoimmune condition is, somewhat ironically, the result of having an immune system that is too strong, too sensitive, that sees everything as a threat, even its own tissue. It's like being a walking ouroboros, eating his own tail.

An autoimmune condition is one in which defense becomes threat; it is the weaponization of security to extreme destabilization. The double bind of care under capitalism is, in a certain sense, autoimmune: the very thing that allows us to survive the onslaught allows for the violence of capitalism to burrow more deeply into us. There is surely something funny (in a gallows-humor sort of way) that AFAB people, disproportionately tasked with social reproduction, are also disproportionately diagnosed with autoimmune conditions—and that, because pregnancy lowers one's immune system (to prevent attacking the fetus, which might otherwise be taken for a parasite), gestation is one of the most effective catalysts for autoimmune remission.

16 Gleeson and O'Rourke, *Transgender Marxism*, 17.

As Mark Neocleous explains:

> The auto-immune disease reveals a large part of immunity's confounding nature: you think you are getting self-defence and instead you get self-destruction; you think your body is being well policed by the immune system, but then the police power turns against you; you find security in immunity and then immunity starts to destroy you.[17]

Might this not describe the labor of care under capitalism?

The autoimmune body confronts itself as a double bind, just as care confronts us as a double bind, a doubled confinement, under capitalism. The household is all of this simultaneously—both refuge and restraint, source of violence and recovery. Because capitalism is committed to the impoverishment of many and the confinement of us all, the interpenetration of social and societal reproduction poses a particular and unique challenge: in reproducing ourselves—that is, in ensuring our survival—we also reproduce a system committed to our confinement. In some cases, the system might be invested quite openly and explicitly in our deaths. That our life entails our destruction or at least the narrowing of our life chances is one of the central contradictions of capitalism; the dual character of home confinement under capitalism constitutes it as a particularly sticky *double bind.*

The fundamental double bind of the home is that it is simultaneously a haven and a site of violence, that socially reproductive care *is also work done out of love*, that in reproducing oneself, one's family, and one's community, one is also doing the work of socially reproducing capitalism. Part of what makes the problem of the home, the family, and care so intractable is that *our survival is mobilized in favor of the system committed to our death, or at least for an anemic version of life.* Because, even despite ourselves, our home work is conscripted into a project that exists specifically *over and against* us, all care work under capitalism is, in the words of Black feminist Joy James, "captive." This work is "captive" because we cannot *but* do it—the choices we are offered are fundamentally constrained in advance. Either we engage in this activity, surviving, renewing, attempting to thrive, and are hence captured by a system of violence, or we literally expire. Your life or your life—a captive choice if ever there were one. That the family does some of its work "for us" and some of its work "for capital" is the very knot of its contradictory constitution and

17 Mark Neocleous, *The Politics of Immunity: Security and the Policing of Bodies* (Verso, 2022), 20.

hence also of its analytic power and political edge. James illuminates the intensity of double bind of social reproduction through the figure of the "the captive maternal."[18]

James understands a wide range of activities as the work of the captive maternal. In addition to the labor normally labeled "social reproduction," she argues that we can also see community organizing *and* collaborationist activities as similarly situated, drawing out the ways that care and violence can be intertwined. James thus understands the ways that the act of care-taking under necropolitical capitalism participates *in* violence as much as it is *subjected* to violence: "Captive Maternals can foster survival skills aligned to obedience and conformity, thus they stabilize political structures that prey upon under-resourced communities."[19] Care for oneself and community are also productive for the very system that profits off of violence, domination, oppression, exploitation.

It is especially interesting to consider her understanding of the continuity between basic social reproduction and the work of activism. Much like the work of social reproduction, the work of organizing and mutual aid can sometimes stabilize the very system we are intending to uproot and fight against. Unfortunately, the more we rely on mutual aid, the more we take on this labor ourselves, the more the state can continue to retreat from its function of collective provisioning. In this way, some elements of organizing have sometimes been accused of buttressing neoliberalism. If care and community can be weaponized against us, if even anti-capitalist organizing can sometimes be captured by the state and capital, the question of resistance becomes eminently more complex.

Here's the thing: autoimmune conditions are chronic, and vexingly difficult to treat. Options are few and far between and generally comprise a few different pathways: first, sometimes we treat symptoms. Knowing that it does not address the root cause, one path of "treatment" is simply to make life more livable, less painful. A reformist approach, if you like. As someone who has, at times in my life, suffered from debilitating pain, I can assure you that making life livable is no small thing, even if it is far from curative.

The other approach, more common with the rise of so-called biologic medications, is to introduce immunosuppressive measures. If the symptoms of these conditions are caused by an overactive immune system,

18 Joy James, "The Womb of Western Theory: Trauma, Time Theft, and the Captive Maternal," *Carceral Notebooks*, no. 12 (2016): 255; Joy James, "The Captive Maternal and Abolitionism," *TOPIA: Canadian Journal of Cultural Studies* 43 (2021): 9.

19 James, "The Captive Maternal and Abolitionism," 14.

these courses of treatment lower the body's ability to fight. A sort of disarming method. The chief problem with this approach is that it disarms the body generally—including its ability to ward off real threats. In the years I was on immunosuppressive medications, I was no longer felled by the direct symptoms of my condition, but I was sometimes bedridden by opportunistic infections a normal immune system would have easily defeated. I spent an excruciating year trying to treat a debilitating chronic ear infection so painful that I spent several weeks in bed, unable to do anything but cry. It took twice weekly ENT visits, an audiologist, two urgent care visits, a rheumatologist, and a primary care doctor fourteen months to finally cure it; I have permanent hearing loss in one ear from the months of chronic infection.

Both of these courses of treatment have incredible, life-changing outcomes for many people who suffer from these conditions, something not to be underestimated. Neither are curative. When I have asked my doctors what would be necessary for a real cure to these kinds of conditions, they have told me that someone would need to find a way to teach the immune system how to more effectively differentiate between friend and foe, to allow the system to continue to function, but to target its opposition more effectively.

It sounds like a political lesson that would be valuable for us all.

Organizing from Care Beyond Complicity

We missed an opportunity to learn this lesson at the height of the pandemic, and it is easy to see why. With the suspension of so many forms of externalized social reproduction, many of us were drowning in an endless spate of care tasks for ourselves and our household. Those with children were transformed overnight into full-time caretakers and teachers, often having to help several children with new technology and long-forgotten school material, all while pivoting to remote work, preparing three meals a day, and trying to keep up with an ever-shifting set of laws and public health measures that often felt arcane and contradictory. In other words, we were unable to show up completely to change the structure of our society because we were fully immersed and stretched thin by increased social reproduction. The endless daily labor of social reproduction made it harder to organize for a different structure of societal reproduction. This is also true more generally of capitalism, a form of repression pursued through social reproduction: the harder it is for most people to survive, the less time they have to organize. The precarity of life is not a bug, it is part of capitalism's systemic design.

We also missed this lesson in the pandemic, in part, because of the way that governments constructed "the family" during the stay-at-home orders. In some places, contact with non-family members was severely restricted for part of the pandemic; as many queer and trans communities argued, states assumed a heteronormative, nuclear concept of the family in creating policy. Policies that allowed visits to "family members" during lockdown often discounted queer forms of kin-making, disrupting life-saving non-nuclear forms of community social reproduction and chosen family.[20] State policies that seek to define and proscribe what "home" and "family" mean are nearly always exclusionary, reproducing a privatized version of social reproduction to the particular detriment of racialized and queer communities who have, against the dictates of capitalism, forged alternative circuits of care. In the face of a repressive, state-sanctioned definition of the family and home, in some circles, collective pandemic response *itself* seemed to be the problem. For some, this must have felt like the heteronormative state's latest disingenuous attempt at queer erasure and meant that any collective COVID mitigation should be met with skepticism or even resisted on queer principle. It pained me to see this response, as it sacrificed the needs of so many queer disabled people like me in the name of supposed anti-heteronormativity. I longed then, as I still do now, for a more comprehensive form of refusal, one that does not pit communities against each other, one that allows us to move from our mutual vulnerabilities.

Organizing in this context must reckon with the long history of these and similar missteps. It is not only that what is "for us" is also "for them" but also, more vexingly, that "us" is already made in advance for us, by capitalism.[21] This is the basic premise of social construction and materialist analysis, all of the things that make us who we are only emerge from the depths of the social—there is no "me" *before* I come in contact with the capitalist world and thus this "me" is a product of that world, a product of conditions I did not choose, indeed, of conditions I *loathe*. "Men make their own history but not always as they choose" is an understatement

20 Mathias Klitgård, "Lockdown Limbo: Reviving Marx's 'Dead Labor' for Queer and Trans Mental Distress during COVID-19," *Forum for Social Economics*, 2024, 1–16.

21 This is perhaps the most enduring insight of Butler's *Bodies That Matter*, nearly three decades on: all the elements of identity are made for me, through me, in a way that means I am always made by others before any process of voluntaristic self-fashioning. Sociality makes us, by definition, creatures of limited agency, even if that agency remains of the utmost importance.

of the problem—it is not only that the external world constrains us, but that this constraint is lodged deep in the heart of what it means to be *us* in the first place.[22] As Sophie Lewis explains, "We are the makers of one another."[23] We make ourselves, each other, and our history, but not as we choose.

In the midst of the pandemic, it became newly clear that the ways we have made one another, and continue to, is unsustainable. The home, with its confining double bind, is not so much a physical place in which we find ourselves but a logic that makes us. Capitalist subjectivity is a constraint, a container—perhaps, even a violence. For his part, Neocleous also sees autoimmune disease in the meeting point of the individual body and the larger body politic:

> What I am interested in with the category of the autoimmune disease, then, is a situation in which the body (and thus *the Self*) is threatened, damaged, and ultimately destroyed from within by its own immunity-security, and a parallel in which the body politic (and thus *the System*) is threatened, damaged, and ultimately destroyed from within by its own security-immunity.[24]

Neocleous demonstrates how, on both the right and the left, autoimmunity is hard to think about, and perhaps even harder to organize around. It is always easier to defend against an intruder than to confront the call that is coming from inside the house. We are always already beholden to the world as it exists, replete with its inequalities, its constraints, its violences.

Alexis Shotwell argues that because we are made by these conditions, we can only ever confront them from inside.

> Since it is not possible to avoid complicity, we do better to start from an assumption that everyone is implicated in situations we (at least in some way) repudiate. We are compromised, and we have made comprises, and this will continue to be the way we craft the worlds to come, whatever they may turn out to be.[25]

22 Karl Marx, *The Eighteenth Brumaire of Louis Bonaparte*, 3rd edition, trans. Daniel De Leon (Charles H. Kerr & Company, 1913), 9.

23 Sophie Lewis, *Full Surrogacy Now: Feminism Against the Family* (Verso, 2019), 19.

24 Neocleous, *The Politics of Immunity*, 27.

25 Shotwell, *Against Purity*, 5.

There is no safe space, no higher ground, no outside. Political transformation has to begin from here, from our constitutive complicity. It is not avoidable, and it cannot be fully exorcized, no matter how ambitious our political program, no matter how ruthless our critique of everything existing. There is no safe position of purity or externality, no place of absolute plenitude, no God's-eye view.

I'll admit this conclusion might initially feel demotivating. If capitalism is lodged deep within every structure, if it is at home even within us, even as we resist, can anything be done at all? Are we doomed to reproduce the conditions of our domination? What are the possibilities of a politics of *non-reproduction*?

Conclusion: Toward a Politics of Abolitionist Non-Reproduction

If reproduction is central to capitalism, if, indeed, reproduction *defines* capitalism, our pathway forward might need to begin from a politics of non-reproduction. But when social and societal reproduction are so intimately intertwined, how can we *refuse to reproduce society without sacrificing ourselves*?

This vision may sound like a Lee Edelman–esque demand to forgo reproduction altogether, to explicitly reject children and embrace a self-immolating cry of "No Future!" for all.[26] This is a strategy, but one that emerges only if we see the future as already foreclosed, itself a product of capitalism's battle cry "there is no alternative." In a certain way, the rejection of the future is sutured into an assumption that the only future available to us is the reproduction of the world we are in.

But on the contrary, most of us experience glimpses of the "something else" of a liberated world in the realm of love, intimacy, desire, and care. The realm of social reproduction, including the realm of community organizing, is where we often have experiences of momentary freedom, the joys of a non-proprietary self, the seductive whisper of a world that may be to come. For those of us who spend time in radical political projects, this experience may feel even more ready to hand. When I think about what a liberated world would look like, I do not really have to conjure a fantasy; all I have to do is it sit in my memories. I think about the roars of laughter sitting around the midnight fire in the Palestinian

26 Lee Edelman, *No Future: Queer Theory and the Death Drive* (Duke University Press, 2004).

village of Sarura, where hundreds of Palestinians and Jewish activists moved a displaced family back into their ancestral caves. I think about the long meetings in three languages, where communities came together across differences to build something together. I think about the joys of comradeship, of walking arm in arm, and of how many times I have gladly placed my body between danger and my comrades. I think of the smiles on Palestinian children's faces when they are asked what they think we should do, seeing the idea wash over them that they are in charge of their own destinies. I think of the taste of za'atar tea in the crisp desert air in Awdah's mother's tent. These moments of resistance, as compromised and impure as they may be, sometimes elicit an exuberant joy in the generalized care of comradeship. They are all too fleeting, too fragile, too few and far between.

The problem of these moments is not their nonexistence, but rather their unsustainability. It is not that alternative communities, positionalities, forms of living do not emerge or contest capitalist society; it is that they have an exceptionally hard time *reproducing themselves over time*. Time and again these experiments fall to targeted state violence and repression, as well as the urgent pressures of survival in the present world. What survives is also a produced outcome. In other words, while many philosophers think the primary question of social theory is "Why don't people resist?," I think the more important question is "How can we sustain and reproduce extant resistance over time?"

What we needed, at the height of the pandemic and still, was to refuse the home as a privatized container for social reproduction. The idea that social reproduction—who survives and on what terms—is a fundamentally individualized, private matter anchored our inability to confront the pandemic conditions for what they were and to mount a campaign to reorganize social relations in the interests of people rather than capital. Reconnecting individual thriving to collective conditions is surely one of the most important tasks of political organizing, and one of the basic demands of communism.

For Neocleous, the inability to make good on this basic demand is grounded in "bourgeois ideals of *self-contained* and self-regulating units"; in liberal schemas, the threat is always from the outside.[27] The privatized self, the idea of contained, impermeable units is part of what makes it so hard to diagnose the autoimmune disorder of collective social life. We live in a political grammar in which this idea forms "a political site of

27 Neocleous, *The Politics of Immunity*, 66. Emphasis added.

enclosure and confinement, training and discipline."[28] Neocleous is more interested in security politics than in care, in the way that the construction of outside threats—immigration, terrorism, national defense, and so on—become deployed against the very people they were nominally intended to protect. But his analysis also illuminates more generally how the capitalist self (rooted in property-in-personhood) predisposes us to think in terms of *immunity* (and hence in terms of contagion, invader, and defense); we actually need to think through political organizing in the face of *autoimmune disease*, in which the systems and social relations we design are dangerous to our survival. In this sense, capital profits not only from the conjunction of social and societal reproduction but also from their ideological separation. At once our private ability to survive is wholly mediated by social conditions and yet the collective character of our lives, our families, and ourselves is constantly denied in the name of private, possessive individualism.

Thus, pushing against the privatizing constraints of social reproduction is a necessary part of creating a world beyond the weaponization of care and the confinement of life. It is not only in activism that the process effects the product; life produced through confinement is itself constrained life.

We must thus find ways of organizing social reproduction that point toward the non-reproduction of capitalist social life. This is why the demand for family abolition has been so central to the communist project since its inception. As Sophie Lewis remarks, "Family abolitionism is, despite what some socialists say, orthodox Marxism."[29] The central premise of family abolition is that tying individual survival to a constrained form of the social will always produce uneven human flourishing; whether and how we survive will be confined to the sheer luck of the family we happen to be born into. Family abolition argues that our survival is too important to be left up to chance. Since social and societal reproduction are so closely aligned, family abolition is foundationally important to a broader politics of non-reproduction. We cannot stop the reproduction of capital and keep privatized social reproduction intact. The fact that families have allowed people to survive capitalist assault does not mean we have to aspire to them, even if we may still find solace in them. Moving away from thinking about care and the self as private brings us one step closer to a politics of autoimmunity, of being able to separate, in the jumble of ideas we receive, which part

28 Ibid., 74. Emphasis added.
29 Lewis, *Abolish the Family*, 46.

of our collective life animates our freedom and which parts further inculcates our subjection.

Neither care nor collectivity automatically clarifies this separation, but understanding the current confinement of social reproduction illuminates where we are and how we must move, love, organize, and structure life in ways more consistent with freedom. As James warns, "The hubris of the Captive Maternal is to think that care can remedy all imbalances."[30] To love and to care often gives us a glimpse, a moment, however fleeting, of what a world very differently organized would *feel like*, even if it cannot, alone, deliver that world. What care can and must do is allow us to survive to fight another day—and to see another world. As already discussed, the collective does not automatically produce more liberatory outcomes. Merely collectivizing care is not enough to remove the double bind of social reproduction. The fact that collective conditions set the terrain for individual lives is not enough to ensure that those collective conditions promote liberation, joy, or flourishing. Many collectives are premised on violent identities—white nationalism, settler publics, fascism, heteropatriarchy, and others. Neither collectivization nor the practice of care on their own will liberate us.

This dual insufficiency discloses why abolition is a necessary framework for mobilizing against the contradictory organization of care that capitalism requires. In M. E. O'Brien's words,

> Instead of destroying the family, we must abolish it by preserving what is crucial to it—human love, connection, care, community, romance—without binding those qualities to the particular form of the household within capitalism. Abolition means radically transforming these qualities, freeing them from relationships of coercion, abuse, isolation, and property. Abolition is a powerful way to describe moving toward the simultaneous destruction of the basis of coercion, and the unleashing of new forms of care. To abolish the family means to free our capacity to care for each other.[31]

As abolitionists learned first in the fight against racialized chattel slavery, social change can sometimes be painfully incomplete, leaving intact an "afterlife" of domination that casts a long shadow. True abolition takes aim at the full range of social relations that emerge from an institution

30 Joy James, *New Bones Abolition: Captive Maternal Agency and the Afterlife of Erica Garner* (Common Notions, 2023), 18.

31 O'Brien, *Family Abolition*, 56–7.

rather than only its present contours. As we think about the conscription of care in domination, we must apply this insight to the family. To truly abolish the family, we must not stop at the *form* that social reproduction takes but also examine the social relations of compulsion that underlie it.

Abolition, then, is both incomplete, and, in Ruth Wilson Gilmore's words, "a fleshly and material presence of social life lived differently."[32] Despite the ruthless power of dominating capital, we *do* experience joy, love, care, and moments of exuberant freedom. Many of us have cherished memories of resistance, of mutual aid projects and riots and barricades, of social movements that breathe into us a form of life we never knew existed. Even when our survival and our organizing *can be* weaponized against us, they also contain liberatory elements; in other words, abolition is also present, also practiced, also tangible, also real.[33] The caricature of abolition describes it as some future, far-off utopia, but Gilmore offers another image: "Abolition is not *absence*, it is *presence*. What the world will become already exists in fragments and pieces, experiments and possibilities . . . Abolition is building the future from the present, in all of the ways we can."[34] Mariame Kaba and Rachel Herzing explain, "There will be no magical day of liberation that we do not make."[35] That process of making will happen, not under conditions of liberation, but under the present conditions of domination. We have to make it, even as the actions we take toward building it are unfree, constrained, confined in advance.

If the future appears foreclosed, we have to bore holes in the walls. We must become corrosive at critical infrastructural joints. We must destroy the family to save ourselves. We must invent a medicine of the future, one premised on treating the autoimmune disease killing us all.

32 Ruth Wilson Gilmore and Clément Petitjean, "Prisons and Class Warfare: An Interview with Ruth Wilson Gilmore," *Verso Blog*, August 2, 2018, versobooks.com.

33 Dylan Rodríguez explains the present tense of abolition in the following way: "Now and long before, abolition is and was a practice, an analytical method, a present-tense visioning, an infrastructure in the making, a creative project, a performance, a counterwar, an ideological struggle, a pedagogy and curriculum, an alleged impossibility that is furtively present, pulsing, produced in the persistent insurgencies of human being that undermine the totalizing logics of empire, chattel, occupation, heteropatriarchy, racial-colonial genocide, and Civilization as a juridical-narrative epoch." Dylan Rodriguez, "Abolition as Praxis of Human Being: A Forward," *Harvard Law Review* 132, no. 6 (2019), harvardlawreview.org.

34 Ruth Wilson Gilmore and Lambert Lo, "Making Abolition Geography in California's Central Valley with Ruth Wilson Gilmore," *The Funambulist*, no. 21 (February 2019), thefunambulist.net.

35 Mariame Kaba, *We Do This 'Til We Free Us: Abolitionist Organizing and Transforming Justice* (Haymarket Books, 2021), 125.

Conclusion

Abolition Communism

I began this book with a story of my dear friend and comrade Awdah, a Palestinian living in Masafer Yatta whose life dream was to see the beach. The same day he spoke about his desire to see the salty waves of the Mediterranean, he also recounted how, perhaps even more than seeing the coast, he wanted to be able to set foot in Jerusalem and to pray in Al-Aqsa Mosque.

Eventually, he did.

It was not because the Israeli system of apartheid has become any less brutal. On the contrary, anyone who has been paying attention has seen the dire acceleration of violence and ethnic cleansing in the West Bank in addition to the genocidal horrors in Gaza.

A couple of years after the day I described in the Introduction, Awdah was able to go to Jerusalem for the first time and to pray in Al-Aqsa Mosque because of a joint project between Palestinians and international activists. It was because of social movements, because of co-resistance, that Awdah was able to do what anyone should be able to do—to travel, to pray, to build community, to experience the pleasure and joy of connection we all deserve. He wrote an extremely moving piece about the experience that I recommend to everyone to understand the very personal and direct human cost of Israeli policies of confinement and the joy and power of moving against it.[1] Awdah's eventual ability to move, even just for one day, was made real because of the transnational, multiethnic, multireligious *social movement for liberation* that he helped to build.

1 Awdah Hathaleen, "An Hour and 22 Years Away: Visiting Jerusalem from the West Bank," *+972 Magazine*, August 15, 2022, 972mag.com.

It's not surprising to me that in many languages—Spanish, English, French Portuguese, Dutch, Afrikaans, Arabic, and Hebrew—collective organizing is figured as "social *movement*."[2] "The connotation in all these languages," Rudolf Heberle explains, "is that of a commotion, a stirring among the people, an unrest, a collective attempt to reach a visualized goal, especially a change in certain social institutions."[3] When so much of the pain and violence in the world is structured by confinement, the form of joining together takes on the character of movement, even when those movements are, like Awdah's, directed toward the right to remain in place, coalescing around forced displacement.

Historians of social movements usually attribute the first use of the concept of social movements to the German sociologist Lorenz von Stein, whose *History of the Social Movement in France, 1789–1850* studied the evolution of resistance in France from the Revolution of 1789 through the uprisings of 1848.[4]

But Marx and Engels were already speaking of social movements two years before the publication of Stein's work. They write in *The Communist Manifesto*, "All previous historical movements were movements of minorities, or in the interest of minorities. The proletarian movement is the self-conscious, independent movement of the immense majority, in the interests of the immense majority."[5]

What does it mean to say that communism is or must be a social *movement*? For Michael Hardt, a movement denotes "a sea-change, the flow of the movements transforming the traditional fixed positions; networks imposing their force through a kind of irresistible undertow."[6] A movement must aim to change against the fixity (confinement) of the current world, and it does so by *pulling people into* the project of liberation.

2 All these languages use terms with root words for "movement": *movimiento* in Spanish, *mouvement* in French, *beweging* in Dutch and Afrikaans, *Bewegung* in German, *movimento* in Portuguese, *haraka* in Arabic, and *tenu'a* in Hebrew.

3 Rudolf Heberle, *Social Movements: An Introduction to Political Sociology* (Appleton Century Crofts, 1951), 6.

4 See, for example, academic sources that make this claim: Greg Martin, *Social Movements and Protest Politics*, 2nd edition (Routledge, 2024), 1; Heberle, *Social Movements*, 4. This claim is reflected in many popular reference works like: Wikipedia, "Social movement," April 18, 2025, en.wikipedia.org; Ralph H. Turner and Neil J. Smelser, "Social Movement," in *Encyclopedia Britannica*, April 19, 2025, britannica.com; Jordi Bonet Martí and Barbara Biglia, "Social Movements," in *Encyclopedia of Critical Psychology*, ed. Thomas Teo (Springer, 2014); Lorenz von Stein, *The History of the Social Movement in France, 1789–1850*, trans. Kaethe Mengelberg (Bedminster Press, 1964).

5 Marx and Engels, *The Communist Manifesto*, 67.

6 Michael Hardt, "Today's Bandung," in *A Movement of Movements: Is Another World Really Possible?*, ed. Tom Mertes (Verso, 2004), 236.

Movements must *move* people, must *mobilize* them against the current order.

As Hagar Kotef explains, social movements thus activate multiple kinds of movement simultaneously:

> The duality of the verb ("to move") is significant. What moves people affectively is crucial not only to moving them physically across empires, or to foster instead their rootedness (feeling at home; staying put) . . . To mobilize people, to move them out of their home and into the streets, certain emotions must be at play (anger, rage, hope, affection and solidarity, perhaps even love). Moving people (to the streets) by moving them (producing emotions) ultimately creates *a* movement, now in a third meaning.[7]

In all these accounts and many more, social movements must involve *action*, not only or primarily political ideas.[8] A social movement must be something more than a trend, a single spontaneous action, or a set of ideas, no matter how broad support for those ideas might be. A social movement requires collective *mobilization.* If the only thing needed for us to win was better *ideas* or a superior *analysis* of the world, the left would have won a very long time ago. Indeed, in *The German Ideology,* Marx argues that communism cannot be a mere "ideal" or utopian set of ideas, it is and must be a real *movement* that pushes against the confines of the capitalist world: "Communism is for us not a *state of affairs* which is to be established, an *ideal* to which reality [will] have to adjust itself. We call communism the *real* movement which abolishes the present state of things. The conditions of this movement result from the premises now in existence."[9]

Communism, in Marx's own words, is the *movement* that *abolishes.*

It is perhaps more correct to say that communism *must be* the movement that abolishes. Too many strands of Marxist thought and praxis have,

7 Kotef, *Movement and the Ordering of Freedom*, 128–9.

8 See, for example, Tilly's famous definition of a social movement: "That political complex combined three elements: 1) campaigns of collective claims on target authorities; 2) an array of claim-making performances including special-purpose associations, public meetings, media statements, and demonstrations; 3) public representations of the cause's worthiness, unity, numbers, and commitment. I am calling that historically specific complex a social movement." Charles Tilly, *Social Movements, 1768–2004* (Paradigm Publishers, 2004), 11.

9 Karl Marx and Friedrich Engels, *The German Ideology* (International Publishers, 2022), 24.

over the centuries, fallen short of embracing the abolitionist philosophy that we so desperately need.

Hopefully this book has shown that capitalism depends on several forms of confinement: property, class, family, gender, slavery, prisons, policing, work, states, borders, white supremacy, colonialism. Understanding capitalism from the standpoint of confinement allows us to see clearly what capitalism is and how it operates—and what must truly be done to move beyond it. Saidiya Hartman's work lends us an important heuristic: the "afterlives" of slavery show how fundamental social relations of domination can be conserved, even with the elimination of their initial form.

The charge for all of us is to make sure that our visions of communism do not conserve forms of domination that would have an "afterlife"—not only the afterlife of slavery, but of all the confinements of land, labor, and life that animate and justify capital accumulation.

To overcome all of these, communism must be and become this total abolition. Thus, it must be more than an *idea* or a *set of politics* that pushes against confinement in all its forms, it must be an actual *movement* that brings people into collective action (of many, diverse kinds) that put these ideas into practice.

I know that I have written a book—that is, a set of arguments—about how we should *think about* capitalism. I am very committed to the principle that the sharper and clearer our analyses, the more strategic our political action will be; intellectual labor is a crucial resource for social movements, one that, especially in these anti-intellectual times of rising fascism and the radical right, must be defended. But these sharper ideas ultimately mean very little if they are not accompanied by the "real movements" that actually *move us* closer toward the world we want to inhabit. If any single idea sticks with readers of this text, I hope it is this one: that since capitalism is saturated with modes of confinement, we need *movement*, specifically *social movements*, to combat it. In these harrowing times, when the forces of the right are coalescing into new barriers for liberation, our only hope is joining with others to move against them and toward the world of joy and liberation.

And we need to do it all the time.

I felt extreme joy in Awdah's trip to Jerusalem, in his ability to see, feel, hear, experience, and enjoy one full day across a barrier that had once felt insurmountable. In the time since that trip, Awdah's village of Umm al-Khair has only faced greater settler encroachment and settler violence. Home demolitions, cattle slaughter, harassment, shootings, arrests, detentions, and hundreds of other forms of anti-Palestinian violence are only accelerating. Awdah's mother, whom many call Umm Awdah (even though he isn't the oldest!), has been a recipient of this violence on more than one occasion. I have fond memories of sitting with her, drinking tea and sharing stories; one particularly cold night, she wouldn't let me leave her tent without accepting the gift of an extra sweater, a lavender hoodie that zipped up the front. In July 2024, she was sent to the hospital after settlers from the neighboring settlement of Chavat Shorashim entered her tent, demanding she make tea for them. When she refused, they shot guns in the air, beat several women, and pepper-sprayed them. In the aftermath of this incident and many others since then, Awdah's five-year-old son has lost the ability to speak.[10] Awdah's wife Hanady had her arm broken by settlers as I was completing this manuscript.

All of this is to say that the movements we need are continuous, that they cannot be one-off mobilizations. Capitalism has entrenched confinement for nearly 500 years; our movements must be robust enough to take real joy in our momentary wins, like Awdah's trip to Jerusalem, and focused enough to see that our work will not be over until all forms of confining violence are abolished.

Abolitionism and/as Communism

So why might we, following Ruth Wilson Gilmore, define abolitionism as "an elaboration (not novel but distinctive) of small-c communism"?[11]

Certainly communism and abolitionism share a certain kind of analysis: to move toward freedom, many institutions must be completely, radically extirpated from our society. They also share at least some continuities in language; abolition, after all, has been part of the communist grammar for hundreds of years. But what I hope to have shown is that each tradition of thinking and organizing complements the other, filling out different parts of the picture of the world and how we got here. They also activate different elements of what we would need to do to get free and what it will look like when we get there.

Any project that is interested *either* in anti-capitalism *or* in abolition must actually be committed to *both* as two sides of the same coin or two

10 Awdah Hathaleen, "In Umm Al-Khair, the Occupation Is Damning Us to Multigenerational Trauma," +972 *Magazine*, July 24, 2024, 972mag.com.

11 Quoted in Robin D. G. Kelley, "Making History, Making Worlds," *American Quarterly* 75, no. 2 (2023): 383.

grammars expressing the same project. That is to say, while there might be important differences between the abolitionist and Marxist traditions with regard to focus, conceptual tools, political history, vernacular, and organizing methods, ultimately these projects converge, and their success are mutually dependent on one another. We cannot achieve communism with private property, police, the state, the family, prisons, or forced labor, and we cannot abolish any of these institutions without an elimination of the capitalist system that motivates them. Ultimately, liberation must mean something like the overcoming of the confinements of land, labor, and life that have been so devastating in so many ways for so long.

Integrating an abolitionist analysis into class politics helps expand the terrain of anti-capitalist struggle. If we think about police as stabilizing both exploitation *and* the oppressions necessary for capitalism's societal reproduction, then communism needs to be abolitionist in its commitment to extirpating all "unfree and unequal hierarchical social relations" that are central to capitalism.[12] Which is to say, if we want to get rid of capitalism, we have to also take aim at patriarchy, racism, colonialism, ableism, heterosexism, Islamophobia, and all other regimes invested with production of unequal life and exposure to violence. When we say that none of us is free until we all are, we are already saying that we need to abolish a form of society whose aim is convincing us that our freedom is predicated on others' confinement, abjection, and subjection. That's the only communism worth the name.

12 Le Baron and Roberts, "Toward a Feminist Political Economy of Capitalism and Carcerality."

Epilogue

I completed this manuscript in May 2025, as the situation in Palestine, both in Gaza and the West Bank, became even more dire. Just a few weeks later, Awdah was supposed to come to the United States for a speaking tour, and I was so excited to see my friend and to give him a copy of the manuscript. Despite having a valid visa, he was detained at San Francisco airport for over twenty-four hours and then summarily deported. As Israel bombed Iran, he was stranded in Qatar, waiting to be able to go home after a harrowing detention. My heart ached that his journey to the United States, to try to tell Americans about the horrifying confinement he lived through in the West Bank, was met with yet another form of confinement.

That summer, five comrades and I went on hunger strike to protest the brutal confinements that the US-backed Israeli war machine was unleashing in Gaza. Over the weeks of consuming no calories, my body learned in new ways what I had already known rationally: food is vital to human survival, but water is even more urgent. For the duration of the strike, my hydration was monitored by a tireless medical team because dehydration, especially in the Chicago summer heat wave, is deadly. As international agencies and leftist news sources covered Israel's food deprivation of Gaza, I was consumed with reports of the lack of clean, potable water, caused in no small part by Israel's targeting of the water desalination plants. As the Lakota water defenders at Standing Rock declared to the world during the 2016–2017 protests against the Dakota Access Pipeline: *mni wiconi*, water is life.

During my protracted recovery from the hunger strike, I received a text message that upended my whole world. Early on July 28, 2025, Awdah messaged that settlers had brought bulldozers into the village of Umm al-Khair, and they were attempting to cut off the village's water pipe. "If they cut the pipe," he wrote, "the community here will literally be without any drop of water."

It was the last text he would ever send to me.

Soon after he sent it, Awdah, a tireless defender of his community, my dear friend, was shot dead by a settler right in front of the community center I described in the Introduction.

There was about half an hour between receiving the phone call that Awdah had been shot and the follow-up call that he had not survived. In that interim, when I thought he was injured, but still breathing, I texted him a phrase I had said to him so many times in the decade we knew each other: "I am with you."

The aftermath of Awdah's murder compounded the brutality. Over a dozen of his friends and family were arrested while his murderer, Yinon Levy, was briefly questioned and then sent home. The Israeli Army declared most of Umm al-Khair a closed military zone, a form of confinement they use to prevent people from gathering, even to mourn. The military destroyed the erected mourning tent and refused to release his body so that he could be buried in accordance with Islamic burial practices. International activists and journalists were barred from entering the village as well. Recalling the confinement of Israeli occupation, Tariq Hathaleen, Awdah's cousin and best friend, said something that I cannot get out of my mind: "I am imprisoned in this reality without him."

On July 31, Hanady and sixty other women of the village launched a hunger strike, demanding they be allowed to bury him. On August 7, after a week of hunger strike, and dozens of protests around the world, Awdah's body was finally laid to rest in Umm al-Khair, in the village he loved so dearly and on the land he defended so bravely.

In the days that followed, it was equal parts devastating and overwhelmingly beautiful to read the outpouring of love for Awdah from people around the world. Reading memories, scrolling through photographs, and watching so many people organize in his name was salve on a permanent wound I will carry with me forever. Awdah was truly the best organizer I was ever blessed to know, and the effort he made to form connections across space, political belief, and identity, and how tenderly he cared for those connections, is truly awe-inspiring. Awdah built such a global community of co-resistors because he believed so deeply that another world was possible, and he showed us all that world in the simple eloquence of his example. I, too, will carry that with me forever.

I dreamed many times of a liberated Palestine, and Awdah was always central to what I imagined. I thought about how joyful it would be when Awdah and I could see each other without the many containments and barriers Israel imposes on Palestinians. I thought of what it would be like to walk with him and his community to gather za'atar or graze the animals, not because international presence granted (some) protection from abutting settlements, but just for the joy of moving through life together. I pictured what it would be like to help the residents build the infrastructure of their collective lives without fears of demolition orders. I dreamed of the day that water was abundant in Umm al-Khair and that all the residents of Masafer Yatta went to sleep without fear that soldiers or settlers would harass them in the night. I am so bitter and devastated that he will never get to see or experience that world.

When Awdah told that story about his desire to go to the beach, he was not yet a father. After he became Abu Watan, he always said that the thing he wanted most in the world was for his children to live in freedom. It is my obligation—it is the obligation of us all—to make sure that his three children will, that all the children of Palestine and all the children of the world, will.

August 15, 2025

Bibliography

Adey, Peter. *Aerial Life: Spaces, Mobilities, Affects*. Wiley-Blackwell, 2010.

Adorno, Theodor W. *Minima Moralia: Reflections from Damaged Life*. Verso, 2020.

Agamben, Giorgio. *Homo Sacer: Sovereign Power and Bare Life*. 1st edition. Translated by Daniel Heller-Roazen. Stanford University Press, 1998.

Akkerman, Mark. *Expanding the Fortress: The Policies, Profiteers, and the People Shaped by the EU's Border Externalization Programme*. The Transnational Institute, 2018. tni.org.

Al-Aly, Ziyad, Hannah Davis, Lisa McCorkell, et al. "Long COVID Science, Research and Policy." *Nature Medicine* 30, no. 8 (2024): 2148–64.

Allen, Theodore W. *The Invention of the White Race*, volume 2, *The Origin of Racial Oppression in Anglo-America*. 2nd edition. Verso, 2012.

Althusser, Louis. *On the Reproduction of Capitalism: Ideology and Ideological State Apparatuses*. Translated by G. M. Goshgarian. Verso, 2014.

Althusser, Louis. *The Spectre of Hegel*. Translated by G. M. Goshgarian. Verso, 1997.

Anievas, Alexander, and Kerem Nisancioglu. *How the West Came to Rule: The Geopolitical Origins of Capitalism*. Pluto Press, 2015.

Arkles, Gabriel. "Correcting Race and Gender: Prison Regulation of Social Hierarchy through Dress." *New York University Law Review* 87, no. 4 (2012): 859–959.

Arkles, Gabriel. "Safety and Solidarity Across Gender Lines: Rethinking Segregation of Transgender People in Detention." *Temple Political & Civil Rights Law Review* 18, no. 2 (2009): 515–60.

Arrighi, Giovanni. *The Long Twentieth Century: Money, Power, and the Origins of Our Times*. Verso, 1994.

Arruzza, Cinzia. "Logic or History?: The Political Stakes of Marxist-Feminist Theory." *Viewpoint Magazine*, June 23, 2015. viewpointmag.com.

Badiou, Alain. "The Neolithic, Capitalism, and Communism." *Verso Blog*, July 30, 2018. versobooks.com.

Balakrishnan, Sarah. "Of Debt and Bondage: From Slavery to Prisons in the Gold Coast, c. 1807–1957." *Journal of African History* 61, no. 1 (2020): 3–21.

Balakrishnan, Sarah. "The Jailhouse Divergence: Why Debtors' Prisons Disappeared in 19th Century Europe and Flourished in West Africa." *Punishment & Society* 24, no. 5 (2022): 1–17.

Balibar, Étienne. "What Is a Border." In *Politics and the Other Scene*. Translated by Christine Jones, James Swenson, and Chris Turner. Verso, 2022.

Bargu, Banu. *Starve and Immolate: The Politics of Human Weapons*. Columbia University Press, 2014.

Barker, Adam J. "Already Occupied: Indigenous Peoples, Settler Colonialism and the Occupy Movements in North America." *Social Movement Studies* 11, nos. 3–4 (2012): 327–34.

Barone, Guglielmo, and Sauro Mocetti. *Intergenerational Mobility in the Very Long Run: Florence 1427–2011*. Temi Di Discussione 1060. Bank of Italy, 2016.

Barrett, Michele, and Mary McIntosh. *The Anti-Social Family*. Verso, 2015.

Barrow, Clyde W. *The Dangerous Class: The Concept of the Lumpenproletariat*. University of Michigan Press, 2020.

Batrlovich, Crystal, and Neil Lazarus, eds. *Marxism, Modernity and Postcolonial Studies*. Cambridge University Press, 2002.

Battistini, Matteo. "Karl Marx and the Global History of the Civil War: The Slave Movement, Working-Class Struggle, and the American State Within the World Market." *International Labor and Working-Class History*, no. 100 (2021): 158–85.

Baucom, Ian. *Specters of the Atlantic: Finance Capital, Slavery, and the Philosophy of History*. Duke University Press, 2005.

Bayley, David H. *Patterns of Policing*. Rutgers University Press, 1990.

Beattie, J. M. *Crime and Courts in England, 1660–1800*. Oxford University Press, 1986.

Beckles, Hilary. "From Land to Sea: Runaway Barbados Salves and Servants: 1630–1700." *Slavery & Abolition* 6, no. 3 (1985): 95–111.

Benner, Derek N. "HSI Academy Launch Memo." n.d. Accessed June 1, 2025.

Bensaïd, Daniel. *The Dispossessed: Karl Marx's Debates on Wood Theft and the Right of the Poor*. Translated by Robert Nichols. University of Minnesota Press, 2021.

Bernault, Florence. "The Politics of Enclosure in Colonial and Postcolonial Africa." In *A History of Prison and Confinement in Africa*, edited by Florence Bernault, translated by Janet Roitman. Heinemann, 2003.

Best, Beverley. *The Automatic Fetish: The Law of Value in Marx's Capital*. Verso, 2024.

Bey, Marquis. "Black Fugitivity Un/Gendered." *The Black Scholar* (San Francisco) 49, no. 1 (2019): 55–62.

Bhandar, Brenna. *Colonial Lives of Property: Law, Land, and Racial Regimes of Ownership*. Duke University Press, 2018.

Blackburn, Robin. *The Reckoning: From the Second Slavery to Abolition, 1776–1888*. Verso, 2024.

Bohrer, Ashley. "Just Wars of Accumulation: The Salamanca School, Race, and Colonial Capitalism." *Race & Class* 59, no. 3 (2018): 20–37.

Bohrer, Ashley J. "Gender Policing the Poor: Toward a Conceptual Apparatus." *Feminist Formations* 33, no. 1 (2021): 74–95.

Bohrer, Ashley J. *Marxism and Intersectionality: Race, Class, Gender, and Sexuality Under Contemporary Capitalism*. Transcript Verlag, 2019.

Bohrer, Ashley J. "To Oppose Zionism, We Have to Deal with Christian Zionism." *Midnight Sun*, February 23, 2024. midnightsunmag.ca.

Bohrer, Ashley J., and Andrés Fabián Henao Castro. "A People's History of Police Exchanges: Settler Colonialism, Capitalism, and the Intersectionality of Struggles." In *The War on Drugs and the Global Colour Line*, edited by Kojo Koram. Pluto Press, 2019.

Bonilla-Silva, Eduardo. *Racism Without Racists: Color-Blind Racism and the Persistence of Racial Inequality in America*. 3rd edition. Rowman & Littlefield Publishers, 2009.

Boyle, James. "The Second Enclosure Movement and the Public Domain." *Law and Contemporary Problems* 66 (2003): 33–74.

Brady, Miranda J., and Derek Antoine. "Decolonize Wall Street!: Situating Indigenous Critiques of the Occupy Wall Street Movement." *American Communication Journal* 15, no. 1 (2013): 1–10.

Brockington, Dan. *Fortress Conservation: The Preservation of the Mkomazi Game Reserve, Tanzania*. Indiana University Press, 2002.

Brogden, Mike. "The Emergence of the Police: The Colonial Dimension." *The British Journal of Criminology* 27, no. 1 (1987): 4–14.

Brown, Elaine. *A Taste of Power: A Black Woman's Story*. Anchor Books, 1994.

Brown, Ian, and Frank Dikötter, eds. *Cultures of Confinement: A History of the Prison in Africa, Asia, and Latin America*. Hurst, 2007.

Brown, Wendy. *Walled States, Waning Sovereignty*. Zone Books, 2017.

Brucato, Ben. "Fabricating the Color Line in a White Democracy: From Slave Catchers to Petty Sovereigns." *Theoria* 61, no. 141 (2014): 30–54.

Brucato, Ben. *Race and Police: The Origin of Our Peculiar Institutions*. Rutgers University Press, 2023.

Brundage, W. Fitzhugh. *A Socialist Utopia in the New South: The Ruskin Colonies in Tennessee and Georgia, 1894–1901*. University of Illinois Press, 1996.

Buck-Morss, Susan. *Hegel, Haiti, and Universal History*. 1st edition. University of Pittsburgh Press, 2009.

Bullard, Alice. *Exile to Paradise: Savagery and Civilization in Paris and the South Pacific, 1790–1900*. Stanford University Press, 2000.

Burnard, Trevor, and John Garrigus. *The Plantation Machine: Atlantic Capitalism in French Saint-Domingue and British Jamaica*. University of Pennsylvania Press, 2016.

Burt, Richard, and John Michael Archer, eds. *Enclosure Acts: Sexuality, Property, and Culture in Early Modern England*. 1st edition. Cornell University Press, 1994.

Butler, James Davie. "British Convicts Shipped to American Colonies." *The American Historical Review* 2, no. 1 (1896): 12–33.

Carney, Mitchell. "Cycles of Punishment: The Constitutionality of Restricting Access to Menstrual Health Products in Prisons." *Boston College Law Review* 61, no. 7 (2020): 2541.

Casarino, Cesare, and Antonio Negri. *In Praise of the Common: A Conversation on Philosophy and Politics*. University of Minnesota Press, 2008.

Castles, Stephen. "Migration, Crisis, and the Global Labour Market." *Globalizations* 8, no. 3 (2011): 311–24.

Castro, Daniel. *Another Face of Empire: Bartolome de Las Casas, Indigenous Rights, and Ecclesiastical Imperialism*. Duke University Press, 2007.

Césaire, Aimé. *Discourse on Colonialism*. Monthly Review Press, 1973.

Chang, Grace. *Disposable Domestics: Immigrant Women Workers in the Global Economy*. South End Press, 2000.

Chapin, Mac. "A Challenge to Conservationists." *World Watch*, December 2004, 17–31.

Cheng, Sealing, and Eunjung Kim. "The Paradoxes of Neoliberalism: Migrant Korean Sex Workers in the United States and 'Sex Trafficking.'"

Social Politics: International Studies in Gender, State, and Society 21, no. 3 (2014): 355–81.

Chomsky, Noam. "My Visit to Gaza, the World's Largest Open-Air Prison." *Truthout*, November 9, 2012.

Churchill, Ward. *Kill the Indian, Save the Man: The Genocidal Impact of American Indian Residential Schools*. City Lights Publishers, 2004.

Clarke, Jennifer G., and Rachel E. Simon. "Shackling and Separation: Motherhood in Prison." *AMA Journal of Ethics* 15, no. 9 (2013): 779–85.

Clover, Joshua. *Riot. Strike. Riot: The New Era of Uprisings*. Verso, 2016.

Collins, Patricia Hill. *Black Feminist Thought: Knowledge, Consciousness, and the Politics of Empowerment*. Revised 10th anniversary edition. Routledge, 2000.

Collins, Patricia Hill. *Black Feminist Thought: Knowledge, Consciousness, and the Politics of Empowerment*. 1st edition. Routledge, 2008.

Conceição Neto, Maria da. "Colonial Incarceration and Selective Memories: What Is Remembered? Who Is Forgotten? The Case of Peasant Women Deported to São Nicolau (Angola, 1969)." *The Journal of Imperial and Commonwealth History* 47, no. 2 (2019): 325–42.

Conlin Casella, Eleanor, and Clayton Fredericksen. "Legacy of the 'Fatal Shore': The Heritage and Archaeology of Confinement in Post-Colonial Australia." *Journal of Social Archeology* 4, no. 1 (2004): 99–125.

Connor, Michael. *The Invention of Terra Nullius: Historical and Legal Fictions on the Foundation of Australia*. Macleay Press, 2005.

Correia, David, and Tyler Wall. *Police: A Field Guide*. Verso, 2018.

Coulthard, Glen Sean. *Red Skin, White Masks: Rejecting the Colonial Politics of Recognition*. University of Minnesota Press, 2014.

Coyle, Andrew. "Prison Privatisation in the African Context." *Review of African Political Economy* 35, no. 118 (2008): 660–5.

Dardot, Pierre, and Christian Laval. *Common: On Revolution in the 21st Century*. Translated by Matthew Maclellan. Bloomsbury, 2019.

Davenport, Rodney, and Christopher Saunders. *South Africa: A Modern History*. 5th edition. Palgrave Macmillan, 2000.

Davidovich, Shay. "For Israeli Soldiers, Some Palestinians Are Little More Than Props." *+972 Magazine*, November 5, 2013. 972mag.com.

Davis, Angela Y. *Are Prisons Obsolete?* Seven Stories Press, 2003.

Davis, Angela Y. *Freedom Is a Constant Struggle: Ferguson, Palestine, and the Foundations of a Movement*. Edited by Frank Barat. With Cornel West. Haymarket Books, 2016.

Davis, Angela Y. "From the Prison of Slavery to the Slavery of Prison."

In *The Angela Y. Davis Reader*, edited by Joy James. Blackwell Publishing, 1998.

Davis, Angela Y. "Political Prisoners, Prison, and Black Liberation." In *The Angela Y. Davis Reader*, edited by Joy James. Blackwell Publishing, 1998.

Davis, Angela Y. "The Approaching Obsolescence of Housework: A Working Class Perspective." In *The Angela Y. Davis Reader*. Blackwell Publishing, 1998.

Davis, Angela Y., and Gina Dent. "Prison as a Border: A Conversation on Gender, Globalization and Punishment." *Signs: Journal of Women in Culture and Society* 26, no. 4 (2001): 1235–40.

Davis, Angela Y., and Cassandra Shaylor. "Race, Gender, and the Prison Industrial Complex: California and Beyond." *Meridians* 2, no. 1 (2001): 1–25.

Day, Iyko. *Alien Capital: Asian Racialization and the Logic of Settler Colonial Capitalism*. Duke University Press, 2016.

De Genova, Nicholas. "A Racial Theory of Labour: Racial Capitalism from Colonial Slavery to Postcolonial Migration." *Historical Materialism* 31, no. 3 (2023): 219–51.

Denning, Michael. "Wageless Life." *New Left Review*, no. 66 (2010): 79–97.

Derrida, Jacques. *Limited Inc.* Northwestern University Press, 1988.

Do Black Lives Matter? Robin D. G. Kelley in Conversation with Fred Moten. Performed by Robin D. G. Kelley and Fred Moten. Critical Resistance, 2014. vimeo.com.

Donahue, Brian. *The Great Meadow: Farmers and the Land in Colonial Concord*. Yale University Press, 2004.

Dowie, Mark. *Conservation Refugees: The Hundred-Year Conflict Between Global Conservation and Native Peoples*. MIT Press, 2009.

Draper, Hal. "The Concept of the 'Lumpenproletariat' in Marx and Engels." *Économies et Sociétés*, no. 15 (1972): 285–312.

Du Bois, W. E. B. *Black Reconstruction in America*. Harcourt Brace and Company, 1935.

Du Bois, W. E. B. *The Souls of Black Folk*. Oxford University Press, 2007.

Edelman, Lee. *No Future: Queer Theory and the Death Drive*. Duke University Press, 2004.

Ehrenreich, Barbara, and Arlie Hochschild. *Global Woman: Nannies, Maids, and Sex Workers in the New Economy*. Henry Holt & Company, 2002.

Emsley, Clive. *Crime, Police, and Penal Policy: European Experiences 1750–1940*. Oxford University Press, 2007.

Engels, Friedrich. *The Origin of the Family, Private Property and the State*. Reissue edition. With Tristram Hunt. Penguin Classics, 2010.

Englert, Sai. *Settler Colonialism: An Introduction*. Pluto Press, 2022.

Fall, Babacar, and Richard L. Roberts. "Forced Labor." In *General Labour History of Africa: Workers, Employers and Governments, 20th–21st Centuries*, edited by Stefano Bellucci and Andreas Eckert. Boydell & Brewer, 2019.

Fanon, Frantz. *The Wretched of the Earth*. Reprint edition. Translated by Richard Philcox. With Jean-Paul Sartre and Homi K. Bhabha. Grove Press, 2005.

Farris, Sara. *In the Name of Women's Rights: The Rise of Femonationalism*. Duke University Press, 2017.

Federici, Silvia. *Caliban and the Witch: Women, the Body and Primitive Accumulation*. 1st edition. Autonomedia, 2004.

Federici, Silvia. "Feminism and the Politics of the Common in an Era of Primitive Accumulation." In *Revolution at Point Zero: Housework, Reproduction, and Feminist Struggle*. PM Press, 2012.

Federici, Silvia. *Re-enchanting the World: Feminism and the Politics of the Commons*. PM Press, 2019.

Federici, Silvia, and George Caffentzis. "Notes on the Edu-Factory and Cognitive Capitalism." In *Toward a Global Autonomous University*, edited by Edu-factory Collective. Autonomedia, 2009.

Fernandez, Fabian Luiz. "Hands Up: A Systematized Review of Polcing Sex Workers in the U.S." Public Health Thesis, Yale University, 2016.

Fields, Gary. "Lockdown: Gaza Through a Camera Lens and Historical Mirror." *Journal of Palestine Studies* 49, no. 3 (2020): 41–69.

Fitzmaurice, Andrew. "The Genealogy of Terra Nullius." *Australian Historical Studies* 129 (2007): 1–15.

Foster, John Bellamy, Hannah Holleman, and Brett Clark. "Marx and Slavery." *Monthly Review* 72, no. 3 (2020): 96–117.

Foucault, Michel. *Discipline and Punish: The Birth of the Prison*. 2nd edition. Translated by Alan Sheridan. Vintage Books, 1995.

Foucault, Michel. "Polemics, Politics, and Problematizations." In *Essential Works of Foucault*, volume 1. Edited by Paul Rabinow. The New Press, 1998.

Foucault, Michel. *"Society Must Be Defended": Lectures at the Collège de France, 1975–1976*. Reprint edition. Picador, 2003.

Foucault, Michel. *The Birth of Biopolitics: Lectures at the Collège de France, 1978–1979*. Reprint edition. Picador, 2010.

Foucault, Michel. *The History of Sexuality*, volume 1, *An Introduction*. Reissue edition. Translated by Robert Hurley. Vintage, 1990.

Foucault, Michel. "The Political Technologies of Individuals." In *Power: Essential Works of Foucault*, volume 3, *1954–1984*, edited by J. D. Faubion. The New Press, 2001.

Foucault, Michel. *The Punitive Society: Lectures at the College de France, 1972–1973*. Macmillan, 2018.

Fourchard, Laurent. "Between Conservatism and Transgression: Everyday Life in the Prisons of Upper Volta, 1920–1960." In *A History of Prison and Confinement in Africa*, edited by Florence Bernault. Heinemann, 2003.

Fraser, Derek. *The Evolution of the British Welfare State*. 4th edition. Palgrave Macmillan, 2009.

Fraser, Nancy. *Cannibal Capitalism: How Our System Is Devouring Democracy, Care, and the Planet—and What We Can Do About It*. Verso, 2022.

Fraser, Nancy. "Contradictions of Capital and Care." *New Left Review*, no. 100 (July/August 2016).

Galeano, Eduardo. *Open Veins of Latin America: Five Centuries of the Pillage of a Continent*. 25th anniversary edition. Monthly Review Press, 1997.

Garfinkle, Adam M. "On the Origin, Meaning, Use and Abuse of a Phrase." *Middle Eastern Studies* 27, no. 4 (1991): 539–50.

Gauthier, Julie. "The Land of the Free." *Country Roads Magazine*, September 23, 2019. countryroadsmagazine.com.

Gavron, Daniel. *The Kibbutz: Awakening from Utopia*. Rowman & Littlefield, 2000.

Gibson, Mary. "Global Perspectives on the Birth of the Prison." *American Historical Review* 116, no. 4 (2011): 1040–63.

Gilles Deleuze, and Felix Guattari. "Capitalism: A Very Special Delirium." In *Chaosophy: Texts and Interviews, 1972–1977*. Semiotext(e), 2008.

Gilmore, Ruth Wilson. "Abolition Feminism." In *Revolutionary Feminisms: Conversations on Collective Action and Radical Thought*, edited by Brenna Bhandar and Rafeef Ziadeh. Verso, 2020.

Gilmore, Ruth Wilson. *Abolition Geography*. Edited by Brenna Bhandar and Alberto Toscano. Verso, 2022.

Gilmore, Ruth Wilson. "Foreword." In *The Jail Is Everywhere: Fighting the New Geography of Mass Incarceration*, edited by Jack Norton, Lydia Pelot-Hobbs, and Judah Schept. Verso, 2024.

Gilmore, Ruth Wilson. *Golden Gulag: Prisons, Surplus, Crisis, and Opposition in Globalizing California*. University of California Press, 2007.

Gilmore, Ruth Wilson, and Lambert Lo. "Making Abolition Geography in California's Central Valley with Ruth Wilson Gilmore." *The Funambulist*, no. 21 (February 2019). thefunambulist.net.

Gilmore, Ruth Wilson, and Clément Petitjean. "Prisons and Class Warfare: An Interview with Ruth Wilson Gilmore." *Verso Blog*, August 2, 2018. versobooks.com.

Gleeson, Jules Joanne, and Elle O'Rourke, eds. *Transgender Marxism*. Pluto Press, 2021.

Global Detention Project. *Annual Report*. Geneva, 2024. globaldetentionproject.org.

Go, Julian. *Policing Empires: Militarization, Race, and the Imperial Boomerang in Britain and the US*. Oxford University Press, 2023.

Goerg, Odile. "Colonial Urbanism and Prisons in Africa: Reflections on Conakry and Freetown, 1903–1960." In *A History of Prison and Confinement in Africa*, edited by Florence Bernault. Heinemann, 2003.

Golash-Boza, Tanya. *Deported: Immigrant Policing, Disposable Labor, and Global Capitalism*. New York University Press, 2015.

Goldberg, David Theo. *The Racial State*. Blackwell Publishing, 2002.

Goodburn, Charlotte, and Soumya Mishra. "Beyond the Dormitory Labour Regime: Comparing Chinese and Indian Workplace—Residence Systems as Strategies of Migrant Labour Control." *Work, Employment and Society* 38, no. 2 (2024): 505–26.

Gooding-Williams, Robert. "Foucault and Modern Racism." *Michel Foucault's College de France Lectures 1970–1984*, November 23, 2015. blogs.law.columbia.edu.

Gordon, Neve. "Civilian Control." In *Israel's Occupation*. University of California Press, 2008.

Graeber, David. *Bullshit Jobs: A Theory*. Simon and Schuster, 2018.

Graeber, David. *Pirate Enlightenment, or the Real Libertalia*. Farrar, Straus and Giroux, 2023.

Gramsci, Antonio. *Selections from the Prison Notebooks*. International Publishers, 1971.

Great Britain Overseers of the Poor. *Abstract of the Returns Made by the Overseers of the Poor: In Pursuance of an Act, Passed in the Twenty-Sixth Year of His Present Majesty's Reign, Intituled, an Act for Obliging Overseers of the Poor to Make Returns upon Oath, to Certain Questions "Specified Therein, Relative to the State of the Poor."* London, 1787.

Greer, Allan. "Commons and Enclosure in the Colonization of North America." *American Historical Review* 117, no. 2 (2012): 365–86.

Greer, Allan. *Property and Dispossession: Natives, Empires, and Land in Early Modern North America*. Cambridge University Press, 2018.

Guha, Ranajit. *A Rule of Property for Bengal: An Essay on the Idea of Permanent Settlement*. Duke University Press, 1996.

Habermas, Jurgen. *The Structural Transformation of the Public Sphere: An Inquiry into a Category of Bourgeois Society*. Translated by Thomas Burger. MIT Press, 1991.

Hadden, Sally E. *Slave Patrols: Law and Violence in Virginia and the Carolinas*. Harvard University Press, 2001.

Hall, Stuart. "Race, Articulation, and Societies Structured in Dominance." In *Essential Essays*, volume 1. Edited by David Morley. Duke University Press, 2019.

Hall, Stuart, Chas Critcher, Tony Jefferson, John Clarke, and Brian Roberts. *Policing the Crisis: Mugging, the State, and Law and Order*. Macmillan Press, 1978.

Hansen, Bue Rübner. "Surplus Population, Social Reproduction, and the Problem of Class Formation." *Viewpoint Magazine*, October 31, 2015. viewpointmag.com.

Haraway, Donna. *Primate Visions: Gender, Race, and Nature in the World of Modern Science*. Routledge, 1989.

Hardin, Garrett. "The Tragedy of the Commons." *Science* 162, no. 3859 (1968): 1243–48.

Hardt, Michael. "Today's Bandung." In *A Movement of Movements: Is Another World Really Possible?* Edited by Tom Mertes. Verso, 2004.

Hardt, Michael, and Antonio Negri. *Assembly*. Oxford University Press, 2017.

Hardt, Michael, and Antonio Negri. *Commonwealth*. Belknap Press, 2008.

Harney, Stefano, and Fred Moten. *The Undercommons: Fugitive Planning and Black Study*. Autonomedia, 2013.

Harris, Cheryl I. "Whiteness as Property." *Harvard Law Review* 106, no. 8 (1993): 1707–91.

Hartman, Saidiya V. *Lose Your Mother: A Journey Along the Atlantic Slave Trade Route Terror*. Farrar, Straus and Giroux, 2007.

Hartman, Saidiya V. *Scenes of Subjection: Terror, Slavery, and Self-Making in Nineteenth-Century America*. 1st edition. Oxford University Press, 1997.

Harvey, David. *A Brief History of Neoliberalism*. Oxford University Press, 2007.

Harvey, David. *Spaces of Global Capitalism*. Verso, 2006.

Harvey, David. *The Enigma of Capital and the Crises of Capitalism*. Oxford University Press, 2011.

Harvey, David. "Value in Motion." *New Left Review*, no. 126 (December 2020).

Hathaleen, Awdah. "An Hour and 22 Years Away: Visiting Jerusalem from the West Bank." *+972 Magazine*, August 15, 2022. 972mag.com.

Hathaleen, Awdah. "In Umm Al-Khair, the Occupation Is Damning Us to Multigenerational Trauma." *+972 Magazine*, July 24, 2024. 972mag.com.

Heberle, Rudolf. *Social Movements: An Introduction to Political Sociology*. Appleton Century Crofts, 1951.

Hernández, Kelly Lytle. *Migra!: A History of the US Border Patrol*. University of California Press, 2010.

Hernández Vidal, Nathalia, and Laura Gutiérrez Escobar. "Resistencias Epistémico-Políticas Frente a La Privatización de Las Semillas y Los Saberes Colectivos." *Revista Colombiana de Antropología* 55, no. 2 (2019): 39–63.

Hernández Vidal, Nathalia, Gabriela Merlinsky, and Paola Bolados. "Defending the Commons: New Frontiers in Latin American Perspectives on Environmental Justice." *Sociological Inquiry* 93, no. 2 (2023): 370–91.

Hester, Helen, and Nick Srnicek. *After Work: A History of the Home and the Fight for Free Time*. Verso, 2023.

Hong, Grace Kyungwon. *The Ruptures of American Capital: Women of Color Feminism and the Immigrant Culture of Labor*. University of Minnesota Press, 2006.

Horrox, James. *Living Revolution: Anarchism in the Kibbutz Movement*. AK Press, 2009.

Innes, J. "Prisons for the Poor: English Bridewells, 1555–1800." In *Labour, Law, and Crime: An Historical Perspective*, edited by F. Snyder and D. Hay. Tavistock, 1987.

INS v. Delgado, 466 U.S. 210 (United States Supreme Court 1984).

International Labour Organization, Walk Free, and International Organization for Migration. *Global Estimates of Modern Slavery: Forced Labour and Forced Marriage*. ILO Publications, 2022. cdn.walkfree.org.

Issar, Siddhant. "Theorising 'Racial/Colonial Primitive Accumulation': Settler Colonialism, Slavery, and Racial Capitalism." *Race & Class* 63, no. 1 (2021): 23–50.

Jaffe, Aaron. "The History and Afterlife of Marx's 'Primitive Accumulation.'" *Historical Materialism* 32, no. 3 (2024): 188–215.

James, C. L. R. *The Black Jacobins: Toussaint L'Ouverture and the San Domingo Revolution*. 2nd edition. Vintage, 1989.

James, Joy. *New Bones Abolition: Captive Maternal Agency and the Afterlife of Erica Garner*. Common Notions, 2023.

James, Joy. "The Captive Maternal and Abolitionism." *TOPIA: Canadian Journal of Cultural Studies* 43 (2021): 9–23.

James, Joy. "The Womb of Western Theory: Trauma, Time Theft, and the Captive Maternal." *Carceral Notebooks*, no. 12 (2016): 253–96.

Jaquet, Chantal. *Transclasses: A Theory of Social Non-Reproduction*. Translated by Gregory Elliott. Verso, 2023.

Jefferson, Thomas. "Letter of Thomas Jefferson to Joel Yancey." January 17, 1819. National Archives (Founders Online). founders.archives.gov.

Jenness, Valerie, Lori Sexton, and Jennifer Sumner. "Sexual Victimization Against Transgender Women in Prison: Consent and Coercion in Context." *Criminology* 57, no. 4 (2019): 603–31.

Johnson, Margaret E. "Menstrual Justice." *UC Davis Law Review* 53, no. 1 (2019): 1–79.

Johnson, Walter. *River of Dark Dreams: Slavery and Empire in the Cotton Kingdom*. Harvard University Press, 2013.

Kaba, Mariame. *We Do This 'Til We Free Us: Abolitionist Organizing and Transforming Justice*. Haymarket Books, 2021.

Kaba, Mariame, and Ashley J. Bohrer. "No Selves to Defend: An Interview with Mariame Kaba." *Red Wedge Magazine* (Chicago), August 19, 2014. redwedgemagazine.com.

Kappeler, Victor E. "A Brief History of Slavery and the Origins of American Policing." *Eastern Kentucky University Police Studies Online*, January 7, 2014. plsonline.eku.edu.

Kauanui, J. Kehaulani. *Paradoxes of Hawaiian Sovereignty: Land, Sex, and the Colonial Politics of State Nationalism*. Duke University Press, 2018.

Kauanui, J. Kehaulani. "The Politics of Indigeneity, Anarchist Praxis, and Decolonization." *Anarchist Developments in Cultural Studies*, no. 1 (2021): 9–42.

Kaye, Jeffrey. *Moving Millions: How Coyote Capitalism Fuels Global Immigration*. John Wiley & Sons, 2010.

Keith, Alexander. *The Land of Israel According to the Covenant with Abraham, with Isaac, and with Jacob*. William Whyte and Co, 1843.

Kelley, Robin D. G. "Making History, Making Worlds." *American Quarterly* 75, no. 2 (2023): 383–90.

Kelly, Alice B., and Nancy Lee Peluso. "Frontiers of Commodification:

State Lands and Their Formalization." *Society & Natural Resources* 28, no. 5 (2015): 473–95.

Khang Chuen, Ong, and William Tng. "CENTURION: Homes for Workers Can't Be Built Fast Enough, so This Company Is Enjoying a Rental Boom." July 20, 2023. Next Insight. Accessed April 20, 2025. nextinsight.net.

Klitgård, Mathias. "Lockdown Limbo: Reviving Marx's 'Dead Labor' for Queer and Trans Mental Distress during COVID-19." *Forum for Social Economics*, 2024, 1–16.

Klockars, Carl. *The Idea of Police*. SAGE Publications, 1985.

Kofman, Eleonore, and Parvati Raghuram. "Gender and Global Labour Migrations: Incorporating Skilled Workers." *Antipode* 38, no. 2 (2006): 282–303.

Kolbert, Elizabeth. *The Sixth Extinction: An Unnatural History*. Henry Holt & Company, 2014.

Konaté, Dior. "Ultimate Exclusion: Imprisoned Women in Senegal." In *A History of Prison and Confinement in Africa*. Edited by Florence Bernault. Heinemann, 2003.

Kotef, Hagar. *Movement and the Ordering of Freedom: On Liberal Governances of Mobility*. Duke University Press, 2015.

Kuhn, Gabriel. *Life Under the Jolly Roger: Reflections on Golden Age Piracy*. 2nd edition. PM Press, 2020.

Lamble, Sarah. "Everyday Abolition." In *Abolishing the Police*. Edited by Koshka Duff. Dog Section Press, 2021, 147–160.

Largent, Mark A. *Breeding Contempt: The History of Coerced Sterilization in the United States*. Rutgers University Press, 2011.

Le Baron, Genevieve, and Adrienne Roberts. "Toward a Feminist Political Economy of Capitalism and Carcerality." *Signs: Journal of Women in Culture & Society* 36, no. 1 (2010): 1–27.

Ledesma, Elida, and Chandra L. Ford. "Health Implications of Housing Assignments for Incarcerated Transgender Women." *American Journal of Public Health* 110, no. 5 (2020): 650–54.

Lehn, Walter. "The Jewish National Fund." *Journal of Palestine Studies* 3, no. 4 (1974): 74–96.

Lewis, Sophie. *Abolish the Family: A Manifesto for Care and Liberation*. Verso, 2022.

Lewis, Sophie. *Full Surrogacy Now: Feminism Against the Family*. Verso, 2019.

Linebaugh, Peter. *Stop, Thief!: The Commons, Enclosures, and Resistance*. PM Press, 2014.

Linebaugh, Peter. *The Magna Carta Manifesto: Liberties and Commons for All*. University of California Press, 2009.

Linebaugh, Peter, and Marcus Rediker. *The Many-Headed Hydra: Sailors, Slaves, Commoners, and the Hidden History of the Revolutionary Atlantic*. Beacon Press, 2013.

Lloyd, David, and Patrick Wolfe. "Settler Colonial Logics and the Neoliberal Regime." *Settler Colonial Studies* 6, no. 2 (2016): 109–18.

Locke, John. "Fundamental Constitutions of Carolina." The Avalon Project, March 1, 1669. Yale Law School Lillian Goldman Law Library. avalon.law.yale.edu.

Locke, John. *Two Treatises of Government*. 3rd edition. Edited by Peter Laslett. Cambridge University Press, 1988.

Lowy, Michael. *Ecosocialism: A Radical Alternative to Capitalist Catastrophe*. Haymarket Books, 2015.

Lukács, Georg. *History and Class Consciousness: Studies in Marxist Dialectics*. Translated by Rodney Livingstone. MIT Press, 1972.

Luxemburg, Rosa. *The Accumulation of Capital*. 2nd edition. Routledge, 2003.

Mac, Juno, and Molly Smith. *Revolting Prostitutes: The Fight for Sex Workers' Rights*. Verso, 2018.

Mackay, Fergus, and Emily Caruso. "Indigenous Lands or National Parks?" *Cultural Survival Quarterly* 28, no. 1 (2004). culturalsurvival.org.

Macpherson, C. B. "The Meaning of Property." In *Property: Mainstream and Critical Positions*, edited by C. B. MacPherson. University of Toronto Press, 1978.

Macpherson, C. B. *The Political Theory of Possessive Individualism: Hobbes to Locke*. 6th Impression edition. Oxford University Press, 1975.

Maddison, Ben. "Radical Commons Discourse and the Challenges of Colonialism." *Radical History Review*, no. 108 (2010): 29–48.

Magdoff, Fred, and John Bellamy Foster. *What Every Environmentalist Needs to Know About Capitalism*. Monthly Review Press, 2011.

Maher, Geo. *A World Without Police*. Verso, 2021.

Malm, Andreas. *Fossil Capital: The Rise of Steam Power and the Roots of Global Warming*. Verso, 2016.

Mann, Michael. *The Sources of Social Power*, volume 2, *The Rise of Classes and Nation-States, 1760–1914*. Cambridge University Press, 1993.

Manning, Peter K. *Police Work: The Social Organization of Policing*. MIT Press, 1977.

Marini, Ruy Mauro. *The Dialectics of Dependency*. Monthly Review Press, 2022.

Mars, Joan. *Deadly Force, Colonialism, and the Rule of Law*. Bloomsbury, 2002.

Marsden, Richard. *The Nature of Capital: Marx After Foucault*. Routledge, 1999.

Martí, Jordi Bonet, and Barbara Biglia. "Social Movements." In *Encyclopedia of Critical Psychology*. Edited by Thomas Teo. Springer, 2014.

Martin, Greg. *Social Movements and Protest Politics*. 2nd edition. Routledge, 2024.

Martinot, Steve. "The Militarisation of the Police." *Social Identities* 9, no. 2 (2010): 205–24.

Marx, Karl. *Capital: A Critique of Political Economy*, volume 1. Reprint edition. Translated by Ben Fowkes. With Ernest Mandel. Penguin Classics, 1992.

Marx, Karl. *Capital: A Critique of Political Economy*, volume 2. Translated by David Fernbach. Penguin Books, 1978.

Marx, Karl. *Contribution to the Critique of Political Economy*. Translated by N. I. Stone. Charles H. Kerr & Company, 1904.

Marx, Karl. *Grundrisse: Foundations of the Critique of Political Economy*. Reprint edition. Translated by Martin Nicolaus. Penguin Classics, 1993.

Marx, Karl. *The Class Struggles in France (1848–1850)*. Martin Lawrence, 1895.

Marx, Karl. *The Eighteenth Brumaire of Louis Bonaparte*. 3rd edition. Translated by Daniel De Leon. Charles H. Kerr & Company, 1913.

Marx, Karl. *The Poverty of Philosophy: A Reply to M. Proudhon's Philosophy of Poverty*. Translated by H. Quelch. Charles H. Kerr & Company, 1920.

Marx, Karl, and Friedrich Engels. "Manifesto of the Communist Party." In *The Marx-Engels Reader*, edited by Robert C. Tucker. W. W. Norton & Company, 1978.

Marx, Karl, and Friedrich Engels. *The Communist Manifesto*. Pluto Press, 2017.

Marx, Karl, and Friedrich Engels. *The German Ideology*. International Publishers, 1967.

Marx, Karl, and Friedrich Engels. *The German Ideology*. Foreign Languages Press, 2022.

Marx, Karl, and J. L. Joynes. *Wage-Labor and Capital*. Twentieth Century Press Limited, 1893.

Mau, Søren. *Mute Compulsion: A Marxist Theory of the Economic Power of Capital*. Verso, 2023.

Maxwell-Stewart, Hamish. "Convict Transportation from Britain and Ireland 1615–1870." *History Compass*, no. 8 (2010): 1221–42.

Maxwell-Stewart, Hamish. "The Rise and Fall of Penal Transportation." In *The Oxford Handbook of the History of Crime and Criminal Justice*. Edited by Paul Knepper and Anja Johansen. Oxford University Press, 2016.

Mbembe, Achille. *Critique of Black Reason*. Duke University Press, 2017.

Mbembe, Achille. "Necropolitics." Translated by Libby Meintjes. *Public Culture* 15, no. 1 (2003): 11–40.

McClintock, Anne. *Imperial Leather: Race, Gender, and Sexuality in the Colonial Contest*. 1st edition. Routledge, 1995.

McGuire, Danielle L. *At the Dark End of the Street: Black Women, Rape, Resistance—A New History of the Civil Rights Movement from Rosa Parks to the Rise of Black Power*. Vintage, 2011.

McKittrick, Katherine. "Plantation Futures." *Small Axe* 17, no. 3 (2013): 1–15.

McWhorter, Ladelle. *Racism and Sexual Oppression in Anglo-America: A Genealogy*. Indiana University Press, 2009.

Mezzadra, Sandro, and Brett Neilson. *Border as Method, or the Multiplication of Labor*. Duke University Press Books, 2013.

Midnight Notes Collective. "Introduction." *The New Enclosures*, no. 10 (1990): 1–9.

Mies, Maria. *Patriarchy and Accumulation on a World Scale: Women in the International Division of Labour*. 2nd edition. Zed Books, 1999.

Mogul, Joey L., Andrea J. Ritchie, and Kay Whitlock. *Queer (In)Justice: The Criminalization of LGBT People in the United States*. Beacon Press, 2011.

Molyneux, John. "Marxism and the Environmental Crisis." *Climate & Capitalism*, November 25, 2011. climateandcapitalism.com.

Montag, Warren. "Toward a Conception of Racism Without Race: Foucault and Contemporary Biopolitics." *Pli*, no. 13 (2002): 111–25.

Montáñez, Daniel. "Colonial Commons and the Decolonisation of the Left." *Guerilla Translation*, November 24, 2020. guerrillatranslation.org.

Moore, Jason W. *Capitalism in the Web of Life: Ecology and the Accumulation of Capital*. Verso, 2015.

Moreton-Robinson, Aileen. *The White Possessive: Property, Power, and Indigenous Sovereignty*. University of Minnesota Press, 2015.

Morgan, Jennifer. *Laboring Women: Reproduction and Gender in New World Slavery*. University of Pennsylvania Press, 2004.

Morris, Norval, and David J. Rothman, eds. *The Oxford History of the Prison: The Practice of Punishment in Western Society*. New edition. Oxford University Press, 1997.

Morrison, Toni. "Home." In *The House That Race Built: Black Americans, US Terrain*. Edited by Wahneema Lubiano and Arnold Rampersad. Pantheon, 1997.

Moten, Fred. *In the Break: The Aesthetics of the Black Radical Tradition*. University of Minnesota Press, 2003.

Moulier Boutang, Yann. *De L'esclavage au salariat: Économie historique du salariat bridé*. Presses Universitaires de France, 1998.

Muir, Diana. "A Land Without a People for a People Without a Land." *Middle Eastern Quarterly* 15, no. 2 (2008): 55–62.

Nadasen, Premilla. *Care: The Highest Stage of Capitalism*. Haymarket Books, 2023.

Nadelmann, Ethan. *Cops Across Borders: The Internationalization of US Criminal Law Enforcement*. Penn State University Press, 1993.

Nail, Thomas. *Theory of the Border*. Oxford University Press, 2016.

Negri, Antonio. *Marx and Foucault: Essays*, volume 1. Translated by Ed Emery. Polity, 2017.

Nemser, Daniel. *Infrastructures of Race: Concentration and Biopolitics in Colonial Mexico*. University of Texas Press, 2017.

Neocleous, Mark. *The Fabrication of Social Order: A Critical Theory of Police Power*. Pluto Press, 2000.

Neocleous, Mark. *The Politics of Immunity: Security and the Policing of Bodies*. Verso, 2022.

Nesbitt, Nick. "Troping Toussaint, Reading Revolution." *Research in African Literatures* 35, no. 2 (2004): 18–33.

Nevada. *The Abolition of Law*. Friends Publishing, 2022.

Newton, Huey P. *To Die for the People: The Writings of Huey P. Newton*. Vintage Books, 1972.

Nichols, Robert. *Theft Is Property!: Dispossession and Critical Theory*. Duke University Press, 2020.

Nietzsche, Friedrich. *Beyond Good and Evil: Prelude to a Philosophy of the Future*. Translated by Helen Zimmern. The Macmillan Company, 1907.

Noiriel, Gerard. *La tyrannie du national. Le droi d'asile en Europe, 1793–1993*. Calmann-Levy, 1991.

O'Brien, M. E. *Family Abolition: Capitalism and the Communizing of Care*. Pluto Press, 2023.

Ocen, Priscilla A. "Punishing Pregnancy: Race, Incarceration, and the Shackling of Pregnant Prisoners." *California Law Review* 100, no. 5 (2012): 1239–311.

Ocobock, Paul. "Introduction." In *Cast Out: Vagrancy and Homelessness in Global and Historical Perspective*, edited by Paul Ocobock and A. L. Beier. Ohio University Press, 2008.

O'Connor, Christopher D., and Phillip C. Shon. "Civilising the Police: Reconceptionalising the Role of the State in Theories of American Policing." *Global Crime* 20, no. 1 (2019): 45–64.

Olúfẹmi O. Táíwò. *Elite Capture: How the Powerful Took Over Identity Politics (and Everything Else)*. Haymarket Books, 2022.

Online Etymology Dictionary. "Abolition." Accessed February 24, 2025. etymonline.com.

Ophir, Adi. "State." *Mafte'akh*, no. 1 (2010): 67–96.

Osterweil, Vicky. *In Defense of Looting: A Riotous History of Uncivil Action*. Bold Type Books, 2020.

Pallister-Wilkins, Polly. *Humanitarian Borders: Unequal Mobility and Saving Lives*. Verso, 2022.

Parton, Dolly, dir. "9 to 5." RCA Records, 1980.

Patterson, Orlando. *Slavery and Social Death: A Comparative Study*. 1st edition. Harvard University Press, 1982.

Pearce, Fred. *The Land Grabbers: The New Fight over Who Owns the Earth*. Beacon Press, 2012.

Pemberton, Sarah. "Enforcing Gender: The Constitution of Sex and Gender in Prison Regimes." *Signs: Journal of Women in Culture and Society* 39, no. 1 (2013): 151–75.

Perelman, Michael. *The Invention of Capitalism: Classical Political Economy and the Secret History of Primitive Accumulation*. Duke University Press, 2000.

Polanyi, Karl. *The Great Transformation: The Political and Economic Origins of Our Time*. Beacon Press, 2001.

Proudhon, Pierre-Joseph. *What Is Property?* Edited by Donald R. Kelley and Bonnie G. Smith. Cambridge University Press, 2008.

Rancière, Jacques. *Disagreement: Politics and Philosophy*. Translated by Julie Rose. University of Minnesota Press, 2004.

Rankine, Claudia. *Citizen: An American Lyric*. Graywolf Press, 2014.

Read, Jason. "The Production of Subjectivity: From Transindividuality to the Commons." *New Formations: A Jounral of Culture/Theory/Politics* 70 (2010): 113–31.

Rediker, Marcus. *Villains of All Nations: Atlantic Pirates in the Golden Age*. Beacon Press, 2005.

Richie, Beth E. *Arrested Justice: Black Women, Violence, and America's Prison Nation*. New York University Press, 2012.

Richie, Bethe. "Queering Antiprison Work: African American Lesbians in the Juvenile Justice System." In *Global Lockdown: Race, Gender, and the Prison-Industrial Complex*. Edited by Julia Sudbury. Routledge, 2005.

Rights and Resources. *Who Owns the World's Land?: Global State of Indigenous, Afro-Descendant, and Local Community Land Rights Recognition from 2015–2020*. 2nd edition. 2023.

Rights and Resources Initiative. *Who Owns the World's Land?: A Global Baseline of Formally Recognized Indigenous and Community Land Rights*. Washington, DC, 2015. rightsandresources.org.

Roberts, Dorothy. *Torn Apart: How the Child Welfare System Destroys Black Families—and How Abolition Can Build a Safer World*. Basic Books, 2022.

Robinson, Cedric J. *Black Marxism: The Making of the Black Radical Tradition*. 2nd edition. University of North Carolina Press, 2000.

Robinson, William I. *The Global Police State*. Pluto Press, 2020.

Rodney, Walter. *How Europe Underdeveloped Africa*. New edition. Verso, 2018.

Rodriguez, Dylan. "Abolition as Praxis of Human Being: A Forward." *Harvard Law Review* 132, no. 6 (2019). harvardlawreview.org.

Roediger, David R., Mike Davis, Michael Sprinker, and Kathleen Cleaver. *The Wages of Whiteness: Race and the Making of the American Working Class*. New edition. Verso, 2007.

Roth, Rachel, and Sara L. Ainsworth. "If They Hand You a Paper, You Sign It: A Call to End the Sterilization of Women in Prison." *Hastings Women's Law Journal* 26, no. 1 (2015): 7–50.

Sahlins, Peter. *Forest Rites: The War of the Demoiselles in Nineteenth-Century France*. Harvard University Press, 1994.

San Jerónimo, Magdalena de. *Razón y Forma de La Galera y Casa Real, Que El Rey, Nuestro Señor, Manda Hacer En Nuestros Reinos, Para Castigo de Las Mujeres Vagantes y Ladronas, Aclahuetas, Hechiceras, y Otras Semejantes*. Francisco Fernández de Córdova, 1608.

San Jerónimo, Magdalena de. "Vagabond Women (1608)." In *Early Modern Spain: A Documentary History*. Edited by Jon Cowans. University of Pennsylvania Press, 2003.

Sartre, Jean-Paul. "Preface." In *The Wretched of the Earth*. Reprint edition. By Frantz Fanon. Translated by Richard Philcox. Grove Press, 2005.

Sassen, Saskia. *Expulsions: Brutality and Complexity in the Global Economy*. Harvard University Press, 2014.

Sayegh, Fayez. "Zionist Colonialism in Palestine." *Settler Colonial Studies* 2, no. 1 (2012): 206–25.

Schling. "(Re)Production: Everyday Life in the Workers' Dormitory." *Society and Space*, November 7, 2017. societyandspace.org.

Schmid, Anastazia. "Crafting the Perfect Woman: How Gynecology, Obstetrics, and American Prisons Operate to Construct and Control Women." In *Abolishing Carceral Society*. Edited by Abolition Collective. Common Notions, 2018.

Schwartz, Stuart B. *Slaves, Peasants, and Rebels: Reconsidering Brazilian Slavery*. University of Illinois Press, 1996.

Scott, James C. *Seeing Like a State: How Certain Schemes to Improve the Human Condition Have Failed*. Yale University Press, 1998.

Seed, Patricia. *Ceremonies of Possession in Europe's Conquest of the New World, 1492–1640*. Cambridge University Press, 1995.

Serge, Victor. *What Every Radical Should Know About State Repression: A Guide for Activists*. Seven Stories Press, 2024.

Sharpe, Christina. *In the Wake: On Blackness and Being*. Duke University Press, 2016.

Shell, Jacob. *Transportation and Revolt: Pigeons, Mules, Canals, and the Vanishing Geographies of Subversive Mobility*. MIT Press, 2015.

Sheller, Mimi. *Mobility Justice: The Politics of Movement in an Age of Extremes*. Verso, 2018.

Shifferd, K. D. "Karl Marx and the Environment." *Journal of Environmental Education* 3, no. 4 (1972): 39–42.

Shoemaker, Robert B. *Prosecution and Punishment: Petty Crime and the Law in London and Rural Middlesex, c.1660–1725*. Cambridge University Press, 1991.

Shohat, Ella. *On the Arab-Jew, Palestine, and Other Displacements*. Pluto Press, 2017.

Shotwell, Alexis. *Against Purity: Living Ethically in Compromised Times*. University of Minnesota Press, 2016.

Smart, Barry. *Foucault, Marxism and Critique*. Routledge, 2013.

Smith, Adam. *Lectures on Jurisprudence*. Oxford University Press, 1978.

Smith, Adam. *On the Wealth of Nations*. Edited by P. J. O'Rourke. Atlantic Monthly Press, 2007.

Spade, Dean. *Normal Life: Administrative Violence, Critical Trans Politics, and the Limits of Law*. Duke University Press, 2015.

Spillers, Hortense. "Mama's Baby, Papa's Maybe: An American Grammar Book." *Diacritics* 17, no. 2 (1987): 64–81.

Sraffa, Piero. *Production of Commodities by Means of Commodities: Prelude to a Critique of Economic Theory*. Vora & Co. Publishers, 1960.

Stanley, Amy Dru. *From Bondage to Contract: Wage Labor, Marriage, and the Market in the Age of Slave Emancipation*. Cambridge University Press, 1998.

Stanley, Eric A., and Nat Smith, eds. *Captive Genders: Trans Embodiment and the Prison Industrial Complex*. 2nd edition. AK Press, 2015.

Stein, Kenneth W. "The Jewish National Fund: Land Purchase Methods and Priorities, 1924–1939." *Middle Eastern Studies* 20, no. 2 (1984): 190–205.

Stein, Lorenz von. *The History of the Social Movement in France, 1789–1850*. Translated by Kaethe Mengelberg. Bedminster Press, 1964.

Stockdill, Brett. "Multiple Oppressions and Their Influence on Collective Action: The Case of the AIDS Movement." PhD dissertation, Department of Sociology, Northwestern University, 1996.

Stoler, Ann Laura. *Duress: Imperial Durabilities in Our Times*. Duke University Press, 2016.

Stoler, Ann Laura. *Race and the Education of Desire: Foucault's History of Sexuality and the Colonial Order of Things*. Duke University Press, 1995.

Sudbury, Julia. "Maroon Abolitionists: Black Gender-Oppressed Activists in the Antiprison Movement in the US and Canada." *Meridians: Feminism, Race, Transnationalism* 9, no. 1 (2009): 1–29.

Taylor, Chloë. "Race and Racism in Foucault's Collège de France Lectures." *Philosophy Compass* 6, no. 11 (2011): 746–56.

Taylor, Christopher. *Empire of Neglect: The West Indies in the Wake of British Liberalism*. Duke University Press, 2018.

Taylor, Keeanga-Yamahtta. *Race for Profit: How Banks and the Real Estate Industry Undermined Black Homeownership*. University of North Carolina Press, 2019.

Taylor, William B. *Landlord and Peasant in Colonial Oaxaca*. Stanford University Press, 1972.

Thompson, E. P. "Customs, Law, and Common Right." In *Customs in Common*. The New Press, 1991.

Tilly, Charles. *From Mobilization to Revolution*. Addison-Wesley Publishing Company, 1978.

Tilly, Charles. *Social Movements, 1768–2004*. Paradigm Publishers, 2004.

Tomlins, Christopher. "Reconsidering Indentured Servitude: European Migration and the Early American Labor Force, 1600–1775." *Labor History* 42, no. 1 (2001): 5–43.

Torpey, John. *The Invention of the Passport: Surveillance, Citizenship, and the State*. Cambridge University Press, 2000.

Tuck, Eve, and K. Wayne Yang. "Decolonization Is Not a Metaphor." *Decolonization: Indigeneity, Education & Society* 1, no. 1 (2012): 1–40.

Turner, M. E. *English Parliamentary Enclosure: Its Historical Geography and Economic History*. William Dawson and Sons, 1980.

Turner, Ralph H., and Neil J. Smelser. "Social Movement." In *Encyclopedia Britannica*. April 19, 2025. britannica.com.

Tutino, John. *Making a New World: Founding Capitalism in the Bajío and Spanish North America*. Duke University Press, 2011.

Valencia, Sayak. *Gore Capitalism*. Translated by John Pluecker. Semiotext(e), 2018.

Vansina, Jan. "Confinement in Angola's Past." In *A History of Prison and Confinement in Africa*. Edited by Florence Bernault. Heinemann, 2003.

Veracini, Lorenzo. *The World Turned Inside Out: Settler Colonialism as a Political Idea*. Verso, 2021.

Vina, Stephen R., Blas Nunez-Neto, and Alyssa Bartlett Weir. *Civilian Patrols Along the Border: Legal and Policy Issues*. Report for Congress RL33353. Congressional Research Service, 2006. sgp.fas.org.

Vukov, Tamara. "Strange Moves: Speculations and Propositions on Mobility Justice." In *The Politics and Erotics of Mobility Justice*. Edited by Liz Montegary and Melissa Autumn White. Palgrave Macmillan, 2015.

Walcott, Rinaldo. *On Property: Policing, Prisons, and the Call for Abolition*. Biblioasis, 2021.

Walia, Harsha. *Border and Rule: Global Migration, Capitalism, and the Rise of Racist Nationalism*. Haymarket Books, 2021.

Ward, Colin. "Editor's Postscript." In *Fields, Factories, and Workshops Tomorrow*. By Peter Kropotkin. Freedom Press, 1974.

Wardhaugh, Julia. "Beyond the Workhouse: Regulating Vagrancy in Goa, India." *Asian Criminology* 7 (2012): 205–23.

Weber, Max. *Economy and Society: An Outline of an Interpretive Sociology*, volume 2. Edited by Guenther Roth and Claus Wittich. University of California Press, 1978.

Weeks, Kathi. "Abolition of the Family: The Most Infamous Feminist Proposal." *Feminist Theory* 24, no. 3 (2023): 433–53.

Whatcott, Jess. "No Selves to Consent: Women's Prisons, Sterilization, and the Biopolitics of Informed Consent." *Signs: Journal of Women in Culture and Society* 44, no. 1 (2018): 131–53.

Williams, Eric. *Capitalism and Slavery*. 1st edition. The University of North Carolina Press, 1994.

Williams, Robert A. *The American Indian in Western Legal Thought: The Discourses of Conquest*. Reprint edition. Oxford University Press, 1992.

Wolfe, Patrick. "Settler Colonialism and the Elimination of the Native." *Journal of Genocide Research* 8, no. 4 (2006): 387–409.

Wood, Ellen Meiksins. *Liberty and Property: A Social History of Western Political Thought from the Renaissance to Enlightenment*. 1st edition. Verso, 2012.

Wood, Ellen Meiksins. *The Origin of Capitalism: A Longer View*. Revised edition. Verso, 2002.

Wordie, J. R. "The Chronology of English Enclosure, 1500–1914." *Economic History Review*, no. 37 (1983).

World Bank. *World Development Report 2023: Migrants, Refugees, and Societies*. International Bank for Reconstruction and Development/ The World Bank, 2023.

World Bank Group. "International Tourism, Number of Departures." Yearbook of Tourism Statistics, UN Tourism. n.d. data.worldbank.org.

Ziegler, Edith M. *Harlots, Hussies, and Poor Unfortunate Women: Crime, Transportation, and the Servitude of Female Convicts*. University of Alabama Press, 2014.

Zinoman, Peter. "Colonial Prisons and Anti-Colonial Resistance in French Indochina: The Thai Nguyen Rebellion, 1917." *Modern Asian Studies* 34, no. 1 (2000): 57–98.

Zinoman, Peter. *The Colonial Bastille: A History of Imprisonment in Vietnam, 1862–1940*. University of California Press, 2001.

Index